ADVOCACY

A Practical Guide

SECOND EDITION

ADVOCACY

A Practical Guide

SECOND EDITION

PETER LYONS
CHRIS TAYLOR

WS
&H

Wildy, Simmonds & Hill Publishing

ISBN: 9780854903139

British Library Cataloguing in Publication Data

A catalogue record for this book is available from the British Library

First edition 2019

This edition published in 2026 by

Wildy, Simmonds & Hill Publishing
Wildy & Sons Ltd
Lincoln's Inn Archway
Carey Street
London WC2A 2JD
www.wildy.com

Printed in Great Britain by CPI Group (UK) Ltd, Croydon CR0 4YY.

Preface to the Second Edition

Peter Lyons was acknowledged as one of the finest advocacy teachers of the last 30 years. He taught thousands of lawyers around the world, from a wide range of backgrounds and experience. This included judges, a number of high-profile commercial solicitors who went on to take silk and the first patent attorney to appear as counsel in the UK Supreme Court.

He spent years reading books by and about the great advocates and acquired an immense – perhaps unequalled – level of learning in the subject. He took great pleasure in pouring that expertise into this book, which was first published by Wildy, Simmonds & Hill Publishing in 2019.

Peter believed that learning should be fun: our minds are most receptive to new ideas when we are happy and relaxed. He always said that his teaching philosophy was to ‘light a fire’ rather than ‘fill a bucket’. Those principles shine through in his writing here.

Peter died suddenly in June 2023 after a short illness. As Peter’s civil partner, his co-owner in our training business CPD Training (UK) Limited and his executor, I am delighted to have been invited by Wildy, Simmonds & Hill Publishing to prepare the text for a second edition.

Whilst this is a book primarily about legal skills, I have taken the opportunity to update references to procedural and conduct rules, and to case law.

Since the first edition was published, we have had a change of monarch, meaning that Queen’s Counsel have become King’s Counsel.

I have taken a pragmatic approach to changing references in the text, depending on the context and the date of the event or quotation.

During the Covid-19 pandemic, Peter had been working with Carol Sowers on a stand-alone publication on online advocacy. Carol is a leading presentation skills coach in the United States and a former main news anchor on the CBS television network. Carol has generously collaborated with me to adapt her work with Peter into a new chapter on online advocacy, which is included in this second edition. I am hugely grateful to Carol and to everyone else I consulted in the preparation of the revised text.

Peter was a modest man. He would be embarrassed, but secretly thrilled, to know that advocates are continuing to benefit from his guidance in the years after his passing.

Chris Taylor
York
January 2026

Foreword to the First Edition

I keep close at hand a cathartic collection of examples of appalling advocacy. After a bad day in court, it is reassuring to be reminded that it could have been so much worse.

When licking my professional wounds, I like to recall that in the United States Supreme Court in 1972, the assistant prosecutor from Louisville, Kentucky was asked in oral argument by Justice Douglas why his argument was so perfunctory. 'Your Honor must realise', the advocate replied, 'I am a very busy man'.[1] In 1981, a court in Tennessee told an advocate during his submissions, 'we shall have no more of this', and issued an injunction to restrain him from bringing any similar cases in the future.[2] In 2005, at Harrow Crown Court, Judge Sanders asked the unfortunate counsel for the Crown in a criminal case how long he had been a barrister. When counsel replied, 'long enough', the judge responded, 'but everything you say is utter rubbish'.[3]

Much more difficult is to find a guide to good advocacy. That is surprising since advocacy – communication with others to persuade them – is vital, not just to the effective presentation of legal argument, but to all aspects of our lives. 'Can I have an ice cream?'. 'I wish to apply for the job vacancy'. 'Will you marry me?'.

---

1 Floyd Abrams, Speech to Graduating Class, University of Michigan Law School (13 May 1990) 3, referring to *Branzburg v Hayes* 408 US 665 (1972) (in which Mr Abrams was the opposing counsel).

2 *State of Tennessee ex rel Inman v Brock* 622 SW 2d 36, 50 (1981) (Supreme Court of Tennessee).

3 Joshua Rozenberg, 'Angry Judge Dismisses Rape Case', *The Daily Telegraph*, 17 September 2005, www.telegraph.co.uk/news/uknews/1498565/Angry-judge-dismisses-rape-case.html

The essential principles of court and tribunal advocacy are, when analysed by a master such as Peter Lyons, surprisingly simple: brevity, clarity, courtesy, integrity and a focus on offering a solution to the problem posed.

Every advocate should bear in mind the advice (quoted by Professor Lyons) from Justice John I Laskin of the Court of Appeal for Ontario: busy judges 'want answers to two questions: can you help us and how fast?'[4] Persuading a court does not mean having an argument with the judge (or with your opponent). It means listening as well as talking. Easy to state, but difficult to accomplish, especially when under pressure from judges, opposing counsel and your client (and not necessarily in that order of impediment).

I have read no better guide to the practicalities of good advocacy than Peter Lyons' book. It is informed by years of experience and by a wealth of illuminating anecdotes that will instruct and entertain all advocates from the novice to the QC. It is easy to understand, comprehensive (from opening submissions, through cross-examination to final speeches) and, as one would expect of a book on advocacy, completely persuasive.

Lord Pannick QC
Blackstone Chambers
Temple
London
EC4Y 9BW
2 January 2019

---

4 The Hon Justice John I Laskin, 'What Persuades (or What's Going On Inside the Judge's Mind)' (2004) 23(1) *The Advocates' Society Journal*, 4–9, http://ellynlaw.com/PDFs/Justice%20Laskin%20-%20What%20Persuades%20(2).pdf.

Contents

About the Authors

Peter Lyons was an Australian barrister and solicitor who spent 30 years living in the UK. From 1995, he taught advocacy across the world to civil, common and arbitration lawyers. He delivered advocacy, litigation and negotiation skills courses to barristers, solicitors and patent attorneys, including programmes for many of the top City law firms in London. He designed and taught the first LLM in Advocacy at the University of Strathclyde, as well as the UK Bar's Public Access course. His company, CPD Training (UK) Limited (www.cpdtraining.net), was founded in 2005. Between 2010 and 2025, the company was authorised by the Solicitors Regulation Authority to train and assess English-qualified solicitors for the Higher Rights of Audience qualification. It continues to provide training in all aspects of advocacy and litigation skills.

Peter Lyons died in June 2023, at the age of 64.

Chris Taylor is an English solicitor and legal skills trainer. He qualified in 1999 and spent many years as a commercial litigator at Addleshaw Goddard and later Eversheds. In 2005, he assisted Peter Lyons to establish CPD Training (UK) Limited, which he continues to run today. He is the co-author of the English law chapter of *Privilege and Confidentiality: An International Handbook*, published by the International Bar Association, has written a chapter on the enforcement of foreign judgments for *The Litigation Practice*, published by Sweet & Maxwell, and was for many years a contributing author to *Blackstone's Civil Practice*.

Introduction to the First Edition

Acutely conscious of Gilbert Gray QC's observation that 'most books on advocacy are unreadable',[1] I hope this book is easy to absorb. It does not purport to be an intellectual tome nor an academic text book. It is designed for those who wish to learn advocacy skills from scratch or those seeking to brush up on what they already know.

I don't want to pontificate or say that my way is the only way. Advocates, like students, are people from all walks of life and with different levels of knowledge and skill. Some will take to the skills easily; some will find them harder to master.

I have heard many a barrister or trial attorney tell me over the years that you cannot teach advocacy. They say, 'Advocates are born, not made.'

These people have usually reached some degree of eminence in their profession. They would have you believe that the great advocates arrived in court on their first day as the finished article.

It is true that some people, like Mozart, are geniuses from a very young age. But the majority of books I have read about advocates or by advocates have disclosed years of enormously hard work and the polishing of persuasion skills in real time on their feet.

No one learns much without making mistakes. The classroom is the best place for making errors, because people can be corrected, and no

---

1 John H Munkman, *The Technique of Advocacy* (Butterworths, London, 1991) foreword.

one suffers. In the courtroom, mistakes are not tolerated; or at least, they are discouraged.

That is why, in my experience, some senior barristers and judges are not effective teachers. They teach to their own level, with all the knowledge they have acquired over the years, even though the students are so green they might never have been in a courtroom before.

Students in those circumstances are often intimidated or overwhelmed as the teacher strives to tell them in painstaking detail how much they know and how much the students got wrong.

It is well meant, but totally ineffective because the student will only hear the first thing that is said and will still be mulling it over when the teacher gets to point 12.

Then the senior barrister or judge will give a demonstration of how it should be done. Students have told me that it often goes one of two ways: either the demonstration will be so good that the student will think 'I could never come up to that standard'; or there will be mistakes by the practitioner that undermine his credibility.

I have been teaching for almost 25 years. I have taught barristers and solicitors, trainees and partners, other trainers and members of the public who want to learn or improve their advocacy skills.

I have made hundreds of mistakes on real people. If I had been a surgeon, I would have been in trouble well before now. But I have learned from those mistakes and I have learned from the mistakes of others. I have also learned by watching and working with accomplished teachers. And the best feeling is watching nervous and sometimes terrified students grow in confidence and skill as the course progresses.

I have also gained much from reading about distinguished advocates and teachers of the past. I used to appear before a wise old judge called Mr Justice Nettlefold. He was known for his memorable turns of phrase. I remember him saying to me in court one day, when he was in effect calling for submissions on the legal problem he was faced with, 'What is the learning, Mr Lyons?'

It is a lovely expression because people tend to forget about the learning and start afresh. This book is full of the learning of people such as Edward Carson, Norman Birkett and Lord Denning. There are also references to contemporary lawyers, such as former UK Supreme Court Justices, Lord Neuberger and Lord Sumption.

The idea for this book came from Jarek Kolkowski, an accomplished Polish lawyer who practised for a large American firm in Warsaw. He said:

> 'We want to know about these techniques – there aren't any books on common law advocacy in Poland; there is nothing to consult when we come up against English or US lawyers using them in international arbitrations.'

In England, several students told me there were no books aimed at solicitors who were seeking rights of audience in the higher courts. I received similar comments in Belfast where I teach a few times a year.

People learn in the following ways:

1 They listen to people telling them what to do or they read about it.

2 They watch others doing it and they learn how it should be done well. Sometimes they see it being done badly and they learn what not to do. But there are occasions when they copy or pick up the bad habits because they don't know any better.

3 The best way to learn is to do it for yourself. Even better is to get a reaction from a trained teacher. You can also learn a lot from watching a video of yourself performing – it is not something that any but the most egotistical ask for, though I strongly recommend it. Just don't show it to your family at Christmas.

Advocacy is a skill, and mastering a skill means acquiring a technique. What I hope you will learn from this book are techniques. Once you have them you will never lose them. It is a bit like driving a car. You will not learn how to drive a Formula One car from this book. That will come from hard work, experience and, dare I say it, a dash of talent.

In my experience, which includes teaching people for whom English is not their first language, it is easier to coax a good performance from a student who knows the basic techniques and is allowed to display them. The best way of teaching advocacy is to correct and encourage, but it is very hard to correct a student who has lost confidence.

This book concentrates on civil advocacy and arbitration, but patent attorneys and criminal practitioners should also find it useful.

At the end of the book is a case study entitled *Cavendish v Downham*.

It is based on a real case,[2] but is entirely fictitious.

I suggest you read the case study first because I use it throughout the book to demonstrate various advocacy techniques.

It is not a bundle of model witness statements. It contains deliberate errors, speculation, hearsay and otherwise inadmissible evidence. It also contains material for cross-examination which only a fool would include in a statement.

Lastly, I would like to acknowledge the established techniques of the National Institute for Trial Advocacy in America (NITA). I have adapted some of its principles for other countries, but NITA's grasp of the most important trial skills remains as sure as ever.

Peter Lyons
December 2018

---

2 *Harlingdon & Leinster Enterprises Limited v Christopher Hull Fine Art Limited* [1989] EWCA Civ 4, [1991] QB 564.

Chapter 1
Presentation Skills

Have you ever been at a wedding where somebody has delivered a good speech? Perhaps not, but we have all been to weddings where there has been a bad speech: long-winded, monotonous, inappropriate jokes or simply dull.

Speaking at weddings is a difficult task. Most people want to get it right. No one wants to spoil the couple's big day.

The pressure on after-dinner speakers is immense. The questions swirl around. Should I lay off the drink? Will a wine or two ease my nerves, or cause me to say the wrong thing and lose my place? I don't want to read it, but what if I miss something out, such as thanking the bridesmaids? Will I be entertaining or boring? Too long or too short? Will I strike the right note with the audience? Will it be remembered for the right reasons?

Yet, the irony is that you will never get a more receptive audience than at a wedding. Nobody wants you to fail. They will forgive you for quite a lot of shortcomings. Unless there is an unbridled drunk in the room, you should get through the experience unscathed.

Think about that good wedding speech you saw. What was it that the speaker did that was effective? Break it down into little pieces. Was the speaker funny; knowledgeable; did he look at the audience; did he vary his tone of voice; pause in the right places; was he prepared? Did he look confident?

These are just a few characteristics of the good speaker. It is worth examining them because, with the exception of being funny, each characteristic is an asset in any courtroom. Let the judge do the jokes. They are usually bad but don't laugh too hard.

1 SUBSTANCE

1.1 Knowledge of subject

It is of enormous assistance if the speaker knows what he is talking about. Preparation is a vital part of presentation.

Former US Secretary of State, James Baker, said that his dad used to talk about the 'five Ps':

> 'Prior Preparation Prevents Poor Performance'[1]

Apart from the redundancy of the first word, it is a memorable aphorism.

The audience has to feel comfortable that the speaker is familiar with the subject. This is even more important in court because the judge is relying on you.

Skilled advocates, especially those who have to cross-examine expert witnesses, become so familiar with the material that they appear to know as much or even more than the expert.

A good advocate anticipates every point that is likely to arise and every question the judge might pose. There are no short cuts. It is a painstaking job.

1.2 Structure

An attractive structure makes things easier to follow. A ramble or stream of consciousness buries the messages.

The ancient Greeks knew the value of presenting things in threes.

Good stories and jokes are usually in threes. You wouldn't look forward to a tale about Goldilocks and the Seven Bears.

---

1 James Baker, *Work Hard, Study ... and Keep out of Politics* (Putnam, New York, 2006) 5.

I heard an otherwise excellent speaker, who was an American judge, stand up in front of a group of admittedly hungover lawyers one Saturday morning and say, 'I want to talk to you this morning about the 17 most important things about cross-examination.'

You could feel the whole room sink.

The same experience occurs when a judge is told that the advocate intends to address her for four days.

The structure has to be logical – it has to make sense. Lawyers are trained to think chronologically and in paragraphs. I have a friend who is an artist and he thinks in images which burst upon him from all directions. A student of mine thought in Venn diagrams.

But the vast majority of lawyers think in neat logical structures. If that is the case, you can be assured the judge also thinks like that. So, present it to her in paragraphs and chronologically.

Your client often wants to tell you the last thing that happened. You always want to know the first thing that happened.

In addition, whereas with a joke you must hide the punch line and deliver it at the end, the situation in court is different.

A submission to a court is not a murder mystery novel. One must announce the murderer or give out the punch line in the first 10 seconds.

1.3 Tell a story

Justice Laskin of the Canadian Supreme Court produced an excellent paper some years ago on what persuades judges. I draw on the judge's observations in this book.[2]

His Honour concluded somewhat strikingly that the best advocates are the best story tellers. By no means did he intend to convey that good

---

2 The Hon Justice John I Laskin, 'What Persuades (or, What's Going On In the Judge's Mind)' (2004) 23(1) *The Advocates' Society Journal*, 4–9, http://ellynlaw.com/PDFs/Justice%20Laskin%20-%20What%20Persuades%20(2).pdf.

advocates make up stories. But your client's case is a story. A well-told story is attractive to most human beings. We were brought up on stories. Most of us had them read to us at bedtime. Why do tabloid newspapers sell so well? Why are novels about sex, violence and intrigue so popular?

The good advocate knows why this is the case and tells his client's story in a compelling way throughout the case: in opening; in examination-in-chief through his own witness; and in cross-examination through his opponent's witnesses.

A good story comprises well-arranged facts. It is easy to follow and enjoyable to listen to.

How many judges drive to work with their partner and say, 'I'm really looking forward to being bored today'?

You want a judge, jury or arbitration panel to be saying to themselves 'Keep going. I'm enjoying this. It's interesting. I want to hear more'.

1.4 Simple words

Using simple words can help to maximise the effect the story has on your audience.

I was intrigued by Tony Blair's success as a politician. I found him compelling to listen to in speeches and interviews. He always seemed to be answering the question but, on reflection, you realised he sometimes dodged it.

But there was more to it than that. I watched him under pressure at Prime Minister's Questions in Parliament and I studied his set-piece speeches at Party Conferences. Clearly, there were many verbless sentences and sometimes he overdid it, but he was a superb communicator.

And then the secret to his success struck me. By and large, Tony Blair used simple words – words of one syllable as often as possible; words that were understandable and easy to absorb.

He never used expressions such as 'fiscal outcomes' or 'driving through the desired policy agenda'. He spoke 'human', which allowed his audience to understand him and relate to him.

So did Winston Churchill. 'We shall fight on the beaches, we shall fight on the landing grounds, we shall fight in the fields and in the streets, we shall fight in the hills; we shall never surrender.'[3]

The longest word is 'surrender'. Apparently, Churchill spent three weeks preparing a speech such as this one, making sure he had just the right words and rhythms. It worked. It was directed to the farm hands and the factory workers. Simple but powerful language, expressed in those growling, defiant tones, inspired and firmed the resolve of the country.

As the famous American journalist, Ed Morrow, put it, 'Churchill mobilised the English language and sent it into battle.'

Lord Denning was another. He had a triple first class Honours degree from Oxford, yet his speeches and his judgments were delivered in the most plain and simple language.

As he put it, 'I had to practise continually … In chambers if asked to advise, I took intimate pains in the writing of an opinion. I crossed out sentence after sentence. I wrote them again and again. Seek to make your opinions clear at all costs.'

Imagine how much Lord Denning would have been assisted by today's technology.

He had a simple philosophy: command of the language is the key to success in any profession where words count.[4]

If you are trying to communicate something and your listener does not understand because of the complexity of your language or the way you

---

3 Winston Churchill, British Prime Minister, 'We Shall Fight on the Beaches' (Speech to the House of Commons, 4 June 1940).

4 Lord Denning, *The Closing Chapter* (Butterworths, London, 1983) 57.

express yourself, you have failed. Simple words are essential to effective communication.

1.5 Picture words

A wonderful advocacy teacher, Professor Irving Younger, told the story of when he was a junior judge in New York. So that he didn't 'screw up' (as he put it), they assigned him to traffic cases. In five years, he said, no attorney ever used the word 'car'.

They chose 'automobile' or 'motor vehicle'.[5]

When someone says the words 'motor vehicle' to you, what do you see? Some people see a bus or a tram; others see a train or a tractor.

But if you use the word 'car', could you see a car? If I said 'black car', could you see a 'black car'? And if I said 'big black car', could you see a 'big black car'? Of course.

Churchill knew this. Can you see people 'fighting on the beaches'? Can you see people 'fighting in the fields and in the streets'? Of course you can.

Today's politicians would say 'We shall engage the enemy at the coastline.'

Picture words create images in the listener's mind. But I'm afraid that most lawyers learn to be drainers. They drain the English language of its colour. They speak in jargon, clichés and legalese.

I remember a lawyer appearing before Mr Justice Underwood in a property dispute. This was the lawyer's question to the witness:

---

5 Irving Younger, 'Ten Commandments of Cross-Examination' taken from *The Advocate's Deskbook: The Essentials of Trying a Case* (Prentice Hall, Upper Saddle River, 1988). 'Irving Younger's 10 Commandments of Cross Examination at UC Hastings College of the Law' (YouTube) www.youtube.com/watch?v=dBP2if0l-a8.

Lawyer:	'On which particular occasion did you form the requisite intention to dispose of the agricultural holding which is the subject matter of the present litigation?'
Witness:	'Huh?'
Judge:	'When did you decide to sell the farm?'

We arc taught legalese at law school, and we hear people speaking the new language in our office and in the courtroom. Being frail creatures, we copy people because we don't want to stand out.

I want to finish this part by telling you of Lord Daniel Brennan KC, one of the finest clinical negligence advocates of the past 50 years. He appeared for the claimant in a complex trial which lasted six weeks. He won. But the silk on the other side sought an order that 'each party bear its own costs'. The silk produced written submissions and a list of authorities and addressed the judge at some length.

When he was finished, the court called on Brennan. He rose and said eight words:

> 'They came. They fought. They lost. They pay.'

'I quite agree', said the judge.

1.6 Putting it into practice

Story-telling, using simple words and picture words were often deployed in Lord Denning's judgments. As a law student, his decisions were the only ones I understood (and enjoyed) at the first reading.

Lord Bingham, generally regarded as the finest English judge of the last 30 years, also liked Denning's judgments. He quoted from several of them in his address during Denning's memorial service at Westminster Abbey.[6]

---

6 Tom Bingham, *The Business of Judging* (Oxford University Press, Oxford, 2004) 409–413. Reproduced with permission of the licensor through PLS Clear.

The much-mocked *Hinz v Berry* is my favourite. This is how it begins, 'It happened on April 19, 1964. It was bluebell time in Kent.' Immediately, the reader wants to know what happened:

> '[Mr and Mrs Hinz] drove out in a Bedford Dormobile van from Tonbridge to Canvey Island. They took all eight children with them. As they were coming back they turned into a lay by at Thurnham to have a picnic tea. The husband, Mr Hinz, was at the back of the Dormobile making the tea. Mrs Hinz had taken Stephanie, her third child, aged three, across the road to pick bluebells on the opposite side.'[7]

Can you see the picture? Can you imagine the happy family picnic?

> 'There came along a Jaguar car driven by Mr Berry, out of control. A tyre had burst. The Jaguar rushed into this lay-by and crashed into Mr Hinz and the children ... Blood was streaming from their heads.'

Is the scene in your mind? All simple words, 'rushed' and 'crashed', but picture words:

> 'Mrs Hinz, hearing the crash, turned round and saw this disaster.'

There is no doubt which way the judge is going. But this case was about damages rather than liability. If you think about it, the facts, although expressed simply, are delivered dramatically. Yet they are all the elements one needs to found a cause of action in nervous shock: negligent behaviour causing severe psychiatric injury.

Lord Justice Dunn wrote an autobiography about his experiences as a soldier, a barrister and a distinguished judge. He often sat with Denning. He said, 'We used to marvel at the way he expressed complex legal propositions in simple language.'[8]

---

7 [1970] 2 QB 40.

8 Sir Robin Dunn, *Sword and Wig: The Memoirs of a Lord Justice* (Quiller Press, London, 1993) 232–235.

2 STYLE

2.1 Beating nerves

You have heard of the 'Fight or Flight' experience. When we are nervous our adrenal gland gives us a rush. Our mouths become dry, our fingers tingle, we perspire and become light-headed, and our hearts pump blood quickly into our arms and legs so we can fight what confronts us or run away.

As Judge Mark Drummond put it, the adrenal gland is incredibly stupid: it cannot distinguish between a joyful wedding reception and an angry polar bear.

The effect on inexperienced public speakers is marked. The most common symptom is speaking too quickly. A resting heart beats roughly once every second. The nervous public speaker whose heart is going ten to the dozen is tricked into thinking they are talking at normal speed.

When I tell my students they are speaking too quickly, they don't believe me. Then I play it back to them on video.

Try it yourself. Get someone to film you and, when you play it back, try to take a note of what you are saying.

For the first 60 to 90 seconds of any speech your heart rate is about 150 beats per minute. The audience, whose hearts are beating at a resting rate of 60 to 80 beats per minute, are acutely aware of a fast-talking speaker.

To the audience this is immensely frustrating. They cannot absorb what the speaker is saying. The speaker's main points are lost and wasted. It's like tipping fine champagne down the sink.

Sometimes people, such as the late Robin Williams, speak fast to make others laugh – a lawyer would say 'for comedic effect'. But Williams was not aiming to inform or persuade the audience; he was there to entertain them.

There are various techniques for slowing yourself down, but first your condition must be diagnosed, and you must accept you are talking too quickly.

The best way of controlling your nerves is to breathe deeply but calmly before you begin to speak. As your performance continues, take larger than normal but imperceptible breaths through your nose. After a while your beating heart will settle down.

Go with the flow. Watch the eyes of your audience. Are they absorbing what you are saying?

Make sure you know your material or you will panic.

2.2 Practice

You would never appear in a play in the West End or on Broadway without practising your lines. Rehearsals are crucial.

I am amazed by the number of advocates who turn up in court without practising what they are going to say. You really have to hear it coming out of your mouth first. Churchill practised his speeches for days until they sounded just right. You don't have to know it word for word. You can always check your notes at the end to make sure that you have not missed anything. The judge will understand if you ask for a moment to do so. Most of them have been in your position themselves.

Ill-prepared, nervous and lazy advocates tend to rely heavily on notes. This gives the speaker the confidence that they will not forget what they are going to say, but it is at the expense of being persuasive.

First, reading tends to make you speak more quickly. It's like the swimming sports at school. The reader wants to get from one end of the pool to the other in as short a time as possible. For the nervous advocate, this only makes their adrenaline-fuelled problem worse.

Second, what is the point of reading to the court? Judges can read for themselves. If you are going to read, you might as well save your breath and rely only on written submissions.

Third, if you are reading you are looking down at the paper in front of you and not at the judge. Many people who read tend to fall into a dull monotone. If you are not making eye contact and not varying your voice, you are not communicating effectively. You are losing the opportunity to persuade.

Practising thoroughly what you want to say will give you the confidence to speak without detailed notes. You may not say every sentence quite as you prepared it, but you will be a lot more convincing. A good idea when you practise is to put your speech into very large, well-spaced bullet points which you can glance at from time to time as you speak. This will remind you of the structure of your speech without the temptation to read.

Sir Patrick Hastings KC never used notes and nor did his pupils. As a struggling young man, he sought pupillage in the chambers of the formidable Theobald Matthew KC. Matthew did not take pupils, but Hastings persisted. When Matthew asked what Hastings could do to help, Hastings replied that he would be able to take a good note of Matthew's conferences.

Matthew was disdainful, saying he had never taken a note in his life. Hastings got the job but followed suit. He trained his memory to become prodigious.

Not all of us can be Patrick Hastings, but I can assure you of this, if you don't rely on detailed notes, you will be forced to rely on your brain. You will have to think before you speak and it will slow you down. You will make eye contact with the judge because you will be looking up instead of reading. You will be more persuasive as a result.

You only need detailed notes if you are dealing with something incredibly technical. Or, horror of horrors, if you don't know your case.

2.3 Stance and gestures

Judges, arbitration panels and juries sum you up in the first 10 seconds. And it is amazing how often first impressions remain.

So, you must dress neatly, tidy your hair, straighten your tie, adjust your wig if you are a barrister and look the part.

You also need to centre yourself. Stand up straight. Imagine that a point inside you about two inches below your belly button is the centre of your body.

Relax your shoulders and let your arms fall by your sides. Your feet should come apart, a bit further than normal so that your ankles are parallel with your shoulders. Make sure your feet are flat on the floor.

You should feel properly balanced and your weight should be evenly distributed. You can stand in this position for a long time.

Now bring your hands up to your lower stomach and rest one hand gently on the other. This position is called 'actor neutral'. It is from this position that you can begin and return.

Let your hands move freely as you speak. Don't become too conscious of them. By the same token don't wave them around because it is distracting. Confine your gestures to an 18-inch square box in front of your stomach.

Telling the court there are three reasons for your submissions and touching a finger in turn is much more persuasive than clasping your hands tightly behind your back or gripping your lapels.

Stance is important to good speakers. It creates authority. Remember President Barack Obama's style. He never slouched. Public speaking is first and foremost creating an impression on your audience. Standing still is easier if you are centred or planted. It also makes it easier to breathe and to watch your audience.

You can also centre yourself when you are sitting. Make sure your back is straight. It depends on the size of your chair. Don't sink into it because you will squash your voice and look too casual. You should sit at the front edge of the chair.

It works in meetings, too. You want to look like you own the room.

Once you have achieved a still, centred stance, stay there. In common law courts, you are not really allowed to move around and in arbitration hearings you remain seated.

A lot of comedians walk up and down the stage when they perform. Sometimes they move very quickly. It is distracting. If moving around annoys the judge, don't do it. You do not want to place obstacles in your own way as you seek to persuade the court.

Try to avoid any other gestures which may distract the judge. Put down your pen when you are speaking, to avoid fiddling with it. Don't hold any papers in your hands. Apart from the risk of disclosing nerves, they also form a barrier between you and the judge.

In all the years I have been teaching, I have noticed a clear correlation between those who don't move their hands and those who speak in a monotone. Gestures bring our voices to life. Just watch people in everyday communication. Everyone uses their hands.

The other thing to note is that if you suppress the movement of your hands the adrenaline will seek to escape from another part of your body. Your legs will jiggle or your shoulders will twitch.

Remember, stance and gesture are vital tools in the art of persuasion. You are not hidden from the audience. They are assessing everything about you.

2.4 Timing

Have you noticed how the celebrated cricketers, golfers, tennis players and pianists seem to do everything at just the right speed? It is almost as if they have loads of time to do things we would find impossible to do.

The elegant Pakistani batsman Majid Khan would face a hard cricket ball being hurled 22 yards away at nearly 100 miles per hour, yet he seemed to have all the time in the world to get into position and hit it for four. He was truly majestic.

Great comedians know the importance of timing and so do actors. They wait to deliver the punch line. They wait for the laughter to subside before speaking again. Their pace is perfect. Watch President Ronald Reagan deliver the Challenger disaster speech. The virtuoso pianist Arthur Schnabel said many people could play the notes of a piano concerto but it 'is in the pauses where the art resides'.

It is the same in court. Sir Rodger Bell, a former High Court judge, used to say 'I haven't heard what you are saying before. I need sinking in time.'

You want the judge to absorb the point before you move on. You can do this in two ways:

1 deliver your speech in small bite-sized phrases or chunks; and

2 watch for any reaction from the listeners.

The Americans call the delivering of speeches in small pieces 'chunking'. It's an unattractive word, but it's accurate and it's memorable.

President Obama is a fan of chunking. Watch one of his speeches. Sometimes, he overdoes it and it becomes an irritation, but generally he has a superb delivery.

The other advantage of chunking is that the chunk can be easily absorbed and remembered then written down by the listener.

I am sure you had lecturers or teachers who spoke so you could make notes of what was said. They were, no doubt, chunking.

I would only recommend the technique for public speakers or teachers. Don't do it in the pub. Imagine saying to your friend 'I'm going to buy you a drink. It will be wine. Sauvignon Blanc. Because I know you like Sauvignon Blanc'.

You would soon find yourself without friends.

Another way of expressing point 2 above is to 'let the penny drop'. I see many students who make a point then immediately look down at their notes. They do not take the crucial opportunity to see how their point has gone over with the court. Nor are they saying to the court, with their eyes, 'Did you like that Your Honour? It was important wasn't it?'

This idea of watching the audience and gauging your impact is crucial. Think of anyone you know who is a good story teller. They watch everyone. They make sure everyone has heard the set-up to the story before they deliver the punch line. They take it very seriously. If people aren't paying attention or there are distractions, the story falls flat. It loses its impact. They take no chances.

2.5 Sounding convinced

Effective public speakers sound convinced, which makes them convincing. They watch the listeners and change the tone of their voice to add to the impact. Try saying the following words in a monotone voice. 'I am sure, ladies and gentlemen of the jury, you'll agree. The evidence is weak. My client is innocent.'

If you speak like this, your client is going down. There are a number of drills to help to practise changing your tone. The best is to repeat the phrase 'Nobody cares what you think'. Each time you say it, emphasise or hang on to a different word. You will see how the meaning can change.

Sounding convinced also gives the impression to your listeners that you know a lot about the subject and are reliable. But this is not all. There must be something in what you say that strikes a chord with the audience.

But there is another side to the coin.

I love the story told by Justice Laskin about the politician who spoke passionately in Parliament for two hours. Someone asked later what he had spoken about and one of the listeners said 'I don't know actually. He didn't say.'[9]

2.6 Paying attention

Judge Mark Drummond delivers an excellent presentation about what audiences pay attention to. He believes they take notice of things in the following order:

1. Actions – if there is a sparrow flying around the auditorium, it doesn't matter what you say. Even though everyone has seen a sparrow before, its actions will always trump what you are saying.
2. Objects – the murder weapon is always the centre of attention.
3. Pictures.

---

9 Laskin, 'What persuades …' (fn 2).

4 Diagrams or charts.

5 The written word.

6 The spoken word.

For these reasons, Judge Drummond advises that when you have finished speaking about an object or looking at a diagram, put it away.

He says that people process information in three main ways:

1 Visual – I see what you mean.

2 Auditory – I hear what you say.

3 Kinaesthetic – this does not feel right.

Good advocates know this instinctively and ask their own witnesses questions such as 'What did you see?', 'What did you hear?' and 'What did you feel?'

I agree with this approach, but I also believe that you must use the technique which makes the point you are putting most memorable.

2.7 The digital age

The law often takes many years to catch up, but judges now have laptops, and documents are arranged by sophisticated computer programmes. You don't have to be Ludwig Wittgenstein to know that courtrooms will soon be dominated by technology.

There were once strict evidentiary rules about showing maps, photographs and documents to a court. These will be relaxed as the equipment becomes more reliable and time is saved.

Online hearings have also introduced specific considerations regarding the use of technology, including the display of documents and other evidence. This is addressed in Chapter 6, 'Online Advocacy'.

A clear and accurate digital representation can be a powerful persuasive tool.

It is crucial that you master the skills in advance and practise your performance so that it runs without a hitch. Arrive at the venue early or practise in the room the night before. Have an IT expert on hand if things go wrong.

I am not a big fan of PowerPoint presentations. Studies have shown that people learn little from them. It's not surprising. The same could be said for TV programmes.

With PowerPoint presentations, you might remember the odd picture or diagram or that the creator of the presentation was able to get a number of letters to fly in from the side, but there is precious little else which will be absorbed and remembered.

I used to work with a lecturer who spent days preparing his PowerPoint slides. Then he would deliver his presentation for six hours with a break for lunch, slide after slide, to his hapless classes.

An average presentation from him comprised 180 slides. His nickname amongst the other teachers was 'Death by Slide'.

He must have had an inkling that people thought him boring because about half way through the show, pictures of his family and him on holiday would appear. But the inkling played no deterrent role.

There are a number of other problems with PowerPoint. Users seem to fill each slide with information and then read it to the audience word for word as if they were blind. And I cannot recall an occasion when there hasn't been a hitch in setting up the equipment or the speaker has pressed the wrong button and skipped a slide or two during the show.

PowerPoint, if it is used at all, should assist the presentation, not dominate it.

Make sure each slide is simple and easy to read. Don't clutter it with silly pictures or quotes or writing that is hard to digest. Are the colours easy to absorb?

Don't use it as a script because the audience can read. Your job is to develop and illustrate the points you make. You as the presenter should be the centre of attention, not the slide show.

You can always hand out a hard copy of your presentation later.

If you wish to deliver a PowerPoint presentation to a court or tribunal, make sure you tell your opponent well in advance. Get the consent of the other parties and the approval of the decision-maker.

Don't break the flow or derail the hearing by causing an argument on the admissibility of your presentation. Trial by ambush rarely works.

Above all, take pains to ensure that what you are presenting complies with the rules (in the case of a court or tribunal) and is fair, reliable and accurate.

Speaking of Wittgenstein, his celebrated aphorism, 'Whereof one cannot speak, thereof one must remain silent' is sound advice in any company, but it aptly describes the power of properly presented visual evidence.[10]

2.8 Sender – message – receiver

This brings me to what I think is the most useful observation about public speaking.[11]

The average speaker focuses on himself. Have I done enough preparation? How do I look? I am so nervous. I hate public speaking. What if I fail? I am the partner in charge. They will listen to me. I am the expert in this area – I'll be compelling.

The better speaker concentrates on the message. What is it that I want to say? How much should I include? Should I use illustrations? Have I covered everything about the subject?

---

10 'Tractatus Logico-Philosophicus', *Wikipedia*, https://en.wikipedia.org/wiki/Tractatus_Logico-Philosophicus.

11 Again, I am indebted to Judge Mark Drummond. To whom he is indebted, I don't know.

Think about flight attendants. They just want to get through the announcement as quickly as they can. They don't think about its purpose – safety – even though they use the expression, 'We are here primarily for your safety'.

If they did think about its purpose they would make sure the passengers absorbed what they were saying.

The best speaker focuses on the receivers – her audience. What will get them thinking? How can I make that happen easily? Is it the right length? What will hold their attention?[12]

If you spend time thinking about the audience, the self-consciousness, arrogance or nerves experienced by the average speaker will disappear.

The observation is so good that I don't need to say any more.

3 PRESENTATION SKILLS: CHECKLIST

3.1 Preparation

- Research your subject properly.
- Think of a message or a theme.
- Think of your audience.
- Write down at random every point you wish to make.
- Put them into a logical order.
- Include ideas for short stories and illustrations.
- Think of a memorable beginning and end.
- Write out the entire presentation (this is optional).
- Use simple words and picture words.
- Reduce it.

---

12 The brother of the Duke of Wellington was a perfectionist who apparently was never happy until he had delivered the finest speech in the House of Lords. Wellington said, 'Now there, I think, he was wrong. The thing to think of is not one's speech, but one's object'.

- Reduce it again.
- Put it into large bold, block-lettered bullet points.
- Practise your speech at least once.
- Visit the venue beforehand or get there early on the day.
- Make sure the visual aids and the equipment work.

3.2 Delivery

- Make sure you can be seen and heard by everyone in the room.
- Centre yourself.
- Wait for the audience to settle down.
- Ignore distractions such as latecomers, but stop speaking until the distraction has gone.
- Take a deep imperceptible breath.
- Smile.
- Grab the attention of your audience in the first 10 seconds.
- Speak in bite-sized chunks, more slowly than usual.
- Watch the audience: are they absorbing what you say?
- Get rid of things that take the attention from your speech, such as pens or mannerisms.
- Don't read.
- Glance at your bullet points.
- Sound interested in your topic.
- Vary your tone of voice and stress or linger on the important words. Take your time.
- Never apologise for your deficiencies.
- Don't end with 'thank you' or 'that's all'.
- End with your message.
- If appropriate, smile again.

Chapter 2
The Qualities of a Good Advocate

For this chapter, I take as my template a speech made in Birmingham in 1954 by Lord Birkett.[1] He identified a number of characteristics that an advocate should seek to develop.

Obviously, some people may not possess certain characteristics at all, and no amount of reading or training is going to succeed in creating them.

It is also clear that few advocates have all the qualities: some, such as integrity, are essential; others, such as a good voice, are desirable.

Lord Birkett spoke of the following characteristics of the advocate's art.

1 INTEGRITY

As soon as an advocate gets to her feet, a court must be able to assume that what she will say is honest and reliable. The advocate must be a person of good character: the court must be able to rely upon the advocate's word.

Lord Birkett speaks of the temptations of ignoring duties. Lawyers are given great power – they can sue people; they can totally disrupt or ruin lives. But with these powers come corresponding duties.

---

1 Presidential Address to the Holdsworth Club in Birmingham in May 1954, quoted in H Montgomery Hyde, *Norman Birkett: The Life of Lord Birkett of Ulverston* (Hamish Hamilton, London, 1965) 551–554.

The administration of justice and the rule of law are essential to a healthy, safe democracy; and advocates play a crucial part in this. As Birkett puts it:

> '… it is essential that there should always be men of honour and uprightness who make the profession of law their livelihood, trained to defend and to plead for the citizen, and zealously guard his rights, his liberties and if need be, his life.'

2 A GOOD VOICE

Not all of us have a good voice to begin with, but with practice it is possible to improve.

Ask people to tell you frankly if your voice needs work. No one likes watching or listening to themselves played back on audio or visual recordings, but it can be quite instructive.

If your voice is annoying – if it is too high or you can penetrate brick walls – you must train it to deepen and become more pleasant.

If the decision-maker is irritated by your voice, much of your good work in producing and delivering submissions will be wasted.

To Birkett, the advocate must speak to be heard, articulate clearly and acquire tone and modulation. For an advocate, he says, 'the spoken word is the breath of life, and it is quite astonishing that … so little thought is given to it.'

You can learn about voice deepening, pronunciation, articulation and projection from many books for actors.[2] However, nothing beats practice.

Margaret Thatcher was trained to deepen her voice because it was considered that her 'shrill' tone put voters off. She was not precious about the advice she was given.[3]

---

2 See Cicely Berry, *Your Voice and How to Use It* (Virgin Books, London, 2000).

3 Charles Moore, *Margaret Thatcher: The Authorized Biography*, Volume One (Allen Lane, London, 2013) 309.

3 PRESENCE

This is a very hard thing to achieve. Some people naturally have presence. Others do not. I suppose one's dignity or bearing helps: straightening your shoulders; centring yourself; looking around the room at the people in it; speaking slowly and carefully while remaining calm and reasonable.

Achieving presence does not depend necessarily on being tall. A lot of people who are tall tend to stoop, perhaps so that they do not draw attention to themselves. That's the whole point: a good advocate *does* draw attention to himself, but only for the right reasons.

Many skilful advocates – Sir Garfield Barwick QC and George Carman QC spring to mind – were not tall, but they still commanded the courtroom.

Presence is often achieved simply by being recognisable. Think of public figures, actors, singers and politicians who you have seen in the street or pubs. They gain their presence because people recognise them for who they are and what they have achieved.

But you can acquire a dignified air without being pompous. Practise keeping a straight face when you hear something funny. Don't do it all the time or you won't have any friends. Stand up straight. Don't slouch. Don't talk too quickly.

4 A QUICK ADAPTABLE MIND

Lord Birkett said:

> 'It is well if the advocate is possessed of a quick mind, alert to seize the unexpected opportunity, to adapt himself to the sudden changes which occur in the conduct of a case, and to be ready to deal with any interventions from the Bench, whether they can be disconcerting or helpful.'

In Oscar Wilde's case, the advocate Sir Edward Carson proved himself extremely adept in this regard.

This is how his cross-examination of Wilde began:

Carson:	'You stated at the commencement of your examination that you were thirty-nine years of age. I think you are over forty, isn't that so?'
Wilde:	'I don't think so. I think I am either thirty-nine or forty – forty my next birthday. If you have my certificate there that settles the matter.'
Carson:	'You were born, I believe, upon the 16th October 1854? [It was then the 3rd April 1895]'
Wilde:	'Yes, I have no intention of posing as a younger man at all. I will try to be correct in the date.'
Carson:	'It makes you somewhat over forty.'
Wilde:	'Very well.'

Carson had caught Wilde lying about his age – a lie of vanity some might say – but it was his first answer in cross-examination.

But then he used the lie to press home his advantage:

Carson:	'May I ask you, do you happen to know what age Lord Alfred Douglas was or is?'
Wilde:	'Lord Alfred Douglas was, I think, twenty-four his last birthday. I think he will be twenty-five on his next birthday.'
Carson:	'May I take it that when you knew him first, he was something about twenty or twenty-one?'
Wilde:	'Yes.'

That little passage,[4] on the basis that people tend to remember the first and last things they hear, was powerful. It established that Wilde was prepared to lie under oath, and it demonstrated the large age difference between Wilde and Alfred Douglas. Carson's theme was that his client, the Marquess of Queensberry (the father of Lord Alfred Douglas) did all he could to save his son from this man. But it also showed Carson's adaptable mind, which allowed him to demonstrate to the court the following: Carson is accurate and therefore reliable. Wilde is not.

5 KNOWLEDGE OF HUMAN NATURE

I think this is very important. An advocate should be self-aware, but also aware of others. A lot of lawyers are self-aware to the point of narcissism. They have no idea of the effect of what they do or say has on others.

A good advocate knows the judge; knows her opponents; knows her client and the witnesses – not in the sense of being an acquaintance, but in being able to predict with some certainty how each will react to various things the advocate does. This is called empathy. However, it is more than this because it involves watching everyone carefully. Is the judge interested in what I am saying? Is she looking unhappy? Bored? Anxious? What is her previous behaviour? Is she behaving as she normally does? Are all 12 members of the jury fast asleep?

Emotion is something that often appeals to juries, but it should be subtle. Judges are trained with legal and forensic skills to put emotion to one side.

---

4 H Montgomery Hyde, *The Trials of Oscar Wilde* (William Hodge & Co, Glasgow, 1960) 120.

6 COURAGE

The former President of the Supreme Court, Lord Neuberger, delivered the Seckford Lecture on 18 October 2012. His topic was Lord Erskine and Trial by Jury.[5]

Erskine is generally regarded as one of the finest advocates in the history of the English Bar.

Lord Neuberger examines four cases in which Erskine appeared. One was his first trial where the Lord Chief Justice, Lord Mansfield, warned Erskine about attacking the First Lord of the Admiralty in his speech – but he did so anyway.

Erskine displayed 'the courage, and the judgement which are possessed by only the best advocates'.[6]

When Erskine was briefed to defend Thomas Paine on a charge of seditious libel, he was urged to hand back the brief. The Prince of Wales, for whom Erskine was retained as Attorney-General, sacked him for continuing to appear for Paine.

In a famous defence of the role of an advocate, Erskine addressed the jury:

> 'From the moment that any advocate can be permitted to say that he will or will not stand between the Crown and the subject arraigned in the court where he daily sits to practise, from that moment the liberties of England are at an end. If the advocate refuses to defend, from what he may think of the charge or of the defence, he assumes the character of the judge.'[7]

---

5 Lord Neuberger, 'Lord Erskine and Trial by Jury' (Seckford Lecture, Woodbridge School, 18 October 2012), https://supremecourt.uk/uploads/speech_ 121018_547b652fdd.pdf.

6 Ibid, 14.

7 Ibid, 31.

Being courageous does not mean being offensive. Advocates who stand their ground may think they are being brave, but what if the court has already ruled on the point?

It is a question of judgement and involves emotional intelligence and listening. There is no point in flogging a dead horse, but nor does there seem to be any reason to waste the court's time.

As Walter Monckton, the distinguished English barrister said:

> 'Don't forget your job at the Bar is to persuade that old man sitting up there that you are right. Be flexible. Don't be tied to your note. But watch him like a lynx. Try to get inside his head and follow his train of thought. Deal with the points that are troubling him.'[8]

Another famous barrister, FE Smith, later Lord Birkenhead, was quite pleased with his ability to be rude to judges. But this is not to be confused with courage or fearlessness. At the outset, I say you should not try to copy Smith's rudeness.

Smith's best friend was a fellow called Winston Churchill. He wrote of the exchange that took place between Smith and Judge Willis in the Southwark County Court:

> 'A boy who had been run over was suing a tramway for damages. FE appeared for the company. The case for the lad was that the accident had led to blindness. The judge, a kindly and somewhat garrulous soul, allowed sympathy to outrun discretion.
>
> "Poor boy, poor boy!" he exclaimed. "Blind! Put him on a chair so the jury can see him."
>
> This was weighting the scales of justice and FE was moved to protest.
>
> "Perhaps your honour would like to have the boy passed round the jury box," he suggested.

---

8 First Lord Birkenhead, *Walter Monckton* (Weidenfeld & Nicolson, London, 1969) 74. Reproduced with permission of the licensor through PLS Clear.

> "That is a most improper remark," exclaimed the judge.
>
> "It was provoked by a most improper suggestion," was the startling reply.
>
> Judge Willis tried to think of a decisive retort. At last it arrived.
>
> "Mr Smith, have you ever heard of a saying by Bacon – the great Bacon – that youth and discretion are ill-wedded companions?"
>
> "Yes, I have," came the instant repartee, "And have you ever heard of a saying of Bacon – the great Bacon – that a much-talking judge is like an ill-tuned cymbal?"
>
> "You are extremely offensive, young man," exclaimed the judge.
>
> "As a matter of fact," said Smith, "we both are; but I am trying to be, and you can't help it."'[9]

Churchill refers to these as 'successive rejoinders, each one more smashing than the former', but Smith's biographer, John Campbell casts doubt on some of the FE Smith remarks, citing one of the barrister's colleagues:

> 'A good many of the paeans of victory were figments of his own imagination. He would invent incidents which never occurred, in order to introduce some especially neat repartee which had subsequently flashed into his mind, too late for actual use, but too good not to be retailed to his admiring audience.'[10]

When I was a young man, I saw a barrister appearing for the defence in contested committal proceedings.

---

9 John Campbell, *FE Smith* (Jonathan Cape, London, 1983) 113. Anecdote also quoted in Winston Churchill, *Great Contemporaries* (Revised Edition, Thornton Butterworth Ltd, London, 1938) 176.

10 John Campbell, *FE Smith* (Jonathan Cape, London, 1983) 113.

During the morning session he insulted the judge on several occasions. In the break, I asked him why and he said because the judge is an idiot and you have to spoon-feed him.

I asked, rather impertinently, because I was much younger than the barrister, 'But don't you want the judge to refuse to commit your client for trial?'

Even then, I don't think it had dawned on him.

A judge in Australia was appealed against successfully for refusing to grant adjournments in certain immigration cases. In fairness, the judge was faced with very long lists.

Here is a short transcript of what occurred in the hearing. It aptly demonstrates the difference between counsel being rude and counsel being courageous:

His Honour:	'I fix the matter for hearing at 9:30am on Tuesday 12 June – sorry – Tuesday 9 June – 9:30 on Tuesday 9 June …'
Counsel:	'Well, Your Honour that's not going to give the applicant any time to prepare for the case. We don't get the court book until the 11th. So there's a chance we won't be in a position to proceed on that date.'
His Honour:	'Well, you'd better be ready, Counsel.'
Counsel:	'Well …'
His Honour:	'Because I won't adjourn it.'
Counsel:	'… Your Honour, there is a …'
His Honour:	'Counsel, you …'
Counsel:	'Your Honour, there are procedural …'
His Honour:	'Counsel …'
Counsel:	'… requirements to have the matter ready for hearing …'
His Honour:	'Counsel, sit down, please.'

Counsel:	'Well, for the transcript, Your Honour.'
His Honour:	'No, no. Sit down …'
Counsel:	'I think it's important …'
His Honour:	'… sit down – sit down, Counsel …'
Counsel:	'… that Your Honour takes note …'
His Honour:	'Counsel. Sit down.'
Counsel:	'… of the procedural requirements in this court.'
His Honour:	'Counsel, if you engage in talking over me again, I will have you removed. Sit down.'
Counsel:	'I will indicate to the court that …'
His Honour:	'No. Please, Counsel, comply …'
Counsel:	'… an application will be made for an …'
His Honour:	'… with what I've said …'
Counsel:	'… adjournment on that day.'
His Honour:	'… Sit down, Counsel, now. Please.'
Counsel:	'Yes, that was for the transcript, Your Honour.'
His Honour:	'Sit down now, Counsel. Your repeated rising to your feet and not complying with my direction is a contempt of court. If you engage in it again, I will have you dealt with for contempt. Do you understand that?'
Counsel:	'May it please Your Honour.'
His Honour:	'I direct the applicant to file and serve any amended application and any affidavit evidence upon which the applicant wishes to rely, together with submissions, by 2 June. The respondent is to file any affidavit in reply and any submissions on which it wishes to reply by 7 June.'
Counsel:	'If the court pleases.'
His Honour:	'Counsel, this is a very busy list. It requires counsel, solicitors and applicants to assist the court in dealing with the list. I really won't

	tolerate the behaviour that you've engaged in just recently. You must cooperate with the court. I understand your desire to advance your client's case but you must do so consistently with the directions made by the court.'
Counsel:	'Can I be heard on that, Your Honour?'
His Honour:	'No.'[11]

In the examples quoted, counsel was courageous and polite. FE Smith was not. (The judge, in this exchange, used counsel's name but I have made him anonymous.)

7 WELL-MANNERED AND IN CONTROL OF TEMPER

Norman Birkett was the epitome of good manners. His clerk of 20 years, AE Bowker, wrote:

> 'Never once did I know him to enter a court without a perfect thorough knowledge of his brief. Nor can I recall any occasion when he had "words" with the Bench or his opponent. Neither, indeed, can I recollect any witness whom he did not treat with courtesy and politeness, even though he might challenge the evidence they gave.'[12]

Of Walter Monckton, Lord Salmon said, 'He was quiet and courteous, but deadly and the victim would emerge discredited without knowing it or realising he had been destroyed.' Monckton's:

> 'manners were impeccable. He never played to the gallery in order to be reported in the press, and unlike Marshall-Hall and other of that generation [he] never tried tricks on his opponent

---

11 Transcript, Ratu Pio Tikovakayalewa Kautoga and Minister for Immigration and Border Protection, Sydney, 28 May 2015, 9:43 am to 9:49 am.

12 AE Bowker, *Behind the Bar* (Staples Press, London, 1947).

> and could be implicitly trusted. He was never rude to witnesses and was adept at keeping the judge in a good mood.'[13]

There is a temptation for many smart young lawyers to see the adversarial system as a points-scoring exercise. There is no denying that to some extent it is, and obviously if your case has strengths and your opponent's case has weaknesses, this should be pointed out. But you should refrain from the desire to make personal attacks on your opponent.

Few judges enjoy bickering between counsel. Intimidation, by virtue of seniority or superior skill, rarely works. It might make the advocate feel empowered for a short while, but that doesn't last. Making enemies unnecessarily is never a good idea.

If you are under a personal attack from a cranky judge, try not to react in kind. Be passive and polite. Think of how it will look on the transcript.

As demonstrated by Walter Monckton and Norman Birkett, a calm, unflappable temperament is an asset in any courtroom.

8 KNOWLEDGE OF THE FACTS AND THE LAW

In his Birmingham address, Birkett said:

> 'the advocate must have made himself master of all the facts; he must have a thorough understanding of the principles and rules of law … and the ability to apply them on the instant; he must gauge with accuracy the atmosphere of the Court in which he pleads and adapt himself accordingly; he must be able to reason from the facts and the law to achieve the end he desires, and he must above all have mastered the art of expressing himself clearly and persuasively …'[14]

---

13 Lord Birkenhead, *Walter Monckton* (fn 8) 74. Reproduced with permission of the licensor through PLS Clear.

14 Hyde, *Norman Birkett* (fn 1) 553–554.

In summary, the successful advocate must possess all the attributes which Lord Birkett mentions and be able to work long but efficient hours.

One of Australia's best advocates, Thomas Eyre Forrest Hughes KC, set out what he saw as the important qualities of a good barrister, 'integrity, courage, competence, resilience and the ability to react to fast-moving situations in litigation'.

To them, he added a need for objectivity, tact, courtesy towards the judge and one's opponents. He highlighted a primary duty, 'complete candour and complete honesty'. It was better to bring a problem in argument to the fore than try to hide it.[15]

The successful advocate must know the facts backwards and apply the law to the facts.

She must know and understand what the decision-maker has to do and how he thinks.

There must be time, as former High Court Judge Sir John Alliott once told my class, for the advocate to brood.

Then the advocate must rehearse what she is going to say, but not learn it by heart.

Lastly, when she gets to her feet in court, she must set out the problem and the solution, and show the decision-maker how to arrive at the decision she wants.

In short, she must be credible, knowledgeable, helpful, nimble and persuasive.

9 NORMAN BIRKETT'S CHECKLIST

- Integrity.
- A good voice.

---

[15] Ian Hancock, *Tom Hughes QC* (Federation Press, Sydney, 2016) 350.

- Presence.
- A quick, adaptable mind.
- Knowledge of human nature.
- Courage.
- Well-mannered and in control of temper.
- Knowledge of the facts and the law.

Chapter 3
Professional Conduct

A dishonest advocate is a pox on the administration of justice.

In the House of Lords, Lord Diplock said:

> 'The acceptance of the Rule of Law as a constitutional principle requires that a citizen, before committing himself to any course of action, should be able to know in advance ... the legal principles that flow from it.'[1]

The system of justice is a series of inter-dependent relationships between various groups: investigative bodies; solicitors; courts; experts; media; clients; and advocates.

An advocate who is untrustworthy not only lets down those who are in direct contact with him, but he also causes a lack of trust in the community of advocates, especially in the eyes of the community at large.

In some respects, we can tolerate the occasional lapse of competence in advocates, but we can never accept a lapse of honesty.

The judge, above all, should be able to rely upon what the advocate says. His word is his bond.

It is in everyone's interests to have honest advocates. If we don't, the administration of justice is in peril.

---

1 *Black-Clawson International Ltd v Papierwerke Waldorf-Aschaffenberg* [1975] AC 591, 638.

1 THE ADVOCATE'S DUTY

The best summary of the advocate's duty was presented by Lord Denning in the case of *Rondel v Worsley*.[2] It's an interesting case because, when it got to the House of Lords, a barrister's immunity for acts of negligence committed in court was upheld. It has since been overturned by the case of *Hall v Simons*[3] on the issue of a barrister's immunity. Nonetheless, it still contains excellent advice.

But Lord Denning was writing in the Court of Appeal and his lucid prose will give you the main duties and responsibilities of the advocate in a nutshell:

> 'As an advocate he is a minister of justice equally with the judge. He has a monopoly of audience in the higher courts. No one save he can address the judge, unless it be a litigant in person.
>
> This carries with it a corresponding responsibility. A barrister cannot pick and choose his clients. He is bound to accept a brief for any man who comes before the courts. No matter how great a rascal the man may be. No matter how given to complaining. No matter how undeserving or unpopular his cause. The barrister must defend him until the end.
>
> Provided only that he is paid a proper fee, or in the case of a dock brief, a nominal fee.
>
> He must accept the brief and do all he honourably can on behalf of his client. I say, "all he honourably can" because his duty is not only to his client. He has a duty to the court which is paramount. It is a mistake to suppose he is the mouthpiece of his client to say what he wants: or his tool to do what he directs. He is none of these things.
>
> He owes an allegiance to a higher cause. It is the cause of justice and truth. He must not consciously mis-state the facts. He must not knowingly conceal the truth. He must not unjustly make a charge of fraud, that is, without evidence to support it. He must produce all the relevant authorities, even those that are

---

2 [1966] 3 All ER 657.

3 [2000] 3 All ER 673.

> against him. He must see that his client discloses, if ordered, the relevant documents, even those that are fatal to his case.
>
> He must disregard the most specific instructions of his client, if they conflict with his duty to the court. The code which requires a barrister to do all this is not a code of law. It is a code of honour. If he breaks it, he is offending against the rules of the profession and is subject to its discipline.'[4]

2 RULES OF CONDUCT

The barrister in England is bound by the Code of Conduct, which can be found on the website of the Bar Standards Board. It is shorter than it used to be. So is the Code of Conduct for Solicitors, which is found on the website of the Solicitors Regulation Authority.

The latest fad is with something called Outcomes Focused Regulation, a phrase which is as obscure as it is ugly.

Solicitors who consult the rules will encounter a series of Principles, Outcomes and Indicative Behaviours. The word 'behaviours' does not appear in the dictionary yet.

Nevertheless, barristers and solicitors must consult the rules wherever they encounter an ethical problem. Quite a lot of practitioners do not recognise when there is an ethical problem, or if they do, they endeavour to do all in their power to get around it or mitigate its effect.

There are two informal tests for recognising an ethical problem. They have varying degrees of efficacy and depend to a large extent on the character of the person employing them.

The first is the Motherhood Test. When faced with a problem you ask yourself, 'Would my mother have said that what I am about to do is wrong?'

The vast majority of us know what is right and what is wrong. It is how we were brought up. It is deeply embedded in our conscience and never goes away.

---

4 *Rondel v Worsley* (1966) 3 WLR 950.

The second is the Fish Test. Ask yourself, 'Does it smell fishy?', because, if it does, it probably is.

The next decision, after you have concluded that you have an ethical problem, is what to do about it.

Whatever you do, do not suffer in silence. Don't carry the burden yourself because it can become intolerable. When in doubt, ask someone, and preferably not the person who is asking you to do it.

First, consult the rules. There is guidance in the Codes of Conduct and the decided cases. Another independent senior practitioner, a well-regarded barrister or a retired judge will always be glad to help you. They don't want to see their profession fall into disrepute.

3 YOUR INSTRUCTIONS

When you make your decision, you must tell the person who is most affected, and it is usually your client. Say that you are bound by the rules of professional conduct. Tell the client, he is entitled to a second opinion.

If the client insists on you going ahead with the unethical behaviour, you must decline to act for him further. At this ultimatum, a client will usually back off.

But you should protect yourself. If you don't trust your client, always see him in the presence of a colleague. Get him to acknowledge and sign your advice. Use your head and watch your back.

If the person asking you to do something unethical is your superior or boss, don't go rushing to inform on her to the Regulator. Give her a chance. Explain the rules to her but do it with tact. She may be unaware of, or have forgotten, the rules on this point.

Whatever you think at the time: one client is not worth your whole career. Nor is one boss.

Professional conduct is often about common sense. What happens if your client is in the witness box and tells what appears to be a lie about a sequence of events? Let us say your client is under cross-examination when the statement is made.

Do you get to your feet and announce to the court that your client has just told a lie?

No, you do not and for a lot of reasons. Even though you believe the court is being misled and, if you remain silent, you are taking part in an active misleading of the court, you would not be doing anyone a service by accusing your client of the criminal offence of perjury in open court.

First, you must ask yourself whether it really is a lie. Or has your client muddled the details or just made a mistake?

Second, can you fix the mistake in re-examination? For example:

Question:	'You were asked in cross-examination about when you spoke to Mr Smith? You replied it was the 14th May which is a Tuesday. Why did you say that date?'
Answer:	'Did I say that? I'm sorry, I meant Wednesday the 15th.'

If the answer is, 'Because that is the date', you must ask yourself whether the date is a material issue. Then it might be serious.

Or, let us say your client has told you in advance that he is going to lie about the date in the witness box.

You should never accuse your client of a crime in open court.

Wait until he is out of the witness box. If the court is adjourning for lunch or a tea break, your task will be easier, but if not, you must ask the court for a short adjournment in order to speak privately to your client.

Make it clear to your client that unless he goes back into the witness box and corrects his evidence, you will no longer be able to appear for him.

Most clients, faced with that dilemma, will not wish to see their lawyer bailing out on them and will correct the error.

The important thing is that you do not inform on your client in the court. You simply seek permission to withdraw on the grounds of professional embarrassment.

There will be complications enough for your client such as having to ask the judge for an adjournment to get another lawyer.

Many people think this is an unsatisfactory arrangement: that by simply withdrawing from the case the lawyer will not be making sure that the witness is telling the truth. But it is better than the lawyer betraying his client and abandoning him. The lawyer is not the judge. By withdrawing he will not take part in the active misleading of the court, but at least the client has been given a chance to correct the false evidence.

As Lord Denning said, counsel is not the mouthpiece of the client. Unless there are valid reasons to put certain questions, you must be careful you do not abuse your role as an advocate.

This includes making statements or asking questions designed merely to insult, humiliate or annoy a witness or any other person. I once heard an advocate say to a police officer who he was cross-examining, 'Your sister is a prostitute and she lives in Melbourne?'

Apart from the problem with the compound question and the latter part being bafflingly unrelated to the first part, the question was put on the instructions of the client, who wanted to unsettle the witness.

It was a bad question and it was an unethical question. Counsel was rightly rebuked by the judge.

It is also necessary for counsel to refrain from making a serious allegation about the witness after the cross-examination has concluded, unless the witness was given a chance to answer the allegation in cross-examination.

Thus, if you wanted to say in your speech that the witness took money from your client (or your client wants to say it in evidence), you must put that allegation to the witness during cross-examination. You will no doubt get a denial, but you will have done your duty.

In *Giannarelli v Wraith*, Mason CJ warned in the High Court of Australia against counsel engaging in irrelevant cross-examination or pursuing unarguable submissions 'even though the client may wish to chase every rabbit down its burrow'.[5]

You are not there to do everything your client instructs you to do. You are responsible for what you say or do in court.

You are also obliged to conduct a considered review of the law and an analysis of the cases. As Justice Estcourt has said, 'To leave the judge to do all the work and then to be caught out overlooking elementary legal principles will result in you being labelled by the court as untrustworthy.'[6]

The Bar Standards Board Code of Conduct is very specific on the questions of honesty, integrity and independence.

For instance, you must not knowingly or recklessly mislead or attempt to mislead anyone.[7]

The last word means it is not just confined to the court and can include a member of the public.

In addition:

> 'you must not draft any statement of case, witness statement, affidavit or other document containing:
>
> a Any statement of fact or contention which is not supported by your client or by your instructions;
>
> b Any contention which you do not consider to be properly arguable;

---

5 (1988) 165 CLR 543, 556.

6 Justice Stephen Estcourt, 'Ethical Advocacy' 'Ethical Advocacy', www.supremecourt.tas.gov.au/publications/speeches-articles/ethical-advocacy, para 7.

7 Bar Standards Board, Code of Conduct, rule C9.1.

c Any allegation of fraud, unless you have clear instructions to allege fraud and you have reasonably credible material which establishes an arguable case of fraud;

d (In the case of a witness statement or affidavit) any statement of fact other than the evidence which you reasonably believe the witness would give if the witness were giving evidence orally.'[8]

As for cross-examination, Justice Estcourt observes that 'you must not put to one witness that his or her evidence is contrary to other witnesses' and expressly or by implication invite an opinion as to the reason. You must not ask a witness to speculate about the reasons someone did or said something. You must not put a hypothetical question to a witness other than an expert.'[9]

4 THE ADVOCATE'S VIEW

You are not permitted to put forward a personal view on the facts or the law unless invited by the court to do so. I have never known or heard of a court doing so. That is why you can't say 'I think' or 'I believe' or 'in my opinion'.

You should say 'I submit' or 'in my submission'. I can thoroughly recommend an interview Lord Birkett gave to the BBC in February 1959 to anyone who wants a neat and persuasive summary of the professional obligations of an advocate. It is entitled 'Face to Face'.[10]

Admittedly, the interviewer, John Freeman, was asking about the advocate's career in criminal law, but the answers have general application:

Freeman: 'Do you happen to remember how many successful murder defences you undertook in your career at the Bar?'

---

8 Ibid, rule C9.2.

9 Estcourt, 'Ethical Advocacy' (fn 6) para 22.

10 See Hugh Purcell, *A Very Private Celebrity: The Nine Lives of John Freeman* (The Robson Press, London, 2015) 138–140.

Birkett:	'If it doesn't sound immodest, it is easier to remember those in which I failed.'
Freeman:	'Well, how many did you fail in?'
Birkett:	'Well, three, I think.'
Freeman:	'Out of many dozens?'
Birkett:	'Yes.'
Freeman:	'Now, I want to ask you, did you yourself always believe in the innocence of your clients when you defended them?'
Birkett:	'To be quite, quite frank, no. I think I ought to say this, that you know, whatever your belief is, you're not allowed to state it in the court. I once remember a man saying, "Now m' Lord, I lay aside my wig. I speak as a man," and the judge said, "And I shall stop you if you do." You're allowed to speak as an advocate, but you mustn't give your opinion.'
Freeman:	'Did you personally have any qualms about defending someone on a murder charge, who you believed to be guilty?'
Birkett:	'None. You see, the view I took of the advocate's duty – and I think it's the right one – is this. He's there to present one side only, and he must do it to the very best of his ability, and do for the man, what he himself would do, had he the ability to do it; what he thinks really is irrelevant, as Dr Johnson said.'[11]

Freeman asked Birkett about whether he had ever got a man or a woman acquitted of a murder charge whom he believed in his heart to be guilty. He replied that he had and he had no regrets about it. When the interviewer went on to ask him whether he had ever defended a person on a murder charge who he *knew* to be guilty, Birkett drew a

[11] H Montgomery Hyde, *Norman Birkett: The Life of Lord Birkett of Ulverston* (Hamish Hamilton, London, 1965) 570–571.

distinction between defending an accused person whom the barrister *believes* to be guilty and someone he *knows* to be guilty:

Freeman:	'How can you defend a man you know to be guilty?'
Birkett:	'The answer is you never do. You are not permitted to do so. You may think that he is guilty, and of course it is really quite impossible for any man of sense to have a brief to defend some man, and read all the facts without coming to some conclusion in his mind. But if he *thinks*, that is quite irrelevant. He is not the judge.'[12]

It is this mixture of principle, clarity and realism which must have made Norman Birkett so persuasive.

In answer to further questions, Birkett admitted that he indeed had got a prisoner acquitted on a murder charge when he believed that prisoner to be guilty:

Freeman:	'Did you ever refuse a brief because of moral certainty that the person who offered it to you was guilty?'
Birkett:	'Never.'
Freeman:	'Have you ever felt sure that someone convicted on a capital charge was innocent?'
Birkett:	'Never.'
Freeman:	'So that you know of no case where a man has gone to the gallows wrongly?'
Birkett:	'Never. I'd like to say. I think possibly I could recall one case during the war where a young man was convicted who ought not to have been convicted, at least in my opinion,

12 Ibid, 428.

	but it's so rare that that's about the only case that stands out in my mind.'
Freeman:	'Did that particular person go to the gallows?'
Birkett:	'No he went to penal servitude.'
Freeman:	'You would never refuse a brief because you disliked the kind of offence alleged?'
Birkett:	'Oh no, indeed. Oh no indeed. Otherwise one would refuse half the cases. But I still think I ought to point out that the criminal side of one's practice is comparatively small with the civil.'[13]

5 BRINGING THE PROFESSION INTO DISREPUTE

Lastly, on the question of professional conduct, the advocate must make sure he does not bring the profession into disrepute.

Many years ago, a complaint made against a barrister for what amounted to a simple story was couched in archaic and somewhat pompous terms.

The barrister faced the following charges of misconduct before the Bar's disciplinary body:

'1. That when instructed as prosecuting counsel:

a. He failed to be in court at the scheduled time (9:30 am) for the commencement of the day's proceedings, thereby failing to use his best endeavours always to be punctual.

b. Having arrived in the court at approximately 10.10 am, he thereafter at various times until approximately 4:30 pm:

(i) Notwithstanding requests by the presiding judge to the contrary, repeatedly interrupted the

---

[13] Ibid, 572.

proceedings by way of inappropriate comments, laughter, gestures and hand clapping;

(ii) Wore sunglasses without reasonable or proper excuse during the course of the proceedings, thereby failing to act with due courtesy to the court before which he was appearing;

c. He appeared in court at approximately 4 pm that day, having consumed alcohol to such an extent as to significantly impair his ability properly to discharge his professional duties as counsel, thereby failing to act with due courtesy to the court before which he was appearing, and breaching his duties:

(i) Not to engage in conduct which may bring the profession of barrister into disrepute;

(ii) To uphold the dignity and high standards of a barrister and his own standing as a member of it.

2. That on or about 10th August …, near the ferry terminal he represented to a newspaper reporter that he had had a sexual relationship with the said presiding judge, which representation was untrue, thereby breaching his duties:

(i) not to engage in conduct which may bring the profession of barrister into disrepute; and

(ii) to uphold the dignity and high standards of a barrister and his own standing as a member of it.'

The barrister was suspended from practice for six months.

Let me conclude this section with some observations made by Sir Owen Dixon to law students at the University of Melbourne in 1953.

Sir Owen, apart from being an outstanding advocate, was a Justice of the High Court of Australia from 1929 to 1952 and Chief Justice from 1952 to 1964. He is still regarded as Australia's greatest jurist.

His Honour distinguished Ethics from Professional Conduct.

'Conduct goes beyond ethics', he said:

> '[It] includes personal behaviour of every description ... In the practice of a profession with which he has grown familiar, a professional man instinctively knows what propriety demands that he should or should not do.'[14]

The first rule of professional conduct, said Dixon, was about the advocate equipping himself for practice:

> 'To be a good lawyer is difficult. To master the law is impossible. But I should have thought that the first rule of conduct for counsel, the first and paramount ethical rule, was to do his best to acquire such a knowledge of the law that he really knows what he is doing when he stands between his client and the court or advises for or against entering the temple of justice. It happens to be a duty the fulfilment of which will serve the self-interest of counsel more than any other.[15]
>
> But counsel needs an equipment that goes far beyond knowledge of the law. He should be able to command the attention of the court. What he says should be treated with respect. He is not likely to command the respect and attention of judges if he cannot stand erect in court, if he cannot bear himself properly, if he cannot express himself in English free from the grosser grammatical errors and mispronunciations. These may appear small things. But they are the things which create the impression of the man.'[16]

Sir Owen concluded his lecture with some persuasive advice. Counsel:

> 'must keep steadily before him the duty of doing all he legitimately can in the true interests of his client ... He must also keep steadily before him the necessity of justly gaining and retaining the confidence of the court. That means that he should feel the court knows it can rely upon him without

---

14 Sir Owen Dixon, *Jesting Pilate* (The Law Book Company Ltd, Melbourne, 1965) 129.

15 Ibid, 131.

16 Ibid, 132.

> misgiving as one who will completely ascertain and present for judicial examination his client's real or strongest case and will do so intelligibly, definitely and with candour. The obligation of candour rests on simple moral grounds. But at the same time, it is a paradoxical if cynical truth which needs no elaboration that in advocacy candour is a weapon.'[17]

6 COURTESY IN COURT

You are a member of an ancient profession. How you behave affects how members of the public view you and the profession.

The courtroom is an important place in the community because it is here that justice is administered. It follows that those who appear in it should behave in a courteous and respectful manner.

The courtroom is an adversarial place, but it is not a place for scoring cheap points. It is not a bear pit.

Take some time to watch how the other lawyers in the court behave. Know how to address the judge.

Never be personal with the court or say things such as 'I am sure you are aware'.

When you wish to address the court, you should stand. If your opponent is speaking at the time, she should sit down when you get to your feet.

Stand up straightaway if the judge speaks to you.

Don't interrupt or talk over the judge. Don't interject if your opponent is delivering an address. Wait till she has finished to reply.

Sometimes your opponent will interrupt you. Sit down and wait.

---

[17] Ibid, 134.

If your opponent cannot find a reference in a case and you have it in front of you, help her.

Be courteous to witnesses and other members of the profession. You are a fool if you are rude to the court staff.

Whatever you do, no matter how formidable their reputation is, don't copy discourteous advocates.

7 PROFESSIONAL CONDUCT: CHECKLIST

- Read the Codes of Conduct thoroughly.
- Know what an ethical problem is and learn to recognise it early.
- Think of the administration of justice.
- If it smells fishy, it probably is.
- Don't lie to anyone in your professional life.
- Mean what you say.
- Deliver what you promise.
- Keep your client's affairs confidential.
- Your starting point for guidance: the rules of professional conduct and the common law.
- Ask someone who is senior, independent and whom you can trust.
- Never mislead the court.
- If you don't know, say so and find out.
- Don't betray your client to anyone.
- Be an ethical tactician: practise ethics first and tactics second.

Chapter 4
Case Analysis

If advocacy is about persuasion, then it must also be about winning. There are those who think this is wrong; that the advocate's only duty is to present the case as well as possible. But what is the point unless you change the mind of the listener, or at least get him to agree with you? A verdict of not guilty; an increase in damages; the development of the law; a reduced sentence – these are all wins.

To win, you have to analyse your case and develop a case theory: the best interpretation of the available facts as to why you should win the case.

A case without a case theory is like a car without a steering wheel.

In this chapter, I use the case study at the end of the book to demonstrate some techniques.

1 THE FACTS

Let's start with the facts. The word 'fact' is not used in its ordinary, everyday sense. If I said to my mother that it is a fact that Christmas Day falls on 25 December each year, she would agree. She would also wonder why she spent so much money on my education. But to mum and all the other normal people, a 'fact' is something that is true.

To lawyers, a 'fact' is a piece of the jigsaw puzzle that is our client's case. It's not necessarily true because you have to prove it.

When you walk into your colleague's office and ask 'What are the facts of your case?', you are not asking 'Is your case true?'

For the purposes of case analysis, a 'fact' is a term of art, in effect an allegation. 'The sculpture is Victorian and not Assyrian' is a fact. You will prove it by calling your expert Mr Worthington. It is a fact of the defendant's case that 'The sculpture is Assyrian'. The defendant will prove that by calling Professor Fournier.

This often confuses people who say, 'How can it be a fact if it contradicts another fact?' Well the answer is that it is a fact or allegation on each side's case and has to be proved.

In a civil case it is the claimant's obligation to prove that a cause of action exists.

Lord Diplock said that a cause of action is simply a factual situation, the existence of which entitles one person to obtain from the court a remedy from another person.[1]

Most causes of action can be broken down into the following elements:

1 Duty.

2 Breach of duty.

3 Causation.

4 Loss or damage.

The claimant must prove at least one fact for each element of the cause of action.

Our job is to look for those facts in the mass of information in front of us. Sometimes the documents in our case and statements of the witnesses are so voluminous and wordy that looking for Lord Diplock's facts is like looking for a needle in a haystack.

---

1 *Letang v Cooper* [1965] 1 QB 232, 243.

The facts we are searching for are what we call the material facts. I often ask my students whether they know the difference between a relevant fact and a material fact. They are often not sure.

A relevant fact is one which relates to the case. A material fact is a relevant fact which is also necessary to the case. In other words, it shows part of the cause of action is made out. In a negligent driving case where the claimant is not injured, there is no material fact relating to damage. There is a hole in the case and it may be struck out.

When we produce a list of the material facts and place them in the right order, we have the first draft of a statement of case or points of claim.

Given that there must be a duty before there can be a breach of that duty, and there must be a breach before loss or damage can flow from that breach, the 'right' order will normally be a chronological one.

2 PARTIES

Are you suing the right person? Is that person an individual citizen or a company? If the company is part of a large corporate group, have you chosen the right one? Has the wrong person been joined as a party? This is a crucial exercise to undertake in the analysis of the case. A mistake will be very costly.

3 EVIDENCE

The evidence is the means by which you prove the facts. So, if it is a fact that 'Jim was driving a car at a speed exceeding 30 miles per hour namely 50 miles per hour', you must ask 'How do I prove that fact?' In other words, what is the evidence of that fact?

There may be many sources of evidence for that fact or ways to prove it:

1 A policeman with a radar gun.

2 A speed camera.

3 A passenger watching the speedometer (Jim will never offer her a lift again).

4 Jim saying to the policeman 'Officer, I was only doing 60' (Jim is not very bright).

5 A police car travelling at the same speed for a fixed distance behind Jim's car.

There are many ways of proving the same fact. You just have to test each one for relevance, admissibility and weight.

Ask yourself the following questions:

1 Is the evidence of the policeman with the radar gun relevant? Yes.

2 Is it admissible? Yes, it has probably been made admissible by regulation or statute.

3 What sort of weight does it carry? Weight means cogency or believability. On a scale of 0–5? Probably 5. What if the radar gun has proved to be inaccurate once or twice in the past month? Probably 3 or 2.

To apply this to our case study:

1 'The sculpture is Victorian and not Assyrian' is the material fact (although it is an opinion).

2 'Mr Worthington, the expert will prove it' is the evidence:

   a Is it relevant? Yes.

   b Is it admissible? Yes, if Worthington's background, education and experience qualify him to give an expert opinion; and

   c What weight does it carry? This depends on the factors in point b and the method of his examination.

Case analysis therefore requires us to separate the facts from the evidence.

4 CONCLUSIONS

We are also required to separate the facts from conclusions or, better still, to break down our conclusions into facts.

Conclusions are inferences drawn from the facts.

Conclusions are inimical to effective advocacy. The only person who should be drawing conclusions is the decision-maker.

Let me show you what I am getting at.

There are two weather presenters on TV. The first one says, 'The weather will be bad today and much worse tomorrow.'

The second weather presenter says, 'Today it will be rain from 3 pm to 5 pm and then it will turn to sleet which will last till 9 pm. Tomorrow, there will be a blizzard from 6 am until 10 am.'

Which weather presenter would you prefer to listen to? The second, obviously, because her statement contains well-arranged facts. The first weather presenter speaks in conclusions. The second presenter allows you to draw your own conclusions from the facts as she presents them. She knows what you will conclude and steers you in that direction.

The world is full of people who speak in conclusions. They are not persuasive.

You see people being interviewed on TV who say, 'The man was angry.' We all know what 'angry' means. But would it not have much more of an impact if the person said 'He was shouting and swearing and waving his arms around. His fists were clenched and his eyes were blazing'?

Do you have friends who say things such as 'The party was such a nightmare'?

You would not dare to reply 'OK' and turn away. Your friend wouldn't like it if you did.

You respond by saying 'What happened?'

In other words, 'Give me the facts. I want to see if I agree with you. I want to draw my own conclusion.'

Good advocates know this instinctively. They arrange the facts so the court will draw the conclusion they want. Case analysis demands that we break down conclusions into constituent facts.

Later, you will see the importance of not putting conclusions in cross-examination.

5 CASE THEORY

The case theory is the best explanation on the available facts logically showing why your client should win. It is short, simple and persuasive. It comprises the three or four best facts and any legal proposition that is relevant. It should address each element of the cause of action: duty, breach and resulting loss.

After the judge has heard your case theory, you want her to say to herself 'I understand the case. If they prove that, they win.' I will explain more about case theory when we have actually created one.

6 CROSS-EXAMINATION

The final reason why case analysis is so important is because it helps us to prepare a cross-examination. Cross-examination, in part, is the arrangement of facts designed to achieve a conclusion and we can only discover those facts when we have carried out a proper analysis of the case for all sides.

There is more about cross-examination, which I know you must be keen to try, later in the book.

7 HOW TO ANALYSE A CASE

Your case may involve a number of areas to be analysed. For instance, the claim may give rise to causes of action in negligence or, alternatively, misrepresentation. In a criminal matter there may be different charges.

The main thing is to take it step by step and analyse the facts in relation to each cause of action, charge, indictment or legal case.

First of all, write down the legal issue or cause of action. You may do this on a piece of paper or computer. It could be done on a flip chart if a team of you is conducting the process.

Next, express your cause of action or charge as a proposition. The proposition will give you context to the facts that follow it.

For example, if the cause of action is negligence, write down the proposition that 'The defendant was negligent.'

If the criminal charge is assault, write down the proposition, 'The defendant is guilty of assault.'

If you are representing the defendant the proposition will be reversed, as in 'The defendant was not negligent' or 'The defendant is not guilty of assault.'

Draw a vertical line down the page from the middle of the proposition. Head one side of the page 'G' for good facts and the other side 'B' for bad facts.

Good facts are those that support the proposition. Bad facts go against the proposition or support the other side's case.

Let us take the *Cavendish v Downham* case study in Appendix 1 as an example. There are two possible causes of action: breach of contract and misrepresentation. We will choose breach of contract.

The proposition to be analysed is 'The defendant breached the contract' or 'Downham breached the contract.' Then think of the facts that are good and bad for that proposition.

8 THE BLITZ

Do it as a 'blitz'. A blitz is my version of a brainstorm: putting down ideas quickly without discussion or debate.

You can edit the results later. Don't stop to analyse each fact because it will retard the process. Here is an example of a typical blitz in this case:

The defendant breached the contract	
GOOD	BAD
C is an antique dealer	D bought sculpture from a reputable auction house
C was talked into it by D	D took her friend with her
Worthing thinks the sculpture is a fake	D accepted £820,000
Sculpture is worth £2,000	D knew about Iraq but not as much as C
C offered £820,000	The sculpture is smashed
C knew less about Iraq than D	D did not describe sculpture over phone
D talked C into buying the sculpture	D's expert says it is genuine
Mr Worthington spent 2 hours, 41 minutes looking at sculpture	C doesn't like D
D knew it was a fake	D's expert compared sculptures to Layard drawings
D's expert only looked at photographs	C didn't get a second opinion
D described it as Assyrian	C relied on his own judgement

These are random facts and some of them will not make it past the cutting room floor. The secret to conducting an effective blitz of the facts is to bear the following in mind but not to the extent that it slows the process down:

1 Think about the elements of your cause of action and what you must prove in law.

2 Tell your client's story fact by fact.

Legal propositions or conclusions will muddy the waters.

9 THE EDIT

When the process is over and the list of facts is exhausted, you must edit the lists fact by fact.

Here are the rules:

1 Is it a fact or a conclusion?

2 If it is a conclusion what facts make it up? For example, 'The defendant was drunk' is a conclusion. The facts that make it up are 'The defendant had seven pints of beer between 6:30 pm and 8:30 pm.'

3 Is it a fact or evidence? In this part of the analysis, the fact is crucial, not how you will prove it. You will say how you will prove it in the opening speech.

4 Does that fact relate to the proposition? For instance, it may be a fact in the case that the defendant is a multi-millionaire. This is an attractive fact as cases go, because you will more likely recover damages should you win; but it does not relate to the conduct of the defendant or more relevantly, to the proposition being analysed. Put simply, does it go to duty, breach, causation or loss?

5 Is the fact expressed clearly and succinctly? In other words, if you expressed it to the judge or any other person, would they know what you were talking about? For example, if I said 'Claimant not happy' would the judge know what I was talking about? Probably not.

6 Lastly, can the fact be combined with another fact in the list? For instance, 'The defendant drove a car' and 'The defendant was doing 60 in a 30 zone' can be combined to 'The defendant drove a car at 60 in a 30 zone'.

It is important that you edit the facts one by one, and systematically. If you are in a group of people, it doesn't matter if you debate as you go along. The blitzing process is over. It is time to think carefully.

Let us take the facts one by one from the column of good facts.

9.1 Fact one: C is an antique dealer

1 Is it a fact or conclusion? Fact.

2 Does it relate to the proposition? Possibly.

3 Is it clear enough? Yes, but it might need more colour such as 'C is a dealer in Middle Eastern antiquities.'

4 Can it be combined with another fact? Maybe. Let's see.

9.2 Fact two: C was talked into it by D

1 Fact or conclusion? Conclusion. Be careful because sometimes 'conclusions' are a shorthand method of expressing a number of facts rather than a value judgement. It may be a fact in the Good Facts column that 'The sculpture is Victorian and not Assyrian'. Some might think this is a conclusion, but for the purposes of case analysis it is really a shorthand way of saying a number of facts that the expert observed about the sculpture. In case analysis, a 'conclusion' is a characterisation, a value judgement or a spin put on the facts such as 'the defendant was drunk'.

2 Does it relate to the proposition? It may relate to the question of reliance.

3 Is it clear enough? Not really. Perhaps it should be expressed 'Mrs Downham wanted to sell the sculpture to Mr Cavendish' and 'She explained all its artistic features in detail to him.'

Let's leave this fact for a moment and move to the next one.

9.3 Fact three: Worthington thinks the sculpture is a fake

1 Fact or conclusion? Conclusion. The word 'fake' is a conclusion. 'Worthington thinks' is evidence.

2 How should it be expressed? 'The sculpture is Victorian and not Assyrian'. As explained, this is really a shorthand expression of all the reasons Worthington gives in his statement. For the purpose of case analysis, it is an effective way to express this fact because it saves paper. It is not a conclusion for our purposes.

3 Does it relate to the proposition? Yes.

4 Is it clear enough? Yes.

5 Does it need to be combined with another fact? No.

9.4 Fact four: Sculpture is worth £3,000

1 Fact or conclusion? Fact.

2 Does it relate? Yes, it goes to damage.

3 Is it clear? Yes.

4 Can it be combined with another fact? Yes, probably. It may be combined with the next fact which is what Cavendish paid for the sculpture.

9.5 Fact five: C offered £820,000

1 Fact or conclusion? Fact.

2 Does it relate? Yes.

3 Is it clear? Not really. It should be firmed up to read 'C paid £820,000 for the sculpture'.

4 Can it be combined? Yes, with the fact above it.

9.6 Last fact: D described it as Assyrian

1 Fact or conclusion? Fact.

2 Does it relate? Yes, if we are relying on a sale by description.

3 Is it clear? Yes, but more needs to be added. 'C described the sculpture over the telephone as being Mesopotamian circa 681–669 BC.'

4 Can it be combined? No, it is such a good fact that it stands alone.

10 FORMING THE CASE THEORY

Once all the facts have been edited and you are satisfied that they are all facts, choose the best three or four and put them in order. I say three or four facts because most causes of action have three or four legal limbs.

The order should be their most persuasive presentation.

A good rule of thumb is to present the facts in the order of the elements of the cause of action. If you choose the description, the purchase, the failure to match the description and the damage, your case theory may look like this:

It is the claimant's case that:

1 The defendant, in a telephone call, told the claimant she had an Assyrian sculpture circa 681–669 BC for sale.

2 As a result the claimant paid £820,000 for the sculpture.

3 The sculpture is not Assyrian but is a Victorian copy worth £3,000.

4 The claimant is owed £820,000 by the defendant.

This is a simple case theory and not the only case theory available to the claimant on these facts. It is short and persuasive.

In delivering this case theory to the court at the outset the advocate does not need to mention the words 'contract', 'sale by description', 'breach' or 'damages'.

It flows chronologically and the facts press buttons in the judge's mind leading to the judge concluding, 'If they prove that, they win.'

What is the defendant's case theory? The bad facts now become good facts. Because the proposition changes to 'The defendant did not breach the contract'.

The claimant must prove all the material facts which make up the cause of action. To defend the claim successfully, the defendant need only show one material fact is missing.

The defendant's case theory may be expressed in the alternative. One American judge I know says the defendant's case theory may be expressed in four words, 'The sculpture is Assyrian'.

However, there needs to be a fall-back position based on the English law of reliance in case the judge finds that the sculpture is not genuine.

For example, 'The sculpture is Assyrian. However, if it is not, the claimant knew more about Assyrian art than the defendant and relied on his own judgement. The description was not sufficiently important to become a term of the contract.'

Note that the last sentence is a legal conclusion and not a factual conclusion. The second sentence is a summary of a number of facts.

11 THE BLITZ AND ITS USES

If you return to the blitz, you can see its value in other areas. For instance, are there enough facts to satisfy the cause of action? Do any of the facts need to be clarified or investigated further? How will you prove each fact? What evidence do you have? What is the relevance, admissibility and weight of each piece of evidence?

12 WHY A CASE THEORY IS IMPORTANT

Your case theory governs your case. Of course, it may change if further facts emerge. But as it stands it can be used in the following ways:

1 Explaining the case to your client or a colleague.

2 In a pre-action letter of claim or letter of response.

3 As the first paragraph in a letter to your expert.

4 Planning your direct examination and cross-examination.

5 As the first thing you say to the judge in your opening speech.

Lord Sumption recognised the importance of a case theory for cross-examination. Before his elevation to the UK Supreme Court, he was asked, 'What is the key to a good cross-examination?':

> 'Know your material backward, preferably better than the witness; spot your opportunities when they arise and *know exactly what it is you are trying to prove*.'[2]

---

2 'Five Minutes With: Jonathan Sumption QC' (YouTube) www.youtube.com/watch?v=I8DlcexQiPw (emphasis added).

The former President of the UK Supreme Court, Lord Neuberger, expressed it this way:

> 'A good lawyer in command of the facts and of the applicable law should, to a reasonable degree, be able to predict the outcome of the litigation. There are, of course, imponderables which might frustrate the prediction: the cantankerous judge who just won't see the force of your brilliant argument; your opponent's unexpected telling point in cross-examination which holes your case; your witness who doesn't come up to proof. By and large though, the more skilled the lawyer, the better prospect that their analysis of a case will be borne out by the result.'[3]

The final word about case theory should go to the late Peter Underwood, former Chief Justice of Tasmania. We were teaching in London together and I showed him this method of case analysis. He was enthused. He said, 'I long for the day when I can say to counsel, please tell me what your case is in two or three sentences and they give it to me. All I ever get is something unclear or long-winded.'

13 PREPARATION AND PROOF

Look at the facts you will be required to prove. What is the most persuasive evidence you have? For instance, a contemporaneous email or letter will always trump the recollection of a witness. Independent evidence is always more persuasive.

What are the issues? What law is relevant to those issues?

What is the applicable law of evidence?

---

3 Lord Neuberger, 'Tomorrow's Lawyers Today – Today's Lawyers Tomorrow' (80 Club Lecture, Association of Liberal Lawyers, 19 February 2013), https://supremecourt.uk/speeches/lord-neuberger-at-the-80-club-association-of-liberal-lawyers.

Chief Justice Peter Underwood said that an advocate who goes into court without knowing the law of evidence is like a carpenter who goes to a building site without tools.[4]

Do you have the evidence? Is it easily obtained?

Is your evidence reliable? Will your witnesses come up to proof?

Do you need to get more or better evidence? Are you missing anything?

Do you need an expert or forensic analysis?

Study your opponent's case thoroughly. What does your opponent have to prove?

What evidence do you have which could lessen the effect or destroy your opponent's case?

What order do you want the court to make? How can you bring that about?

Get to court early.

There is more about preparation in the following chapters, but here are some general thoughts to help you.

It was said of George Carman QC that 'his soundbites glistened with midnight oil'.

What looks effortless and off-the-cuff is usually the result of hours, maybe days of preparation.

Sir Garfield Barwick QC adopted the 'no stone unturned' approach to preparation:

---

4 Justice Underwood, Lecture to Law Students, University of Tasmania, 6 January 2014.

> '... I would always work from the ground up. I would examine closely the relevant accepted wisdom of the day but not take it for gospel; I would verify it from original sources. In this way, in later days, I often found a principle which was misunderstood in its current application, or one that had been forgotten or overlooked. Following this course, I sometimes achieved results that in themselves appeared novel but which were simply built on the fundamentals of the law.'[5]

He was once consulted about the defence of people who were alleged to have committed perjury before an extended Royal Commission in Sydney.

His response was to question the validity of the government's extension of the Royal Commission. He argued that as a consequence of the abdication of Edward VIII, it had been done using the wrong seal.

The trouble was that the same wrong seal had been used to commission a number of the State's judges.

As he wrote in his autobiography, 'It was quite a point, but unfortunately it was too large a point. This is always a dangerous thing for a lawyer.'[6]

Peter Wood, who became a distinguished construction lawyer in Melbourne, was able to confine the point he made in an appeal to a judge. His client, a racehorse trainer, had been warned off every racecourse. The stewards had seen him at a race meeting in apparent contravention of the ban.

Wood knew the judge was very proud of his knowledge of property law and quite pedantic. He searched the title of the land where his client had been standing and was able to prove that it was just (a few feet) outside the land controlled by the racing club.

---

5 Garfield Barwick, *A Radical Tory* (Federation Press, Sydney, 1995) 19.

6 Ibid, 42–43.

14 CASE ANALYSIS: CHECKLIST

- Identify the legal issue or cause of action.
- Write it down as a proposition, e.g. 'the respondent breached the contract'.
- List the facts good and bad underneath it. At this stage, the facts are merely the pieces of your client's story. You still must prove them. Good facts support the proposition; bad facts damage the proposition. Some facts may be both good and bad and some may be neutral.
- Edit the lists:
  - Separate facts from conclusions or evidence. Well-ordered facts are more persuasive than a conclusion. What facts make up the conclusion? E.g. 'the respondent was drunk' is a conclusion. But 'the respondent drank five large vodkas in 25 minutes' is a fact.
  - Separate the facts from the evidence. Evidence is the means by which you prove facts.
  - 'The contract shows he signed it' is evidence; 'He agreed to the terms' is a fact.
  - Are the facts relevant to the proposition?
  - Are the facts specific and clearly expressed?
- Choose the four best facts and put them into a persuasive order. Add the legal proposition if you wish.
- What you have created is the case theory: the best explanation on the available facts logically showing why your client should win.
- You are not determining the truth. You are working out what each party's story is.
- The case theory may change. But a case theory drives an advocate's case.
- How good is your evidence?
- Leave no stone unturned.

Chapter 5

Interim Applications (Motions)

Interim applications, which are called motions in some countries, are a vital part of a young advocate's training. They used to be called interlocutory applications, 'interlocutory' meaning a dialogue or conversation. To 'interlocute' is to interrupt someone speaking.

In civil cases, they take place on an application being made to the court and can occur at any time up to the day of the trial.

In a lot of cases they are used for court housekeeping. These sorts of applications include summary judgment, strike out, applications for specific disclosure, extensions of time and so forth.

In England, the court uses its case management powers to further the 'overriding objective' in Part 1 of the Civil Procedure Rules.

The whole thrust of Part 1 is that the court, the parties and their representatives must reduce the expense of proceedings by defining and narrowing the issues, avoiding unnecessary steps and delay, and allocating a proportionate share of the court's resources to the cases which deserve it.

Interim applications may be heard by a senior judge, especially in complex cases, but they are generally heard by a District Judge, Master or a part-time judge. They are best recognised by the fact that most applications take no more than 30 minutes to hear and rarely take more than a day.

There is a lot of procedural rubbish talked about what you can and cannot say in an interim application. A lot of law schools teach it as a tick-box exercise, as if the role of the advocate is reduced to that of a person applying to the council for a parking permit.

Arbitration lawyers are frequently faced with procedural problems such as another party dragging its feet or being uncooperative.

In making an application to the arbitration panel for an interim measure, you must be acutely aware of any powers which appear in the arbitration agreement, relevant institutional rules and applicable legislation.

You should also read the International Arbitration Practice Guidelines, particularly the sections on Interim Measures and Challenges to Jurisdiction. These helpful notes appear on the website of the Chartered Institute of Arbitrators.

Remember, the decision-maker is bound by the rules, so you must pitch your application according to the rules.

If you do not, you are wasting your breath, the decision-maker's time and your client's money.

1 PREPARING THE SUBMISSION

The court will always be assisted by a thoroughly prepared advocate who knows what she wants and knows how to get it. In other words, a credible advocate.

Let us begin with a little psychology. Judges who hear interim applications are often very busy. There are 10 or more cases in the list. The judge is faced with a number of problems.

We forget that judges are also human beings. Some of them might have had an argument with their partner on the way to court. They might have found out that their daughter is seeing someone they don't like or a colleague has rung in sick and they must take over his list.

The last thing the judges want to see is an unprepared and disorganised advocate in their courtroom saying 'I don't know, Judge. I was only given this file half an hour ago.'

I did that once. Never again. It was in the Federal Court before a lovely old judge called Mr Justice Northrop. He said calmly but witheringly,

'The court is entitled to expect that once counsel gets to his feet he knows all about his brief.'

It was said in front of two of our trainees. As I left the building I said, 'I hope you learned something. That's exactly how you don't do it.'

So let us talk about preparation. You must know the file or brief backwards. If the procedural history is complicated, make a chronology. If you think it will assist the court, make a copy for the judge, but whatever you do, make sure your opponent agrees with its contents first.

Judges hate it when counsel proudly produces a chronology only to find out that opposing counsel disputes things in it or, worse, has not seen it.

1.1 Structure

As you prepare your submission, think about what will be attractive to the judge at the outset. Put your best foot forward. That is when the judge is paying the most attention.

Narrow your submissions down to one, two or three points. There's nothing worse than an advocate who says, 'I have 17 submissions to make.' The judicial heart sinks.

Use the relevant procedural test as your structure. Ask yourself, 'What is the judge looking for?', 'What does she need in order to make the order I want?' and 'What facts does she need and what law?'

A submission is the application of the relevant legal or procedural test to the facts of your case, inviting the decision-maker to conclude that the applicant has – or hasn't – satisfied the test. When we say, 'I submit', what we are really saying is, 'I invite you Judge to conclude that …'. Choose your best facts to support each submission you will make.

Then ask yourself, 'Will it further the overriding objective?[1] Will the order I am seeking save time and costs or narrow the issues between the parties?'

---

1 English Civil Procedure Rules, Part 1.

1.2 Know all of the facts

You must know your client's story backwards. This is not so that you can tell the court the full story, for that would be foolish. It is in case your opponent mistakes the facts or the judge asks you a question about them. An advocate who does not know his client's case will not attract the confidence of the decision-maker. Be deadly accurate about the facts. A wrong or mis-stated fact could be lethal to your credibility.

1.3 Know the procedural history

When was the claim served? Has there been a case management conference? Have witness statements been exchanged? You should scour the file for the milestones just in case the judge wants to know.

1.4 Know where your documents are

A disorganised advocate wastes the court's time and, frankly, does not inspire confidence. If the court asks to see a copy of a letter you have referred it to and you flap around to find it, you will lose valuable credibility points.

Mark the documents with coloured Post-it notes or put them into labelled files so that you can find them quickly. For everything you say, have a page reference ready if the judge asks, 'Where will I find that in the bundle?'

1.5 Anticipate your opponent's arguments

Anticipate the arguments opposing counsel will make but don't make them for them. In other words, have a reply up your sleeve in case your opponent raises a good argument. Don't say 'My friend will probably submit there is no evidence of consideration in this contract.'

The chances are that your opponent might not have thought of it at all, and will be sitting there thinking, 'Gee that was a good point. I think I'll raise that.' Never give your opponent a free kick.

1.6 Find out about the judge

Try to discover as much about the judge as you reasonably can. Is the judge fussy or silent or genial? Does she hate hearing submissions on the law? Is she bored with life on the Bench? What things should you not say? What sort of submissions does she like?

I know this sounds rather personal, but it is crucial. You want to say the things that will win the case, not things that will be obstacles to success.

If you don't know about the judge yourself, then ask people in your office or colleagues from other firms.

Lastly, make it your business to get to know the judge's assistants and court staff. If they like you, they will help you. They might even offer a friendly critique of your performance. I know. I used to work for judges while I studied law.

1.7 Research the law and the judge's powers

It is essential that you know the law that applies to the case. It is also vital that you know what the court is entitled to do. Don't patronise the judge by telling her at length what she is empowered to do. But do have those powers at your fingertips if she asks.

I used to appear before a judge who had been on the Bench for nearly 30 years. He often asked counsel, 'What is my power to do that?' or 'Am I entitled to make that order?'

I knew that he knew full well he had the power he was asking about. I think he was just testing me, but I was ready for him.

1.8 Have submissions on costs ready: win or lose

In the English civil courts, if the hearing is to last less than a day, you must file and serve a schedule of your costs at least 24 hours before. What happens if you win? What form of order will you seek? What do you say if you lose?

2 MAKING THE SUBMISSION

2.1 Address the court appropriately

No one looks more out of place than an advocate who doesn't know how to address the court.

Two tips: listen to how other advocates address the court before you speak; and the best way to ensure you don't go wrong is to say, 'May it please the court.' It is the equivalent of saying hello or goodbye to the judge and you don't get tripped up by the level of the judge.

In an interim application the judge is likely to be a District Judge or a Master. Both should be addressed simply as 'Judge'.

If in doubt, I suggest that you refer to the judge as 'the court'. This will solve all the problems and be sufficiently respectful. Just avoid calling the judge 'You'.

2.2 Announcing your appearance

If you appear for the applicant, and the judge doesn't know you, tell the judge your name and your opponent's name. It's a matter of courtesy.

The best idea is to let the clerk or associate know the names before the court commences.

If the judge calls you by name as in 'Yes Mr Smith', it's not generally a good idea to stand and say 'My name is Mr Smith'. I see nervous students do this regularly. It means they are not listening. Some even write their name down so they won't forget who they are. Tell the judge how you would like to be addressed, especially if you are a woman – 'Miss', 'Mrs' or 'Ms', for example – to avoid embarrassing the judge. You want her to be concentrating on your case and not social niceties.

2.3 Outline the application and the requested relief

The judge will be at her best in the first 30 seconds of your submission. That is when she is paying attention the most. She is sizing you up. She wants to know precisely what you are asking her to decide.

An average advocate begins as follows:

> 'May it please the court. My name is Ms Jones and I appear for the applicant. My friend Mr Patel appears for the respondent. This is an application for security for costs.'

A better advocate begins like this:

> 'May it please the court. My name is Ms Jones and I appear for the applicant. My friend Mr Patel appears for the respondent. This is an application for security for costs on the basis that the claimant will not be able to pay the defendant's costs should it lose at trial.'

The best advocate begins in this way:

> 'May it please the court. My name is Ms Jones and I appear for the applicant who is the defendant in the main action. My friend Mr Patel appears for the respondent.
>
> This is an application for security for costs on the basis that the claimant will not be able to pay the defendant's costs should it lose at trial. The claimant company, an art dealer in antiquities, is in considerable financial difficulty and has operated at a loss for the past 3 years.'

The third advocate not only introduces herself and her opponent, she outlines the application, says why she is making it and gives a factual reason why an order should be made. This is all done in the first 30 seconds. It will be memorable.

2.4 Structure your submission

Because it is an interim application and the court is busy, I don't hold with the theory that you should tell the court what you are going to say, tell it and then tell the court what you said. You don't have time.

After you have introduced the application, say 'I have three submissions. The first is that the claimant is not in a position to pay the defendant's costs. This is because ...'.

The judge will be assisted because she will be able to write down a heading, 'Unable to pay costs'. Then as you develop your submission she can make notes.

Numbering and headlining each submission will help the judge follow your structure and indicate how far through your submissions you have reached.

At the end, give a brief summary as to why you say the order should be made.

2.5 Make the judge's job easier

A number of Legal Practice Courses, paying homage to the tick-box method of advocacy, teach young law students to say the following:

> 'Have you read all the papers in this matter, Judge?'

It's tantamount to saying 'Have you done your job?'

I think it's better to make sure the judge has all the papers by checking with her clerk before court commences or, if it is important, going through the papers with the judge one by one. But this is using up valuable time.

A more effective and polite way is to say to the judge:

> 'Judge, you should have the following papers …'

Judges often tell you whether they have had a chance to read the papers. Be flexible and base your approach on what you can see and hear.

The second thing students are taught is to take the judge to every document or piece of evidence to which they will refer and then start speaking about it. This is to ensure the student is not referring to something outside the papers. But as a style of advocacy, it is clunky. It breaks the flow of the submission. Often the judge is going back and forth through the papers.

If the judge prefers this method, and you will soon find out if she does, then by all means you should employ it. However, I think 'point-first' advocacy is better. This starts from the premise that the judge is accepting everything you say as truthful and accurate, and that the evidence to support it is contained in the papers. But have a page reference ready, if challenged.

The court can only rely on the evidence that is before it, which is usually in the form of witness statements and documents.

With 'point-first' advocacy you make your submission first and if you want to draw the court's attention to the evidence which supports it, then do so. But only do so if you think it is important enough.

2.6 Respond directly to questions

An inexperienced counsel, who is stopped mid-flow by a judge's question, usually blurts out the first thing on her mind, such as, 'That's a very good question.'

Or she says, slightly irritably, 'I'll be coming to that later; bear with me, Judge.'

This is not good advocacy. If the judge is thinking about the point at the time you should answer, then and there. Like Diana Ross and the Supremes, you don't want to keep him hanging on.

But whatever you do, pause and think before you answer. Judges like that. A pause is not showing weakness. It is a signal to the judge that he has asked a good question.

Try to answer succinctly. If the judge is satisfied with your answer, you will know. Whatever you do, don't say when you resume your submission, 'As I was saying ...' or 'As I was saying before the interruption ...'.

If you don't know the answer to the question (and most times, being on top of your brief, you should), say to the judge, 'I don't know the answer to that question, but I will research it in the break (or overnight) and provide an answer to the court and my opponent.'

Finally, don't see a judge's question as an attack on your submission. The judge may be largely with you, but just need a little further assistance before deciding in your favour.

As an officer of the court, you have a duty to assist the court, and the judge is entitled to ask for counsel's assistance.

2.7 Be flexible and make concessions if appropriate

There is nothing so unpersuasive as an advocate who sticks doggedly to an unmeritorious point or who says, 'I have 12 submissions and they are all equally strong.'

You lose credibility. You dilute your argument and you weaken your best points.

2.8 Be courteous and professional

A court appearance featuring two advocates is not a debate. It's not like the Prime Minister and the Leader of the Opposition standing across the gangway in the House of Commons.

Your submissions (and think of the passive nature of that word) must be delivered to the judge, not your opponent.

The temptation to knock spots off your opponent is often hard to resist, especially if you think he is talking rubbish. It is not the judge's job to referee spats between opposing counsel. The judge is already trying the issues between the parties to the case.

Be courteous to the court and courteous to your opponent. Don't lose your cool or you will cede ground.

Keep to 'I submit' or 'in my submission'. Avoid 'as discussed': it is not a discussion. Avoid 'I think', 'I believe' or any other language suggesting a personal view. Your role is to present a legal argument, not to express an opinion.

Whatever you do, do not speak while someone else is addressing the court and never speak over the judge. Be quiet and listen.

2.9 Make a note

Some young lawyers sit down at the end of a submission and relax. They think to themselves 'I'm glad that's over. I can't wait to tell Mum how good I was.' They sit in a wide-eyed reverie as their opponent is going merrily along making the most appalling submissions.

You must make a note of everything that is said by your opponent and the court. First, you may have to respond and, second, someone else might be appearing for the client next time this case comes to court, who will want to know what was said. If you haven't got time for a full note, do something more detailed when you get back to the office.

2.10 Read the judge

Watch the judge like a hawk. If her arms are folded, she has probably made up her mind. If she's looking out the window, she's probably thinking of lunch. If she's writing furiously, slow down.

I once appeared before a judge who was paying no attention to my utterly brilliant and well-crafted submissions. He appeared to be looking at something on the bench, so I stood on tiptoes and saw to my horror, that he was playing chess. I was young and he had been a judge for 25 years. He had heard it all before.

If you don't think the judge is paying attention, then stop talking. He will soon ask you to continue. But read the signals.

In the UK Supreme Court not long ago, a judge told counsel he had got the point. Undeterred, counsel kept talking. It's poor advocacy. It's almost as if counsel is thinking, 'I'm going to make my point whether you are persuaded or not'. But after the Supreme Court, you cannot go any further.

2.11 Using a skeleton

Don't read the skeleton argument out word for word. Everyone in court, especially the judge, can read. Try to say things from a fresh perspective. Make it interesting. Remember, you are putting flesh on the bones. See Chapter 8, 'Skeleton Arguments'.

2.12 Reply if necessary

Judges get silently, and sometimes openly, annoyed if you reply just because you can. As I said, this is not a parliamentary debate.

Only reply if there is something your opponent said that needs to be corrected or if you have a submission which is going to blow your opponent's case out of the water.

Going over your original submissions again wastes the court's time and, more importantly, doesn't endear you to the decision-maker.

2.13 After the decision

In preparing your submissions, be ready to make the appropriate submission on costs should you win or lose.

After the Court of Appeal's decision in *Denton v TH White Limited and Another*,[2] consider whether it is appropriate to ask the judge to add a sanction to the order. If the sanction has some bite, it might be hard for your opponent to escape from it should his client default on the main order. An example would be:

> 'If by 4 April the defendant does not file and serve a witness statement from Professor Fournier which contains a statement of truth, the defendant will not be permitted to call Professor Fournier at the trial.'

Lastly, make sure that the orders and directions you are seeking from the court are clear.

2.14 Knowledge of the rules

In preparing for and appearing in any interim application, you must know more about the rules and practice directions than your opponent or the judge.

---

[2] [2014] EWCA Civ 906.

Never patronise the court but give them the confidence to rely upon you.

As you walk back to your chambers or your office, whether you have won or lost, ask yourself 'How could I have done that better?'

3 INTERIM APPLICATIONS: CHECKLIST

3.1 Preparing the submission

- Your approach: concentration and simplification.
- Know the procedural rules.
- Know the facts.
- Apply the procedural rules to the facts.
- Know your procedural history.
- Know where your documents are.
- Anticipate your opponent's arguments.
- Put yourself in the shoes of the judge.
- Find out about the judge.
- Be nice to the court staff.
- Research the law and the judge's powers.
- Have submissions on costs ready should you win or lose.

3.2 Making the submission

- Address the court appropriately.
- If you appear for the applicant, introduce yourself and your opponent and say for whom you both appear.
- Outline the application and the requested relief.
- Say:
  - what you want;
  - why you want it; and
  - how the court can give it to you.

- You are neither a witness nor a party. The court can only rely on evidence before it.
- Don't refer to things that are not in the court's papers.
- Don't use expressions such as 'I think' or 'I believe'. Say, 'I submit', 'in my submission' or 'it is submitted'.
- Don't make up facts.
- You have a duty to assist the court.
- You have a duty to do the best for your client whilst not deceiving or misleading the court.
- Make sure the court is informed of all relevant decisions.
- Give the judge a solution which suits your case.
- Respond directly to questions.
- Be flexible and make concessions if appropriate.
- Be courteous.
- Read the judge.
- Make a note of what your opponent and the court say.
- Reply if necessary.

3.3 After the decision

- Are the order and directions clear?
- Have sanctions for non-compliance been included?

Chapter 6
Online Advocacy

Thank you to Carol Sowers[1] *for her significant contribution to this chapter.*

The Covid-19 pandemic of 2020–2022 rapidly changed the conduct of court hearings around the world. Within weeks, advocates had to learn new online presentation techniques, and to grapple with previously unimagined technical challenges. You may remember the viral clip of the Texas attorney who, thanks to a filter, appeared on screen before the court in the form of a kitten. With admirable sincerity he informed the judge, 'I am not a cat'.[2]

In subsequent years, most substantive hearings have returned to the physical courtroom. In-person trials have distinct advantages, affording the decision-makers the opportunity to assess credibility and the interaction between counsel and witnesses. However, many interim hearings, in both court and arbitration proceedings, remain online for the sake of cost-effectiveness and convenience. Shorn of travel and accommodation costs, and with decision-makers, counsel and parties available to appear simultaneously all around the world, online hearings are going to remain attractive. The modern advocate must adapt.

---

1 Carol Sowers is a leading presentation skills coach and former broadcaster with over 30 years' experience. A graduate of the Missouri School of Journalism, she has held senior roles at CBS/ABC affiliate KHQA, including Vice-President for Public Affairs, Main Anchor, Executive Producer and News Director. She now trains advocates, broadcast professionals, law enforcement organisations and government departments in poise, delivery, speaking without notes, using gestures and voice control.

2 '"I'm not a cat": lawyer gets stuck on Zoom kitten filter during court case' (YouTube) www.youtube.com/watch?v=lGOofzZOyl8.

1 PRESENTING ONLINE

There is both bad news and good news about online advocacy. The bad news is that you lose the ability to use some communication skills. You no longer have a commanding physical, three-dimensional presence in front of the judge and jury. Your body language is viewed mostly from the shoulders up. Your gestures are largely invisible to the court. Your voice quality and vocal expressions, which served you well inside the courtroom, can lose some of their effectiveness when the sound must travel through a variety of technical hardware and software to reach your audience. You lose some control over your presentation to the court when you have to rely on sometimes tenuous internet connections, and that loss of control can increase your nervousness.

The good news is that many of your strongest communication techniques remaining in the two-dimensional online courtroom can become even stronger. Your eye contact can be more focused. Your facial expressions can become easier to read. Your effective use of pausing, phrasing and other language techniques can become more noticeable and persuasive. But you must minimise the distractions of remote advocacy in order to make the most of your communication to the court.

2 SET-UP

2.1 Remove distractions

First, find a suitable location in your office or home for your remote advocacy. Strive for as much privacy as possible, both for the court's sake and for yours. Set up a schedule with other people in your office or home so you won't be disturbed during online court proceedings. Carol Sowers, who lives in New York City, has gone so far as to put a note on her front door, asking that people making deliveries do not use the doorbell during certain hours. She says it doesn't always stop the insistent buzzing of delivery drivers, but it helps.

Our brains help us tune out background noise. Microphones don't have that ability. You may not notice the sound of traffic outside your office or a clanking radiator inside your home because you've grown accustomed to them. Those distracting noises can come through loud and clear over your computer. Voices carry more than we realise. Is your spouse working in the next room? Can you hear them? Seek as much silence around you as possible.

What if there is distracting noise around you that you can't silence? Is using headphones or earpieces permissible, or will the sight of them be even more distracting to the court? Carol recalls coaching an advocate who was wearing large headphones at the start of an online session. When asked why, the advocate explained that workmen were using a pneumatic drill outside her window. She wouldn't be able to hear if she didn't use the headphones. Her explanation eliminated Carol's potential distraction. Transparency with the court will have the same result. Explain your need for an out-of-the-ordinary technical set-up at the start of the hearing. Better yet, seek permission in advance to avoid potential controversy with the court.

2.2 Choose your location

When choosing a remote advocacy set-up space, smaller is better. Large rooms with high ceilings are not ideal for audio quality. Your voice may sound hollow, as if you're speaking from an indoor stadium. If your computer set-up must be in a large room, face towards a corner and away from a wide, open space. Podcasters sometimes set up their remote studios inside a cloakroom for two reasons. First, it's a smaller space so the sound doesn't bounce around and echo. Second, the hanging coats help to muffle the sound, similar to foam muffling material hung on the walls of a professional radio booth. Try placing a bath towel underneath your laptop during online presentations, for the same reason.

Once you've selected the space for your remote set-up, look around. Remember, your goal is to minimise distractions. The court will be able to see inside your office or home. Does the background look professional? Does it look tidy? Even if the only available spot for your remote court presentations is your child's bedroom, you can and should remove the toys and straighten the books on the shelves. The most professional backgrounds are visually interesting but not busy. A plain, light-coloured wall behind you is not distracting but it's not very interesting. Being seen on screen only from the shoulders up against a solid grey wall tends to look like a criminal mug shot.

Once you have tidied the space behind you, consider the distance between you and the background. The more distance between you and your background, the better. The court should not be able to read the titles of the books on your shelf or see if your artwork is signed. The items behind you should be slightly out of focus. Your face should be the most sharply focused object on the screen.

2.3 Lighting

Your face must be the most well-lit part of the screen. Avoid sitting with your back to a window or door with natural light coming into the room. Strong natural or artificial light behind you will cast your face in shadow. Worse, you could appear in silhouette like a person trying to hide their identity on a news interview. If the room behind you is light and bright, you may have to add more lighting in front of you, so that your face is at least as bright and well-lit as the background.

Don't rely solely on natural light for your remote set-up, because it could change dramatically during a lengthy court hearing as the sun moves or if the weather changes. In the Northern Hemisphere, a north-facing window will give the most consistent level of light during the day. Experiment with closing curtains or blinds behind you.

The most flattering light is balanced on either side of your face. Place a lamp on either side of you, perhaps with the lampshade removed to provide brighter light. Depending on other light sources in the room, such as overhead lighting in the ceiling, you can adjust the lamps' height and distance from you. The most flattering lighting can come from ordinary household lamps positioned with their unshaded bulbs slightly above your head height, placed no more than two feet from the sides of your computer but slightly behind it. Avoid using spotlights aimed directly at your face. It is difficult to concentrate with light shining in your eyes. Your computer screen will also cast some light on your face as you look into it, but it is not bright enough alone.

2.4 Your appearance on screen

You must place your computer's camera at eye level. We are used to looking people in the eye when we speak to them. If your camera is lower than eye level, it will appear as if you are looking down at the camera and at everyone with whom you are communicating, including the judge. If your camera is higher than eye level, your gaze upward into the camera can appear strained and awkward. A good rule of thumb: if you can see the ceiling or overhead lights onscreen in the room behind you, your camera is pointing up. Therefore, you are looking down into the camera. If you can see the floor, your camera is probably too high.

Check the framing of your body on the screen. You should be centred in the frame, with a small amount of space visible above your head like a portrait. Your shoulders and upper arms should be visible, like that of a bust sculpture. We are used to having a certain amount of physical distance when we speak to people in person. Placing your face too close to the screen can feel intrusive to those watching you.

Advocacy students often ask if they should sit or stand during remote court presentations. If you are used to standing in the courtroom, you may be more comfortable and give a better presentation if you stand during the remote hearing. If you choose to stand, your entire remote set-up must be raised to your height, including your camera and lighting.

If you choose to sit, your choice of chair matters. If your chair rocks or swivels, it is almost guaranteed that you will too. Your movement will be pronounced on camera. Sit towards the front of your chair. Straighten your back. Put your feet flat on the floor. Placing the computer camera at eye level will help your posture, as will placing a small pillow behind your back.

Think about your clothing. If possible, wear shaded plain-coloured clothing and avoid patterns which may jump or strobe. Unless you are required to, don't wear a white shirt or light-coloured clothing, as it tends to be dazzling. If you must wear white, cover it substantially with a jacket. Aim for a degree of contrast between your clothing and your background. Don't take risks with wearing informal (or no) clothing below the waist.

In summary, the best video set-up does nothing to distract from the person and their communication.

2.5 Virtual backgrounds

Some remote courts require the use of virtual backgrounds for advocates, witnesses or both. The reasons vary, but it is usually a desire to level the visual playing field among all parties in a case. If you must use one, your choice of actual background remains important. A solid, plain background behind you is best. Then, avoid choosing a virtual background which is too exotic or busy and try to keep any corporate branding discreet.

Your lighting must closely match that of the scene in the virtual background. If it doesn't, you can look out of place in the virtual scene. Ideally, your on-screen appearance with a virtual background should look as realistic as a photograph taken in front of a real background.

Even then, movement on screen will change light and shadows. Unless you have a sophisticated set-up, like a green screen used by television weather presenters, you will probably have auras, halos, or parts of the face or body 'disappearing' into the background. The same problems can occur when someone uses the 'blur' function to hide their home or office behind them.

With most computer-generated or blurred backgrounds, the risk is that your audience will be focusing on problems with the background rather than listening to what you are saying. For that reason, they are best avoided.

2.6 Multiple screens

How you set up the hearing for yourself is important. It is a good idea to have one screen for the bundle, one screen for your notes and one screen for the live hearing. You may be able to put those screens in a minimised form on one computer screen. See also para 4.5, 'Referring to notes'.

2.7 Test your set-up

Your remote set-up is not complete until you sit (or stand) in front of your computer camera to test it. Take screenshots to check the background, lighting and framing. Arrange a practice session with a trusted colleague, friend or family member who has a good eye and ear for detail. Once you have achieved the look and sound that you want, take more screenshots and photos for reference so you can replicate the set-up.

3 HEARING PREPARATION

As with any hearing, consider whether a preliminary conference should take place to determine the rules of procedure. As a party's representative, you should anticipate what problems, from technical to substantive, might arise and argue firmly to get orders which will smooth the progress of the hearing. You must be a pessimist and think about all the things that could go wrong.

3.1 Procedural considerations

Check the court or tribunal's practice directions on virtual hearings. If the rules are silent on a certain point, consider seeking the agreement of the decision-maker and other parties to additional requirements in advance. Relevant considerations might include:

- Placing an express obligation on each party to ensure they have the correct IT equipment for the hearing.
- Expressly confirming that witnesses must not be prompted by another person or by any other means.
- Providing that a person (whether advocate or witness) should only speak if invited to do so by the judge or the panel.
- Prohibiting the proceedings from being recorded or photographed, or any screenshots being taken.
- Skeleton arguments or written submissions delivered in advance may assist the decision-maker and support the oral advocacy (see Chapter 8, 'Skeleton Arguments'). Consider whether a direction is required.
- Do you wish to deliver a pre-recorded speech? If so, you may require permission.

Check local customs for the court or tribunal you are appearing before. For instance, some English courts require barristers to be wigged and gowned online; others may dispense with wigs for online hearings.

3.2 Bundles

It is important that you prepare an electronic bundle that is user-friendly and complies with any relevant practice direction.

The bundle should usually be in pdf format and employ optical character recognition (OCR), which makes all text machine-readable. This will mean that the court or any of the parties can search and find someone's name or an issue quickly.

The index or contents page should contain hyperlinks to the listed documents. Documents should be bookmarked, and pagination should be electronic. All of this is time-consuming and should be factored into the costs of the hearing.

Think about how you will transmit the bundle to the court or tribunal. If using email, be aware there will be limits on the size of files that can be received.

An alternative is to use a cloud-based evidence management system. Be careful to download your own copy, so others can't read any notes that you make on it. In one early online case during the Covid-19 pandemic, a judge had not downloaded his own copy and was making remarks on the documents which everyone could see.

Check deadlines for filing and serving documents, and make sure you comply with them.

3.3 Witnesses

Ahead of the hearing, you should send a standard fact sheet to any witnesses explaining the procedure at the online hearing and how it will work.

Make sure your witnesses have a clean copy of the trial bundle and not one that is marked up. It is much better for the witness to use an electronic copy, but sometimes it may be that one of the witnesses only has a paper copy. Ideally, when examining the witness, you should have the same document in the same format in front of you, so check in advance.

Factor in breaks, because it is very tiring conducting hearings online. Tell the witness they should request a break if a problem occurs outside the room they are appearing in. Make sure they turn off cameras and microphones during breaks, so the decision-maker and other parties cannot hear what they are saying. In a case in Northern Ireland, a witness took his laptop to the toilet with him during a break but forgot to mute his microphone. The flushing toilet was heard by the rest of the court.

The witness may wish to use headphones. Headphones can be helpful, because they give a witness some privacy. If a witness wants to say something personal while giving evidence, he or she may feel more secure if they are wearing headphones. As mentioned earlier, consider whether a reason for wearing headphones should be provided, or permission sought.

Ensure there is no one in the room with the witness who may be guiding or influencing them.

Before the witness is sworn in, make sure the witness knows the wording of the oath or affirmation. Remind them that they must not record the hearing.

Encourage the witness to say if there is a problem during the hearing: for instance, if they are not following the evidence or cannot hear the questions properly. Agree in advance how they should do that, perhaps by raising their hand.

Instruct your own witnesses that if they are referred to a document by opposing counsel during cross-examination, they should ask to see the entire document. Remember the witness will not be in control of the display of the document, so this approach will help to avoid excerpts being shown out of context (see para 4.6, 'Use of visuals').

3.4 Practical considerations

At least the day before, check your Wi-Fi is working; but check again an hour before the hearing. Glitches, although sometimes unavoidable, look unprofessional. If your computer decides to download an IT update just before the start of the hearing, you will be stressed and may be delayed. Check that morning whether any updates are pending.

You will be given a link by the court to access the hearing. Copy and paste the link into a saved document, so that if the hearing is disrupted in any way you can go back to the link quickly rather than trawling through emails looking for it.

Take time to familiarise yourself with the online platform being used for the hearing. Do you know how to turn your camera on and off? Can you mute yourself quickly? Do you know how to share documents on screen?

If you plan to use the screen-share function, make sure you have opened and formatted the documents you wish to display.

Have an alternative device ready should yours fail. Make sure it is charged. Provide at least one other person with access to the documents you wish to refer to, so they can display them for you if for any reason you can't.

Your online account name should describe you appropriately. It is helpful to the other participants at the hearing for you to display your full name, including your title. If you have a screen-saver image when you turn off your camera, make sure it is appropriate.

Each advocate should have their own computer and own camera, so that they are individually visible and identifiable on screen. They should each be in a separate room. A group of people in a meeting room sharing one computer and camera is not effective, even if permitted by the court or tribunal. Individuals will be sitting further away from the camera and will not be seen or heard clearly. It may also not be obvious who is speaking. Make sure that no one other than an authorised person is in each room during the hearing.

Check that your phone is charged and keep it handy in case you need to seek urgent instructions from your client. You might wish to have a personal WhatsApp group for you and members of your team, including the witnesses. This will make it easier to communicate with them during the day. It will also go some way to replicating how you would conduct an in-person hearing, with meetings before the hearing starts, in the lunch hour and after the hearing finishes. Turn your phone on to silent mode.

Go online well before your session is due to start. Switch off any other programmes on your computer which are not required.

4 AT THE HEARING

4.1 Etiquette

Be patient when joining the appointment. Wait for the host to speak to you. This may be the court clerk, but it could be the judge.

If you are remotely attending a hybrid hearing where some of the participants are appearing in person, be aware that the court's camera may not reveal everyone in the courtroom. Be careful not to talk informally to the court staff when you join the hearing, as the court may already be in session. Others, including the judge, may hear you.

Do not interrupt or talk over people, especially the judge. The judge may be asking a question, but if you are also talking, you are drowning it out and may miss it.

Listen and watch carefully.

If you don't hear something, ask for it to be repeated.

It is good practice to use the mute facility when you are not speaking. This will avoid any background noise being heard by other hearing participants, especially if you are typing. Make sure you know how to unmute quickly, if asked a question by the tribunal. For instance, some online platforms allow you to unmute temporarily by holding down the space bar.

Be aware that it is more difficult to control a witness during an online cross-examination. Your physical presence is removed. The witness will be in a familiar setting rather than in a physical courtroom. They will be more relaxed. They will not feel as pressured under cross-examination when looking at an advocate on screen. They may feel more confident in holding to a particular position. It is therefore even more important that questions are precise, clear and easy for everybody (not just the witness) to understand.

4.2 Handling the camera

The greatest challenge of communicating effectively during remote presentations is remembering to look into the lens of the camera when speaking. We are used to looking at our listeners' faces when we speak. It therefore feels natural to look at the screen. Doing so makes it appear that you are, in fact, not looking at your audience. To give the impression of making eye contact you must look at the camera, not your screen.

There are a variety of ways to remind yourself to focus your attention on the camera. First, make sure you know exactly where the lens is – especially if it is built into your device, as it may be very small. You can mark Post-it notes with arrows pointing towards the camera and place them on either side of the lens to draw your attention to it.

If you will be the sole speaker during the remote presentation, it can be helpful to cover the screen with a piece of paper. This eliminates the distractions of movements made by your listeners and helps you focus only on the camera. This may be appropriate when making a submission or trial speech.

It is tempting to spend a large portion of your time looking at your own face on the screen rather than focusing on the lens of the camera. Most remote platforms have an option to hide the view of yourself on your screen, which will eliminate the temptation.

When another person is speaking, watch the screen to observe their facial expressions and body language. This is especially important when cross-examining a witness. Before you speak again, change your focus to the lens of the camera, then begin.

If the judge is speaking, occasionally look into the camera to show that you are engaged and listening.

4.3 Gestures and body language

We are used to gesturing when we speak. Gestures make us more eloquent and descriptive and should be used when presenting online. However, your camera set-up will prevent most gestures from being seen. The gestures shown on the screen should be defined. They must help describe the information you are sharing; for instance, counting three points on your fingers. They must be fully visible on the screen. Random gestures and gestures that are only partly visible will be distracting.

Be aware that body language seen on camera can appear magnified or exaggerated. Your observers may pick up more from your facial expressions than they would in the courtroom, so try to remain impassive. Conversely, using the camera to give the impression of eye contact can feel quite penetrating, and pauses can carry greater dramatic effect.

4.4 Voice control

Oral persuasion relies in part on our use of voice. We naturally change the volume, pace and tone to emphasise arguments. Microphones used during remote presentations can limit the ability to speak in higher or lower than normal ranges. Some microphones will automatically limit volume that reaches a certain level. Others will not, which can result in a grating sound to the voice. It is best to speak at a consistent mid-range level during remote presentations.

To create more energy and interest in your argument, you may change the pace, tone and intensity of your speech, as you would when speaking in person.

4.5 Referring to notes

Using electronic notes on the screen or on paper during a remote presentation is a personal preference. If you choose to use electronic notes, practise in advance so that you can access them smoothly and quickly. When reading from notes on the screen, scroll so that the information you read is always at the top of the screen, closest to the lens of the camera.

Remote presentations allow us to see eye movements more closely. Looking from side to side to check notes and view additional screens can make you appear distracted and unprepared. It is therefore better to keep anything you will use or refer to on only one side of the screen. This includes paper notes, a notebook and pen, your phone, and a glass of water.

In a multi-screen set-up, choose your main screen then arrange all additional screens to the same side of the main screen, rather than on either side of it.

Paper notes are better kept on a vertical stand to the side of your screen, rather than laid horizontally on the desk in front of you. This will avoid you having to look down repeatedly. The notes should be elevated to eye level, so you don't have to drop your gaze (and your chin) to see them.

If you don't need extensive notes, consider writing bullet points on an index card or Post-it note and attaching it to the side of your screen at eye level.

4.6 Use of visuals

Remember that when documents are shared online, they will take up most of the screen. The advocate will only be visible in a thumbnail image at best. During a speech or submission, a shared document will have the full attention of the tribunal. Ideally, its displayed content should make your client's case for you.

Equally, documents shown to a witness are more important than during in-person hearings, as they take up the full screen. Arbitrator Simon Gabriel suggests that advocates should make their case in cross-examination by showing a selection of document excerpts which the witness cannot deny. A more sophisticated approach to online cross-examination may prove difficult.

If you take some time to locate a document, resist the urge to provide an ongoing commentary about your progress in finding it. Instead, look for it silently and quickly. A commentary adds nothing and can be annoying.

When taking the court or a witness to multiple references in the same document, try to present the information in the same order as it appears in the document, so you only have to move in one direction. Have page and paragraph references ready, in the order in which you will rely on them. Avoid scrolling up and down.

Resist the urge to display too much information on screen at one time. Make sure you know how to highlight a sentence or a paragraph to draw attention to it.

Finally, consider pre-recording your closing submission. You can make it look good by rehearsing and re-recording. The panel can view it at their leisure and re-watch it if they wish. A 20-minute online session can then be scheduled for any questions the panel has.

5 ONLINE ADVOCACY: CHECKLIST

5.1 Set-up

- Remove distractions.
- Choose a small space with a professional, tidy background.
- Your main light source should be in front of you.
- Place your camera at eye level.
- Position yourself so that only your head and upper body are visible on screen.
- Arrange multiple screens and notes to one side of your main screen.
- Test your set-up.

5.2 Hearing preparation

- Consider whether any agreements or directions are required for the conduct of the hearing.
- Check local customs.
- Ensure the bundle is user-friendly and prepared according to applicable practice directions.
- Brief witnesses on how the online hearing will work. Ensure they will be alone while giving evidence.
- Familiarise yourself with the functions of the online hearing platform.

- Prepare and format documents to be displayed at the hearing.
- Have a back-up plan if your system crashes.
- Check your online account name and screen saver are appropriate.

5.3 At the hearing

- Speak only when invited. Do not interrupt.
- Use the mute facility when not speaking.
- When speaking, look at the camera, not at the screen.
- Keep gestures within camera shot.
- Speak at a consistent mid-range level of volume.
- Keep notes to one side, at eye level.
- Let documents make your case for you.
- Limit the amount of information displayed in a document on screen at one time.
- Consider pre-recording closing submissions.

Chapter 7
Written Advocacy

When you draft a document for the court, you are starting the process of persuasion.

English barrister Iain Goldrein KC was fond of asking his students:

> 'What was written on the cakes in Alice and Wonderland?
>
> "Eat me!"
>
> Your documents should have "Read Me" written on them.'

I am sure you have received an email (usually from the Human Resources or Marketing Department of your firm) which has no paragraphs and is full of jargon. My practice was to save it to read later. Then, invariably, I forgot. None of the emails had 'Read me' on them.

A person I worked with would write very long and very turgid emails to his staff. The really important message that he wished to convey was buried in a sentence on line 56. No one reading his emails would make it that far, and he would get really cross that people had not heeded his order.

I have seen witness statements that run to hundreds of pages. They are written by lawyers who are very bright and who don't miss a single important fact – it's just that those important facts are lost in a sea of verbiage. The witnesses just sign the statement. It's not in their own words. Everything is covered but nothing is distilled.

It is manna from heaven for a smart cross-examiner.

I often think of the judge sitting in her chambers and looking at a mountain of badly drafted pleadings and witness statements. Decision-makers must despair.

But there is hope. We can learn from some distinguished writers.

The first one who can help us is the memorably named Professor Betty Sue Flowers from the University of Texas.

Professor Betty Sue changed my life and she will change yours.

This is for all those people who feel like giving up as they look at a blank piece of paper or a blank screen and have no idea what to write. It is also for all those people who get half way through a document and dry up. Lastly, it is for all those people who have a deadline looming and think they are not going to make it.

Professor Flowers says that there are four roles to be played in the writing process: madman, architect, carpenter and judge.[1] Sacrilegiously, I have changed carpenter to builder because I remember it better.

When you prepare to write you must think about these roles and play them properly. The technique is to play them in the right order and not move to a new role until you have completed the responsibilities of the role you are playing.

1 MADMAN, ARCHITECT, BUILDER, JUDGE

Let's begin, as we must, with the madman. Playing this role requires you to write down everything you want to include or cover in the document you are to write. The word 'random' is best used to describe this process. It's a personal 'brainstorm' or 'blitz'. You may have all the thoughts already at your fingertips, but the madman remembers other thoughts while shopping or walking along the street, or even, as we shall see in due course, whilst in the shower.

---

1 Betty S Flowers, 'Madman, Architect, Carpenter, Judge: Roles and the Writing Process' (1981) 58 *Language Arts*, 834–836.

The madman process could take anything from 10 minutes to 10 days. Don't put the thoughts in order and don't even think about writing in sentences: just words or short phrases to capture the point. Remember, no other role can interfere with this process.

When the madman is exhausted, you can then play the role of the architect.

The architect's job is to put all the random thoughts into the right order. In advocacy, unlike murder mystery novels or jokes, it's a good idea to put the punch line or the solution first. After that, a chronological order is usually helpful.

Can any of your thoughts be grouped into headings? Are they logically arranged? Do you think the readers will find the arrangement of thoughts persuasive?

The third role is what I call the builder. The madman has supplied all the material; the architect has designed the house; now it is the time to start building. It is the builder's job to create sentences from the arranged thoughts of the architect.

I will spend more time on the construction of the sentences in due course.

Once the sentences have been created, the judge can take over. The judge is the building inspector. He is pedantic and fussy. It is his job to check on the work of the architect, but more particularly, the builder.

The judge is not creative. He has little time for the sloppy thoughts of the madman. He has very definite views about the structure of sentences, their arrangement and the words used in them.

When he has finished his work, your document should be comprehensive and easy to read. With some polish it will be persuasive.

Most writers begin the process with the builder – or a rough draft of sentences. It works for some, but not many. The other roles interfere. The madman says, 'You have forgotten to include this!' The architect says, 'Don't put it there!' and the judge says, 'That's a very clumsy sentence!'

No wonder, after 10 minutes of this constant interference, most writers give up.

Think about how it is for lawyers. We go to university and learn lots of long and pompous words and some pretty indigestible jargon. My cynical friends call them 'money words' because we can charge more for explaining them. 'Hereinbefore', 'thereafter' and 'furthermore' are just a few.

When I was a first-year lawyer my colleagues and I met in the pub to talk about our experiences in court that day. After a while, I noticed that one of my best friends was speaking in a foreign language. He'd spoken plainly at university, but now he was saying things such as, 'I appeared this morning in the civil jurisdiction in respect of an application to amend particulars of claim pursuant to a notice served on the respondent ...'.

Back at the office, you had a Dictaphone shoved into your hand and you were expected to dictate letters to your secretary, making them up as you went along. Although they rarely showed it, it can't have been much fun for the poor secretary.

But back to Professor Flowers. Her formulation is so neat and easy to remember that it makes writing no longer a chore.

2 CONSTRUCTING THE SENTENCES

The builder phase is no doubt the most difficult. You must make it easier by shutting out the madman, architect and judge.

But many writers have given us guidance so it would be foolish not to listen to them.

2.1 Lord Denning

The first is Lord Denning, the legendary English judge. He had three first class honours degrees from Oxford; he took a law degree in seven months; he was a pre-eminent advocate and he became a High Court judge at 42, writing some of the most outstanding judgments in history.

It was his view that command of the language is the key to success in any profession where words count. He said the main problem with written documents was that the writer was thinking about himself and not his reader. 'He uses a word in the meaning which he himself puts on it: whereas he should be using it in the meaning which his [readers] put upon it.'[2]

Lord Denning cited the following example. A village had asked for a bus shelter to be provided near the school. This was *one* sentence in the reply by the council:

> 'The stated requirement for a shelter at this location has been noted, but as you may be aware shelter erection at all locations within West Yorkshire has been constrained in recent times as a result of instructions issued by the West Yorkshire Metropolitan County Council in the light of the Government's cuts in public expenditure and, although it seems likely that the capital budget for shelter provision will be enhanced in the forthcoming financial year, it is axiomatic that residual requests in respect of prospective shelter sites identified as having priority, notably those named in earlier programmes of shelter erection, will take precedence in any future shelter programme.'[3]

Denning had very firm ideas about writing. He believed in using simple, picture words and short sentences.

A lot of writers, he said, did not appreciate the simple truth that short words are better. He said they use long words so as to show off. It gives them a feeling of superior knowledge or at any rate a superior vocabulary.

If the purpose of the document is to communicate something to the reader and the reader does not understand it, the writer has failed. Denning recommended an average of 20 words or fewer in a sentence. He used simple words. He believed a massive unbroken page of print

---

2 Lord Denning, *The Closing Chapter* (Butterworths, London, 1983) 57–58.

3 Letter from West Yorkshire Transport Executive (1982), cited in ibid, 62.

is ugly to the eye and repulsive to the mind. A long, unbroken paragraph is indigestible.[4]

You know what it is like when you read books. If you have to keep stopping and re-reading sections because you did not get the sense of what the writer was saying, the exercise becomes tedious.

Think of the books you enjoy and how the writing just flows. The writer who does not make himself plain may either not understand the topic he is writing about or may not be thinking of his readers.

People say, well, the judges or the arbitrators are clever people: they will understand. But your job is to make their job easier.

Here are some examples of Lord Denning's style. These passages are how two distinguished Law Lords began their speeches in *Barclays Bank v Inland Revenue Commissioners*:[5]

> Lord Simonds: 'This appeal once more demands your Lordships' consideration of section 53 and 58 of the Finance Act 1940.'
>
> Lord Denning: 'My Lords, Tom Shipside died on December 15, 1955. The question is whether during the last five years before his death, he "hid the control of" a company called T. Shipside Ltd: for the amount of estate duty depends upon it.'

Denning's exposition is an excellent case theory. The words are simple and the problem is expressed succinctly with just the right touch of humanity.

Here is another example:

> 'Broadchalke is one of the most pleasing villages in England. Old Herbert Bundy, the defendant, was a farmer there. His

4 Ibid, 57–65.

5 [1961] AC 509.

home was Yew Tree Farm. It went back 300 years. His family had been there for generations. But he did a very foolish thing. He mortgaged it to the bank. Up to the very hilt.'[6]

Lord Denning was 100 when he died. At his memorial service in Westminster Abbey, the senior law lord, and the man who is regarded as the best English judge of the last 30 years, Lord Bingham, read out excerpts from Denning's famous judgments.

Lord Sedley wrote that Denning's 'literacy style, in fact, is perhaps his most underrated achievement':

> 'While in his many books simplicity is studied and embarrassingly overdone, Denning's judgment in case after case performed the feat achieved by no other judge, of speaking directly and compellingly to ordinary people in well-constructed and lucid prose. Concepts which lawyers had struggled to articulate, clashes of doctrine which seemed insoluble, would emerge in his judgments as crystalline statements of principle.'[7]

Here is my favourite passage from Lord Denning, which I mentioned in Chapter 1. It tells the tale of a tragic family outing:

> 'It happened on April 19, 1964. It was bluebell time in Kent. Mr and Mrs Hinz had been married some ten years, and they had 4 children all aged 9 and under. The youngest was one. Mrs Hinz was a remarkable woman. In addition to her own four, she was foster-mother to four other children. To add to it she was two months pregnant with her fifth child.
>
> On this day they drove out in a Bedford Dormobile van from Tonbridge to Canvey Island. They took all eight children with them.
>
> As they were coming back they turned into a lay-by at Thurnham to have a picnic tea. The husband, Mr Hinz, was

---

6 *Lloyds Bank Ltd v Bundy* [1974] EWCA Civ 8.

7 Stephen Sedley, 'Lord Denning Obituary', *The Guardian*, 6 March 1999.

> at the back of the Dormobile making the tea. Mrs Hinz had taken Stephanie, her third child, aged three, across the road to pick bluebells on the opposite side.
>
> There came along a Jaguar car driven by Mr Berry, out of control. A tyre had burst. The Jaguar rushed into this lay-by and crashed into Mr Hinz and the children. Mr Hinz was frightfully injured and died a little later. Nearly all the children were hurt. Blood was streaming from their heads.
>
> Mrs Hinz, hearing the crash, turned around and saw this disaster. She ran across the road and did all she could. Her husband was beyond recall. But the children recovered.'[8]

Let's analyse the writing in this judgment:

1 By beginning with the sentence 'It happened on April 19, 1964' the judge captured your attention. What happened? You want to keep reading.

2 The judge tells an almost complete story in five sentences. But he uses words which are simple, 'rushed', 'crashed', 'disaster', and there are a large number of picture words. You can see the scene of the accident.

3 Critics ask why he had to say 'It was bluebell time in Kent?' Because it sets up the happy and tranquil scene of the mother picking bluebells with her three-year-old daughter. They are blissfully unaware of what is about to happen.

4 Denning mentions all the elements or material facts necessary to found an action in nervous shock. Understandably, the mother suffered a psychiatric injury as the result of the negligent driving of the defendant.

One of his colleagues in many cases on the Court of Appeal wrote this about Denning:

> 'He was quite simply, a genius. He had the amazing facility of expressing complicated thoughts in clear, simple English ... He

---

8 *Hinz v Berry* [1970] 2 QB 40.

> always ... gave judgment ... in his characteristic way, making the facts come alive and linking the law to them in a way which was comprehensible to everyone.'[9]

Denning was asked to review the book in *The Daily Telegraph*. In his twinkling and not-so-modest style Denning wrote '… Sir Robin Dunn is a first-rate observer and he was one of the best judges of our time.'

2.2 George Orwell

Another great writer, George Orwell, posed the following questions:

1 What am I trying to say?

2 What words will express it?

3 What image or idiom will make it clearer?

4 Is this image fresh enough to have an effect?

5 Could I put it more shortly?

6 Have I said anything that is avoidably ugly?[10]

2.3 Bertrand Russell

Bertrand Russell exhorted writers to compose each sentence fully in the head before beginning to write it out.

Russell, who won the Nobel Prize for Literature, was also a physicist, mathematician, philosopher, logician and teacher. His brain was the size of Jupiter. If you can't compose the sentence fully in your head before writing it out, go back to basics. Madman, architect, builder, judge.

---

9 Sir Robin Dunn, *Sword and Wig: The Memoirs of a Lord Justice* (Quiller Press, London, 1993) 232–233.

10 George Orwell, *Why I Write* (Penguin Books, London, 1984) 113.

3 STATEMENTS OF CASE AND POINTS OF CLAIM

Drafting statements of case or points of claim is a difficult skill to master. In what appears to be a contradiction, they must be brief but detailed enough to do your case justice.

Their main purpose is to assist the court by identifying the issues and facts which frame the cause of action. The court will not go outside these issues and facts. The dispute is confined and therefore the court's resources will not be wasted.

The second purpose is to inform each party of the case it has to meet and prepare for.

You should consult the relevant rules, practice directions and court guides first.

The judges usually write the rules for their convenience.

What are the formal matters? How should the case be headed? Are there any rules about spacing or font size?

Should there be subheadings? Should there be a glossary? Must you attach any evidence such as the relevant sections of the contract?

What are the material facts? You will get these from your case analysis. Who are the parties? How does their relationship give rise to legal consequences?

You must plead a cause of action for every claimant and a legal liability for every defendant. Your pleadings on behalf of the claimant should mirror the cause of action.

Every time you plead a breach you should give details of the breach or what are called 'particulars'. Ask yourself, 'If I were defending this would I know what case I had to meet?' Parties should not have to dig for information from their opponent.

Unless you are required by the rules to do so, do not plead evidence (or how you intend to prove the fact).

Use uncontentious headings. Don't argue the case. Let the facts speak for themselves. Avoid annoying phrases such as 'Without prejudice to the foregoing' or 'Clearly'.

Don't plead law unless the rules demand it. Don't anticipate the defence.

What remedy or relief are you seeking? If it is damages, have you given sufficient details of the damage suffered? Are you entitled to interest? On what basis? Is it governed by the contract or a statute?

Who signs the document? Is there a statement of truth?

Read it over. Are there any holes in it? Is your opponent likely to ask for further information? Can you prove all the facts you have pleaded?

Is it easy to read?

4 WITNESS STATEMENTS

Many decision-makers form a view about the case by reading the witness statements before the hearing begins. This represents a huge opportunity for the drafter to make an early and good impression.

The witness statement should be in the witness's own words. It may well be that a nurse or a shopkeeper might use the phrase '*res ipsa loquitur*', but I doubt it.

As the editor of the statement, correct it for grammar and punctuation and remove slang or jargon. But do not change the character of your witness.

Don't include technical terms that the witness would not use. But if the witness does use those terms (such as an expert), make sure he explains what they mean.

Your witness must be happy with what he is saying otherwise his credibility and your case are in trouble.

The worst answer that your opponent can extract in cross-examination is 'I didn't say that. My lawyer wrote it for me'.

Keep the content focused. It should be the witness's account of the relevant facts of the cause of action, as experienced by them. Confine the statement to your witness's knowledge; usually what he saw, heard or believed. Think of the senses. If he believes something to be the case, get the witness to state the source of his knowledge, information or belief so that the judge can test it.

Avoid exaggeration, argument and conjecture. Present the statement in simple language, short sentences and uncontentious headings. Only include an opinion if the witness is qualified or entitled to give that opinion.

Usually, a chronological structure will be appropriate.

The witness statement should not be a commentary on the contents of documents. The judge can read them for herself.

Check that there are no inconsistencies in the statement.

Make sure you have complied with the procedural rules. In particular, Practice Direction 57AC in the Business and Property Courts of the High Court lays down detailed requirements for the preparation of trial witness statements. Non-compliance risks strike-out.[11]

5 AND FINALLY

The ability to tell a complete story succinctly is rare. Charles Moore, the former editor of *The Daily Telegraph* and biographer of Margaret Thatcher, has that ability.

He told an interesting story in *The Spectator*. It has humanity, simple words, some drama and a nice twist in the end, all in 152 words. Here it is:

---

[11] See *KSY Juice Blends UK Limited v Citrosuco GmbH* [2024] EWHC 2098 (Comm), [22] and *Fulstow and Another v Francis* [2024] EWHC 2122 (Ch), [21]–[36].

'I had not been to Honfleur since 1972 when, one cold spring, a school friend and I drove our mopeds there. We were so poor that we ate in a restaurant only once in the whole trip, choosing a modest place away from the town's main tourist attractions.

At the table next to us, a man eating alone ordered a bottle of cider and left having drunk only half of it. We could not believe that anyone could be so rich as to do this, and incited one another to take what remained of the bottle, but didn't dare.

My companion's name was George Robinson. Today he appears in the *Sunday Times* Rich List, where it alleges that he earns enough each year to buy himself 20 million bottles of cider. Sadly, I have not achieved this happy state, but my wife and I ordered cider, and dashingly left half of it.'[12]

---

[12] Charles Moore, The Spectator's notes, *The Spectator*, 1 August 2015.

Chapter 8
Skeleton Arguments

The purpose of a skeleton argument is to assist the court.[1]

It is amazing how many practitioners ignore this basic truth and produce documents that are verbose, impenetrable and infuriating.

The rules were created when Lord Donaldson was Master of the Rolls. In his autobiography, Lord Justice Kerr said that Donaldson was the leader of a 'long overdue efficiency drive' in the Court of Appeal:

> 'It was decided to do more pre-reading, to do away with lengthy opening of cases and reading from authorities, and to require the delivery of "skeleton arguments" in advance. For this I claim some credit, in particular for the name, but I am sure that John Donaldson as MR would claim the original copyright for a word which has now passed into the legal language throughout the English-speaking forensic world.'[2]

As is the problem with a number of skeleton arguments, Lord Justice Kerr leaves it at that and we are tantalised as to why he claims 'some credit'.

The skeleton 'should provide the court with a reasoned justification for finding in your favour':

> '... It allows the advocate *two* shots at persuading the court of his case. It is the golden opportunity for ... the advocate to

---

1 English Civil Procedure Rules, Practice Direction 52A, para 5.1(1).

2 Michael Kerr, *As Far As I Remember* (Hart Publishing, Oxford, 2002) 317.

persuade the judge of the merits of [the case] before [he opens] his mouth.'[3]

Practice Direction 52A of the English Civil Procedure Rules says that skeleton arguments must:

- '• be concise;
- both define and confine the areas of controversy;
- be set out in numbered paragraphs;
- be cross-referenced to any relevant document in the bundle;
- be self-contained and not incorporate by reference material from previous skeleton arguments;
- not include extensive quotations from documents or authorities.'

Documents to be relied upon must be identified. Where it is necessary to refer to an authority, a skeleton argument must:

1 state the proposition of law the authority demonstrates; and

2 identify the parts of the authority that support the proposition.

If more than one authority is cited in support of a given proposition, the skeleton argument must briefly state why.

The parties should consider what other information the (appeal) court will need. This may include a list of persons who feature in the case and glossaries of technical terms. A chronology of relevant events will be necessary in most appeals.[4]

Each court has different rules or peculiarities regarding skeleton arguments, and it is essential that you abide by the relevant practice

---

3 Michel Kallipetis KC and Lady Justice Andrews, 'Skeleton Arguments, A Practitioner's Guide' (The Honourable Society of Gray's Inn, London, 2004).

4 English Civil Procedure Rules, Practice Direction 52A.

direction and court guide. If you don't, you might attract criticism from the court and not get the costs of preparing the skeleton argument.

In *Inplayer Ltd v Thorogood*, Lord Justice Jackson said the message had not got through to the profession:

> 'As anyone who has drafted skeleton arguments knows, the task is not rocket science. It just requires a few minutes' clear thought and planning before you start. A good skeleton argument (of which we receive many) is a real help to judges when they are reading (usually voluminous) bundles. A bad skeleton argument simply adds to the paper jungle through which judges must hack their way in an effort to identify the issues and the competing arguments. A good skeleton argument is a real aid to the court during and after the hearing. A bad skeleton may be so unhelpful that the court simply proceeds on the basis of the grounds of appeal and whatever counsel says on the day.'[5]

Lord Justice Jackson said skeleton arguments should not exceed 25 pages. Many practitioners read this as meaning the skeletons must be 25 pages. His Lordship said, 'Usually it will be much shorter. In a straightforward case like this the skeleton argument would, or at least should, be much less than 25 pages'.[6]

The skeleton argument is there not only so that you can set out your case with precision and style, but also to help the judge find in your favour.

Make sure you don't present obstacles to the judge: too many words; bad grammar; trite or obvious law, such as 'you are bound by the overriding objective'; poor layout; long sentences or paragraphs; burying the main point in a morass of propositions. These are all irritants.

Before his elevation to the UK Supreme Court, Jonathan Sumption QC was interviewed in Inner Temple Hall about skeleton arguments.

---

5 *Inplayer Ltd v Thorogood* [2014] EWCA Civ 1511, [55].

6 Ibid, [52]–[57].

He was reported as saying, 'Judges start with an instinctive view and work backwards to justify it.'[7] He advised:

- 'The first paragraph of a skeleton should grab the judge with an interesting legal principle or interesting facts. It should not begin: "This is the hearing of ..."
- Bad points drive out good points. List your points in order of merit and briefly set out your position on them.
- Make it as pithy as possible. Use unusual turns of phrase.
- Forget your skeleton once the hearing begins. Don't make your oral presentation a mere commentary on your skeleton, but say things freshly so the judge listens to you rather than reads.
- Add historical or social context to make what you say more interesting.'

The 2004 paper by Michel Kallipetis KC and Lady Justice Andrews entitled 'Skeleton Arguments, A Practitioner's Guide' is essential reading. In it, they bring together three papers on effective skeleton arguments by Sir John Mummery, Sir James Hunt and Edmund Lawson QC.

Their conclusion is stark:

> 'Many a judgment has been handed down which owes its clarity and swiftness in delivery to a good skeleton argument. It is a good test when you have finished and before you hand it in to look at the skeleton and ask yourself: "If I was giving judgment in this case, how can I use this to produce it?"
>
> If you follow the guidance in this paper, you will produce a skeleton argument which is a valuable aid to oral advocacy – and the bones will flesh themselves out, with luck in a judgment.'[8]

---

7 Jonathan Sumption QC, 'Appellate Advocacy' (SEC's Masters of Advocacy series of lectures), 29 September 2009.

8 Kallipetis and Andrews, 'Skeleton Arguments' (fn 3), 12.

1 SKELETON ARGUMENTS: CHECKLIST

1.1 Purpose

An adverse reaction is a negative own goal.

What it should be:

- The key to opening the judge's mind.
- Short, pithy and persuasive.
- An aid to the court.
- Concise and user friendly.
- Accurate and reliable.
- Presented well.

What it should *not* be:

- A written submission.
- A US-style brief.
- Notes for a lecture.
- A commentary.
- The first draft of an article.
- A script.

1.2 Technical content

- Define and confine the areas of controversy.
- Cross-reference any relevant document.
- Make it self-contained, not referring to other skeleton arguments.
- Don't include extensive quotations from documents or authorities.

- 'We should not have to hack our way through a paper jungle to find the issues and competing arguments.'[9]
- Lord Justice Jackson: mild rebukes and gentle comments for non-compliance have not worked. As a result, expect non-compliance to mean no costs.

1.3 Referring to authorities

- State the proposition of law the authority demonstrates.
- Identify the parts of the authority that support the proposition.
- No trite law.
- Cite authorities succinctly, even ones against you.

1.4 Formal matters

Kallipetis and Andrews:[10]

- Not in excess of 25 pages.
- Printed on A4; 12- or 14-point font and 1.5-line spacing.
- One side of page only. Leave wide margins for notes by the judge.
- Headings and sub-headings.
- Numbered paragraphs.
- Avoid footnotes.
- If dates are important, use a chronology.
- Avoid confusing terminology.
- Conclude with what you want.
- Sign and date it.

---

9 *Inplayer Ltd v Thorogood* [2014] EWCA Civ 1511.

10 Kallipetis and Andrews, 'Skeleton Arguments' (fn 3).

1.5 Style

Lord Sumption:[11]

- Grab the judge with an interesting legal principle or interesting facts, not 'this is the hearing of ...'.
- Bad points drive out good points.
- Use unusual turns of phrase.
- Discard the skeleton at the hearing. Say fresh things.
- Add historical or social context.

---

11 Jonathan Sumption QC, 'Appellate Advocacy' (fn 7).

Chapter 9
Preparing Witnesses

This is a vexed subject. In some countries, lawyers hold expensive full-scale dress rehearsals of upcoming trials: complete with mock juries and judges.

In other places, witnesses are prepared for trial by videoing and voice coaching.

But in countries such as England and Wales the ability to prepare witnesses for trial is strictly controlled.

I remember the first time I briefed an English barrister. About an hour before court began, I asked him if he wanted to meet our witnesses. He recoiled in horror. He wasn't allowed to. I compounded the faux pas by saying 'Don't you want to see what they look like? One might have a facial tic. It might throw you if the witness box was the first time you saw him twitch.'

Nowadays the rules are more relaxed. In the Guidance Notes to the English Bar Standards Board's Code of Conduct it says that a barrister is:

> 'entitled and it may often be appropriate to draw to the witness's attention other evidence which appears to conflict with what the witness is saying and [the barrister] is entitled to indicate that a court may find a particular piece of evidence difficult to accept. But if the witness maintains that the evidence is true, it should be recorded in the witness statement

and [the barrister] will not be misleading the court if [he or she calls] the witness to confirm their witness statement.'[1]

1 ENCOURAGING FALSE EVIDENCE

The rule in England for barristers is that they 'must not encourage a witness to give evidence which is misleading or untruthful'.[2]

It goes further in Australia. 'A barrister must not advise or suggest to a witness that false or misleading evidence should be given; nor condone another person doing so ...'.[3]

In the United States, under the title of *Candor Toward the Tribunal*, the rule is that 'a lawyer shall not knowingly offer evidence that the lawyer knows to be false. If a lawyer ... has offered material evidence and comes to know of its falsity, the lawyer shall take reasonable remedial measures'.[4]

Look at the loopholes: 'knowingly'; 'he (the lawyer) knows to be false'; 'material evidence'.

2 COACHING

The English rule is stark. A barrister must 'not rehearse, practise with or coach a witness in respect of their evidence'.[5]

The original Middle English definition of the word 'rehearse' means to repeat aloud, and we all know what it means to rehearse for a play. The word 'practise' means to perform (an activity) or exercise (a skill) repeatedly or regularly in order to acquire, improve or maintain proficiency in it. To 'coach' means to train or instruct.

---

1 Bar Standards Board, Code of Conduct, guidance note gC7.

2 Ibid, rule C9.3.

3 Legal Profession Uniform Conduct (Barristers) Rules 2015, rule 69(a).

4 American Bar Association, Model Rules of Professional Conduct, rule 3.3(a)(3).

5 Bar Standards Board, Code of Conduct, rule C9.4.

In Australia, a barrister 'must not coach a witness by advising what answers the witness should give to questions which might be asked'.[6]

To the English and Australian positions, there are certain qualifications.

2.1 England

You must not knowingly or recklessly mislead or attempt to mislead anyone.[7]

You must not draft any statement of case, witness statement, affidavit or other document containing:

> 'a. any statement of fact or contention which is not supported by your client or by your instructions;
>
> b. any contention which you do not consider to be properly arguable;
>
> ...
>
> d. any statement of fact other than the evidence which you reasonably believe the witness would give if the witness were giving evidence orally.'[8]

You must not ask questions which suggest facts to witnesses which you know, or are instructed, are untrue or misleading.[9]

2.2 Australia

A barrister:

> 'does not breach [the main rule] by expressing a general admonition to tell the truth, or by questioning and testing in conference the version of evidence to be given by a prospective witness, including drawing the witness's attention to inconsistencies or other difficulties with the evidence, but

---

6 Legal Profession Uniform Conduct (Barristers) Rules 2015, rule 69(b).

7 Bar Standards Board, Code of Conduct, rule C9.1.

8 Ibid, rule C9.2.

9 Ibid, rule C6.1.b.

> must not encourage the witness to give evidence different from the evidence that the witness believes to be true.'[10]

In addition, a barrister may not confer with more than one lay witness at a time or condone another legal practitioner for doing so:

> '(a) about any issue which there are reasonable grounds for the barrister to believe may be contentious at a hearing; and
>
> (b) where such conferral could affect evidence to be given by any of those witnesses,
>
> unless the barrister believes on reasonable grounds that special circumstances require such a conference.'[11]

Note the loopholes again: 'reasonable grounds'; 'may be contentious'; 'could affect evidence'; and 'special circumstances'.

The barrister may not talk to a witness who is being cross-examined, except in special circumstances. [12]

2.3 United States

Things are starkly different in America. It is not called witness coaching – it is called witness interviewing. Federal judges must give the jury the following direction on this issue:

> 'It is proper for an attorney to interview any witness in preparation for trial.'

The leading case is *United States v Torres*.[13] The defence attorney accused the prosecutor of 'spending 8 or 9 hours' with the witness and 'juicing up the case'. He said, 'call that what you want.'

---

10 Legal Profession Uniform Conduct (Barristers) Rules 2015, rule 70.

11 Ibid, rule 71.

12 Ibid, rule 73.

13 *United States v Torres*, 28 F3d 1463, 1463 (7th Cir 1994).

It is perfectly proper for a lawyer to interview a witness in preparation for trial, and an attorney who does not question, rehearse and prepare his witnesses before trial, said the court, is not properly prepared for trial.

The prosecutor in this case was supported by the court. The defendant went to prison and the prosecutor became the Chief Judge in the district of North Illinois.

3 EXPERT WITNESSES

The question of preparing expert witnesses is interesting. In *Whitehouse v Jordan*,[14] Lord Denning noted that there were two long conferences between counsel and the professors who were expert witnesses. He said the joint expert report was actually settled by counsel.

'In short', said Denning:

> '[The report] wears the colour of a special pleading rather than an impartial report. Whenever counsel "settle" a document, we know how it goes. "We had better put this in, we had better leave this out" and so forth.'[15]

Lord Wilberforce, in the same case, thought there should be some degree of consultation between counsel and experts, but taking the practice too far is not only incorrect, it is self-defeating.

In an excellent paper entitled 'Can counsel settle expert reports?',[16] written by two Australian barristers, there was a watering-down of the Denning approach. They reviewed the changes in the rules and the authorities since Denning's decision in 1979 and concluded:

- counsel may (and *should*) identify and direct the expert witness to the real issues;

---

14 *Whitehouse v Jordan* [1980] 1 All ER 650.

15 Ibid, 655.

16 Garth Blake SC and Philippe Doyle Gray, 'Can Counsel Settle Expert Reports?' (2013) 199 *Precedent*, 16–20.

- counsel may (and *should*) suggest to the expert witness that an opinion does not address the real issues when counsel holds that view;
- counsel may (and *should*), when counsel holds the view, suggest to the expert witness that an opinion does not adequately:
  - illuminate the reasoning, leading to the opinion arrived at; or
  - distinguish between the assumed facts on which an opinion is based and the opinion itself; or
  - explain how the opinion proffered is one substantially based on his specialised knowledge.
- counsel may suggest to the witness that his opinion is either wrong or deficient in some way, with a view to the witness changing his opinion, provided that such suggestion stems from counsel's view after an analysis of the facts and law and is in furtherance of counsel's duty to the proper administration of justice, and not merely a desire to change an unfavourable opinion into a favourable opinion;
- counsel may make an expert report comprehensible and legible and compliant with the rules.

The leading English case is *R v Momodou*, a Court of Criminal Appeal decision.[17] A training firm presented a course for witnesses in an upcoming trial and used identical facts in the training case study to those in the trial.

The court said 'there is a dramatic distinction between witness training or coaching and witness familiarisation':

> 'Training or coaching for witnesses in criminal proceedings (whether for prosecution or defence) is not permitted.
>
> This is the logical consequence of the well-known principle that discussions between witnesses should not take place, and

[17] [2005] EWCA Crim 177.

> that the statements and proofs of one witness should not be disclosed to other witnesses.
>
> The witness should give his or her own evidence, so far as practicable uninfluenced by what anyone else has said and equally avoids any unfounded perception that he may have done so. These risks are inherent in witness training.'

The court went on:

> 'An honest witness may alter the emphasis of his evidence to accommodate what he thinks may be a different, more accurate, or simply better remembered perception of events.
>
> A dishonest witness will very rapidly calculate how his testimony may be improved.'

It is a tricky area. What if the training is done to ensure the witness speaks clearly and slowly? Surely this is of benefit to the court.

The court in *Momodou* seemed to acknowledge that some kind of witness familiarisation was advisable:

> 'familiarisation with the layout of the court; the likely sequence of events when the witness is giving evidence and a balanced appraisal of the different responsibilities of the various participants in the forum of a pre-trial visit to the court [were] to be welcomed.'

Later cases have followed *Momodou*.

In *Republic of Djibouti v Boreh*,[18] Flaux J said that witness training:

> 'is to be discouraged, since, as this case demonstrates, it tends to reflect badly on the witness, who, perhaps through no fault of his or her own, may appear to be evasive because he or she has not been "trained" to give evidence in a particular way.'

---

[18] [2016] EWHC 405 (Comm).

In *Harlequin Property (SVG) Ltd v Wilkins Kennedy*,[19] Coulson J remarked that he 'was unsurprised that Mr MacDonald had had witness training … In my view, the training he received exacerbated Mr MacDonald's natural tendency to avoid any difficult questioning.'

The other problem is where the examination-in-chief or direct examination has been dispensed with and the witness statement stands as the evidence-in-chief. The witness is cross-examined immediately and may be asked questions about facts which occurred years ago. Some civil cases take a long time to get to court. It is unfair to make the witness turn up in court cold. It does not assist the court either.

In short, get your witness ready for court but do not tell them what to say.

4 HOW JUDGES SEE WITNESSES

There is a lot of talk about how judges assess the demeanour of witnesses. Demeanour is important but cold, hard, even boring evidence is usually what tips the scales.

The English judge Lord Bingham said:

> 'Faced with a conflict of evidence on an issue substantially affecting the outcome of an action, often knowing that a decision this way or that will have momentous consequences on the parties' lives or fortunes, how can and should the judge set about his task of resolving it?
>
> How is he to resolve which witness is honest and which dishonest, which reliable and which unreliable?
>
> … The normal first step in resolving issues of primary fact is, I feel sure, to add to what is common ground between the parties (which the pleadings in the action should have identified, but often do not) such facts as are shown to be incontrovertible.

---

19 [2016] EWHC 3188 (TCC), [2017] 4 WLR 30.

> In many cases, letters or minutes written well before there was any breath of dispute between the parties may throw a very clear light on their knowledge and intention at a particular time. In other cases, evidence of tyre marks, debris or where vehicles ended up may be crucial.
>
> To attach importance to matters such as these, which are independent of human recollection, is so obvious and standard practice, and is in some cases so inevitable, that no prolonged discussion is called for.
>
> It is nonetheless worth bearing in mind, when conflicts of oral testimony arise, that these fall to be judged against the background not only of what the parties agree to have happened but also of what plainly did happen, even though the parties do not agree.'[20]

Lord Pearce wrote perceptively about witnesses. To him it was all about credibility.

'Credibility' involves wider problems than mere demeanour which is mostly concerned with whether the witness appears to be telling the truth as now he believes it to be:

> 'Credibility covers the following problems. First, is the witness a truthful or untruthful person?
>
> Secondly, is he, though a truthful person, telling something less than the truth on this issue, or though an untruthful person, telling the truth on this issue?
>
> Thirdly, though he is a truthful person telling the truth as he sees it, did he register the intentions of the conversation correctly and, if so has his memory correctly retained them?
>
> Also, has his recollection been subsequently altered by unconscious bias or wishful thinking or by over much discussion of it with others? Witnesses, especially those who

---

[20] Lord Bingham, 'The Judge as Juror: The Judicial Determination of Factual Issues' (1985) *Current Legal Problems*, 1–27 (reprinted in Tom Bingham, *The Business of Judging* (Oxford University Press, Oxford, 2004)). Reproduced with permission of the licensor through PLS Clear.

> are emotional, who think that they are morally in the right, tend very easily and unconsciously to conjure up a legal right that did not exist.'[21]

Anyone who has had clients knows this. They have developed a case theory before they meet you and all the facts are sifted, chosen and sometimes twisted to suit that theory under the guise that they have been wronged or they are in the right. It is hard to shift them from their theories. When a sober, dispassionate judge rejects their version they feel terrible wrong has been done. How are they going to save face with all the family and friends to whom they have propounded their theory in the preceding months, or sometimes years?

Lord Pearce went on, 'It is a truism, often used in accident cases, that with every day that passes the memory becomes fainter and the imagination more active.'[22]

5 CONTEMPORARY DOCUMENTS

> 'For that reason a witness, however honest, rarely persuades a judge that his present recollection is preferable to that which was taken down in writing immediately after the accident occurred.
>
> Therefore contemporary documents are always of utmost importance.'

Lord Pearce wrote this judgment in 1968. Nowadays, often the best evidence a lawyer can obtain is in emails, tweets, Facebook remarks or texts. This evidence is not only contemporary; it is almost immediate. It is often emotional or knee-jerk and is of great value in assessing the maker's state of mind at the time.

Lord Pearce concluded his remarks by saying:

---

21 *Onassis v Vergottis* [1968] 2 Lloyd's Rep 403, 431.

22 Ibid.

> 'Although the honest witness believes he heard or saw this or that, is it so improbable that it is on balance more likely that he was mistaken?
>
> On this point it is essential that the balance of probability is put correctly into the scales in weighing the credibility of a witness. And motive is one aspect of probability.
>
> All these problems compendiously are entailed when a judge assesses the credibility of a witness; they are all part of one judicial process. And in the process contemporary documents and admitted or incontrovertible facts and probabilities must play their proper part.'[23]

Lady Justice Arden said that contemporaneous documentation can be significant in checking the witness's account:

> 'It can also be significant if written documentation is absent. For instance, if the judge is satisfied that certain contemporaneous documentation is likely to have existed were the oral evidence correct, and that the party adducing oral evidence is responsible for its non-production, then the documentation may be conspicuous by its absence and the judge may be able to draw inferences from its absence.'[24]

6 PRACTICAL MATTERS

It is not coaching a witness to advise them to dress smartly and to turn up on time. It is not rehearsing a witness to tell them to become thoroughly familiar with their witness statement in good time for the hearing.

And it is not training a witness to let them know in advance that they will be cross-examined and that they should give succinct, polite and relevant answers, speak loudly enough to be heard, address their answers to the judge, and say so if they did not understand the question.

---

23 Ibid.

24 Arden LJ, *Wetton v Ahmed* [2011] EWCA Civ 610, [14].

Just don't tell your witness what to say.

To conclude, one of Australia's most distinguished barristers was Chester Porter QC, who was known as 'The Smiling Funnel Web'. [25]

In his memoirs he wrote, 'In 52 years of experience at the Bar, the best witness of conversations I ever saw and heard was a crooked developer.'[26]

---

[25] A poisonous Australian spider.

[26] Chester Porter, *Walking on Water* (Random House, Australia, 2003) 266.

Chapter 10
Examination-in-Chief or Direct Examination

Examination-in-chief, which for the purposes of convenience I call 'direct examination' from now on, is the process of asking questions of your own witness. The aim is to get the witness to give answers which help prove your case.

Direct examination is not used in quite a few countries; it has largely been dispensed with in civil cases in England and Wales and it is rarely if ever used in arbitration.

Why do you need to know about it then? Well, in those courts where it is used, such as criminal courts, the advocate must be familiar with the basic technique.

But in learning advocacy generally it is helpful for three main reasons:

1 It helps you to be a better interviewer if you are required to take a witness statement.

2 The same techniques are used in re-examination or re-direct examination.

3 It reinforces a recognition of the sort of questions you should not use in cross-examination.

The idea of advocacy as story telling still applies. In this case you are facilitating your witness to tell his story to the court. So, to be effective, the facts must be attractively arranged.

In civil cases in England and Wales some witnesses do not appear in court to give evidence until months, if not years, after the event that they speak of. Historically, direct examination was becoming a memory test and all sorts of rules cropped up to deal with situations where the memory of the witness was exhausted.

To avoid these problems and mainly to save time, in 1999 the Civil Procedure Rules brought in a change of approach. The witness is now called, introduced, asked if his statement is true, given the opportunity to make any additions or corrections, and then the statement is tendered. [1]

In effect, a witness in civil proceedings in England and Wales does not now have much to say at all before being subjected to cross-examination.

This 'reform' caused some resentment, especially among witnesses who were parties to the case, because they did not feel they were having their say.

It also means that the drafting of the statement has become much more important. The English rules demand that the statement be written in the witness's own words, but not many witness statements escape the dead hand of the lawyer.

One of my students told me of a witness statement that had been delivered to her by her opponent in a matrimonial case. It read 'My boyfriend took me to Paris where we shagged all weekend. Then I returned to London where I resumed normal marital cohabitation with my husband.'

You can learn a lot about direct examination from watching interviewers on television. The good ones put the spotlight on the guest and listen to the answers. The bad ones put the spotlight on themselves and ignore the answers.

The TV interviewer wants the guest to talk for reasons of entertainment. Direct examination is a more difficult skill because the advocate is not having a conversation with the witness. The advocate is asking questions designed to get the witness to give answers to the court. The advocate does not want the witness to talk too much or go off the point. The witness must be controlled to give relevant probative evidence.

---

1 English Civil Procedure Rules, rule 32.5(2).

Here are some simple rules which will enable you to carry out a successful direct examination.

1 NO LEADING QUESTIONS

A leading question puts words into the mouth of the witness. It contains the facts the witness should be saying. For example:

Advocate: 'You are wearing a blue, woollen suit?'

Witness: 'Yes.'

Leading questions are forbidden for a very good reason. The advocate is not a witness and she cannot be cross-examined. Anyway, she was not at the scene.

If the lawyer were to state all the facts, there would be no need for the witness to be there. But it would be highly unpersuasive.

2 START YOUR QUESTIONS WITH THE WORDS 'WHAT', 'WHEN', 'WHERE', 'WHY', 'HOW', 'WHO', 'PLEASE DESCRIBE', 'TELL THE COURT'

So, using the first example again, the question should be:

Advocate: 'What are you wearing?'

Witness: 'A suit.'

Advocate: 'What colour is it?'

Witness: 'Blue.'

Advocate: 'What is it made of?'

Witness: 'Wool.'

Be careful. Even if your question begins with one of these words, it may still be leading. For example:

Advocate: 'Why do you always wear blue?'

This question is still leading because it proceeds on the assumption that the witness always wears blue.

However, generally these words are at the beginning of what we call 'open' questions: those which invite a descriptive answer. Good journalists use them. A well-written news item will normally have answered these questions. If a train crash has been reported we would be very frustrated if we were not told where it happened, when it happened, how it happened and so on.

The English poet, Rudyard Kipling, put it succinctly:

> 'I keep six honest serving men,
> (They taught me all I knew.)
> Their names are What and Why and When
> And How and Where and Who.'[2]

3 SIMPLE WORDS AND SHORT QUESTIONS

Because they are nervous, a lot of advocates speak their thoughts out loud as they ask a question. The real point gets lost.

For instance, an advocate might say:

> 'Now I am going to ask you a few questions, for the purposes of clarification, on the subject of the suit, in particular its colour ... what is it, and by that I mean what colour is it?'

Resist the temptation to speak before you ask your question. Think quietly and not aloud. Then say:

> 'What colour is your suit?'

It is important to concentrate on one fact per question. The first question comprised 37 words, most of which were unnecessary to elicit the fact. The second question contained five words.

---

2 Rudyard Kipling, 'I Keep Six Honest Serving Men', www.kiplingsociety.co.uk/poem/poems_serving.htm.

Despite this, some form of the first question is often seen in courts.

In my experience, the shorter the question, the more impact is contained in the answer.

4 STYLE

Speak clearly, in simple language and try to limit your questions to six words or fewer. Above all, make sure the spotlight is on the witness and not you.

Watch the witness carefully. Does he understand what you are saying? Did he hear you correctly? Is he talking too fast for the court to make a note?

Watch the judge, court, jury or arbitration panel like a hawk.

Are they going to sleep? Can they keep up? Are your best facts getting home? If not, you are wasting your time.

None of these things will be achieved if your head is down, reading the question.

5 ARRANGE YOUR FACTS

An attractive arrangement of facts goes a long way to persuading the court. You have a couple of options in arranging your facts. It could be done chronologically, which is the traditional method. What happened first, up to what happened last?

The other way is to arrange the facts into subject: the agreement; the breach; and the damages. You have to work out which is the most effective arrangement and the one that will bring out the best in your witness.

It is easier for the decision-maker if you use 'headlines' when you introduce a new topic.

For example, 'I'm now going to ask you some questions about the sculpture itself.'

These headlines not only direct the witness and the court to the area being examined, but also make it easier for the decision-maker to record a note of the evidence.

6 SOURCES OF EVIDENCE

Most witnesses get their information from one of their five senses, most typically what they saw or what they heard.

There are other sources such as what they believed, 'I believed he was trying to sell it to me', or what they knew, 'I had been told to be careful of the dog'.

A court likes to test the source of the information, so a good examiner listens to the answer and asks himself 'Is that good enough for the judge?'

For example, 'I walked into the house and saw an angry man.'

The signal to the examiner is the word 'angry'. It is a conclusion and it is also the opinion of the witness. Is it good enough? No.

We know the source. It was what the witness saw. But what is the source of his opinion that the man was so angry?

An average advocate would ignore the answer and move to the next point.

A better advocate would think out loud and say, 'Now you used the word angry. It's not quite clear what you mean. What were you intending to convey?'

The most effective advocate would simply ask:

	'What do you mean by angry?'
Answer:	'He was shouting and swearing, clenching his fists etc ...'.

Always be on the lookout for a conclusion. They are rarely persuasive.

Here is another example:

Advocate: 'What did you see?'

Witness: 'I saw a man in a blue suit who was very drunk.'

Ask yourself: would a better answer contain more facts? Is 'very drunk' good enough for the judge? No.

Advocate: 'What do you mean by "very drunk"?'

Witness: 'Well, he was staggering. His eyes were bloodshot, his speech was slurred and his breath smelled strongly of liquor.'

Now an average lawyer might be tempted to say what is in her mind:

Witness: 'I saw a man in a blue suit who was very drunk.'

Advocate: 'Would you care to elaborate on that for the court?'

Witness: 'On what?'

Advocate: 'Well you've said in your answer the man was very drunk. What do you mean when you say that?'

This is a clumsy way to tease out the answer. The question in the first example, 'What do you mean by "very drunk"?', is seven words long.

The second series of questions is 29 words to get to the same result.

7 CONTROLLING THE WITNESS

The guest on the talk show is there to entertain. The witness is there to help prove the case. Michael Parkinson wanted his guests to talk. But a loquacious witness is rarely popular in the courtroom. Then again, someone who clams up in the witness box is not much better.

Your job, as the director of the show, is to get the witness to be like Goldilocks' porridge: just right.

There is a wonderful story about a well-known barrister in Tasmania who later became a Supreme Court judge.

His client was in the witness box: a nervous woman in her mid-50s. He established her name and address then the woman blurted her evidence out word for word, for three minutes, without stopping. Then she said, 'Did I get all that right Mr Cosgrove?'

There are a number of techniques for controlling a witness and they all involve signposts.

Let's just imagine you are driving a car. The judge is in the back seat and your witness is in the front. Some pieces of evidence are much more important than others.

You can slow down for these sections, taking them piece by piece. As top New York advocate Ben Rubinowitz puts it, 'frame by frame' – like the pictures on those, dare I say it, old reel-to-reel movies.

For other topics you can move more quickly because they are not so important. But you can use signposts to guide you. Let me give you an example using the *Cavendish v Downham* case study in Appendix 1:

> Advocate: 'Mr Cavendish. May I take you to 28 November? What were you doing that afternoon?'

Note the signpost or headline and the open question of six words.

> Witness: 'I was in my shop when I got a phone call.'

The following evidence may be very important because it involves the description of the sculpture. You must slow the car right down. Take care to see that the judge can take a note. Slowing down signifies to the court that the next passage is important.

Advocate:	'Who called?'
Witness:	'A woman called Mrs Downham.'
Advocate:	'What did she say?'
Witness:	'She said "I have a Mesopotamian sculpture for sale. It is of a soldier and two horses. Circa 681–669."'
Advocate:	'What did you do?'
Witness:	'I wrote down what she said on a piece of paper.'
Advocate:	'Why?'
Witness:	'Because it was important.'
Advocate:	'Where is that piece of paper today?'
Witness:	'I don't know. I lost it. But I remember what she said.'

The second way to control a witness is to take them to an actual period of time.

If you were to ask a witness, 'What did you do after you left work yesterday?', you might get an answer that is so long it takes you up to the time he went to bed. Yet you might only be seeking to establish what he saw on the train on his way home from work. Let's say he witnessed an assault.

You should put a time limit on any question which you hope would apply to his answer:

Advocate:	'What did you do in the 15 minutes after you left work yesterday?'
Witness:	'I walked to the train station.'
Advocate:	'Which station was that?'
Witness:	'Blackfriars.'

Advocate: 'What time did you arrive at Blackfriars station?'

Witness: '5:30. I always get the 5:35 train.'

Advocate: 'Where were you going?'

Witness: 'Home.'

Advocate: 'What did you do when you got to Blackfriars?'

Witness: 'I got on the train.'

Advocate: 'Which carriage?'

Witness: 'The third from the back.'

Advocate: 'Describe the carriage.'

Witness: 'It had about 100 seats. Some facing forwards and some backwards. All the seats were taken. It was standing only.'

Advocate: 'In which part were you?' (Or 'Where were you?')

Witness: 'I was standing near the door closest to the back of the train.'

Now look how short and simple the examiner's questions are and how the answers have an impact. You want to know what happened next. So will the judge.

The third method of control is a transition – a movement in time. It also comes in the form of a signpost:

Advocate: 'Let me take you back to when you arrived at Blackfriars. Describe the scene as you entered the station.'

Witness: 'It was packed with people. It always is. Everyone was in a hurry.'

Or you could move the witness forward, being careful not to ask a leading question:

Advocate:	'I want to ask you about the end of your journey. Where was that?'

So transitions are movements in time. Remember, you are controlling the speed and the amount of information that the witness is giving.

Signposts are also useful to focus the witness's and the court's attention in cross-examination.

8 WHAT HAPPENED NEXT?

One of the things an advocate should avoid is repeating the question 'What happened next?' It becomes jarring after a while and sometimes takes the impact from the answers given by the witness. Yet often it is unavoidable.

The problem can be lessened by what American advocates call 'looping'. Looping is the process of including part of the answer in your next question. For example:

Advocate:	'Where were you?'
Witness:	'I was standing near the door closest to the back of the train.'
Advocate:	'Which side of the train?'
Witness:	'The right-hand side as you face the driver.'
Advocate:	'From the right-hand side what could you see?'
Witness:	'I could see both sides of the entire carriage.'

Be careful that you do not overdo the looping technique because it might become a gremlin. (See para 13, 'Avoid gremlins'.)

9 KNOW THE ANSWER

As we have seen, a lot of techniques of advocacy involve story telling. In direct examination, you are getting a witness to tell her story in the most appealing way possible.

It is therefore assumed that you know what the witness is going to say. The witness might not be allowed to read her witness statement. In preparing for the performance, you will have to frame the questions carefully to elicit the right facts in the best order.

Here is a transcript of a radio interview which took place in Belfast on 8 January 2014. It was held on the anniversary of the Kegworth Air Disaster. Many people were killed when a plane headed for Northern Ireland crashed on a motorway near Nottingham at a place called Kegworth.

The interviewee was a survivor.

Question one

Interviewer:	'Now it's 25 years ago today. Does that seem like a long time or a short time or hasn't it left your mind at all?'
Survivor:	'I'll never forget it.'

Question two

Interviewer:	'Now you were sitting down the front of the plane, is that right?'
Survivor:	'No it's not. I was down the back.'

Question three

Interviewer:	'Now isn't it true that most of the passengers who were killed were sitting up the front of the plane?'

Try to analyse what is wrong with each question. The overwhelming impression is that the interviewer does not know what the answers are going to be because he does not know what happened.

10 AVOID COMPOUND QUESTIONS

A compound question contains more than one fact or thought.

There is a compound question in the Kegworth interview:

> 'Does it seem like a long time or a short time or hasn't it left your mind at all?'

The interviewer gets a good answer, but it is more from luck than anything else:

> 'I'll never forget it.'

The problem with compound questions is the witness may choose which part of the question he wishes to answer and ignore the others:

> 'What did you do at 5 pm, 6 pm and 7 pm last night?'
>
> 'Well at 7 pm I went to dinner.'

The question should have been broken up into bite-sized pieces:

> 'What did you do at 5 pm?'
>
> 'I left work and headed home.'
>
> 'When did you get there?'
>
> '6 pm.'
>
> 'Between 6 pm and 7 pm what did you do?'
>
> 'I prepared a chicken stir-fry.'

11 LISTEN TO THE ANSWER

Apart from making sure the question is open, this is the most important skill in examining witnesses directly. I saw an interview with the late Max Clifford and Ted Francis many years ago. It was just after the world-famous novelist Jeffrey Archer had been convicted of perjury.

Clifford, a publicist for celebrities, was being asked about Archer. Ted Francis was Archer's co-accused and he had been acquitted.

The gist of the interview, as much as I can recall, was this:

Interviewer: 'Everyone wants to know why Mary Archer stands by her husband.'

Clifford: 'I agree there is a lot of speculation. Is it a financial reason? Is it for the sake of the family? Does he have some hold over her? There have been many answers to this question. I know the real answer.'

Interviewer: 'Ted, you've got a book coming out soon ...'

Now, in fairness to the interviewer, he might have considered it not a good idea to have invited what may have been a libellous answer, but I was so frustrated, I wanted to throw a shoe at the telly.

The witness's answers are what the judge is recording, not your questions.

You must ask yourself after every question, 'Was that answer good enough for the judge?' and 'Does it need to be clarified?'

The usual characteristic of an unsatisfactory answer is a conclusion or a value judgement (see para 6, 'Sources of evidence').

Say you have a nervous or uncommunicative witness and the following occurs:

'What did you do at 6 pm?'

'Not much.'

It's not a satisfactory answer. Remember to include the witness's words (looping) and ask:

'What do you mean by not much?'

'I was standing outside the kebab shop.'

'What could you see?'

12 TAKE THE STING OUT OF THE CROSS-EXAMINATION

If there is a weakness in your witness's evidence or a string of bad facts, it might be a good idea to ask for your witness's version first.

Belfast advocacy trainer Fiona Donnelly says it is a bit like the child who gets into trouble. Would it be better for the child to tell his mother first or wait until his sister informs on him?

But be careful. Do this only if you think that it is necessary in order to take the sting out of the approaching cross-examination, and do so especially if your client has a plausible explanation.

13 AVOID GREMLINS

A gremlin is a verbal tic which, after a while, annoys the listener. It appears in direct examination and cross-examination. You will usually not know you have a gremlin until you are diagnosed.

I put people into categories according to their particular gremlin or gremlins. They can be anders, echoers, ummers, thankers, okers, smilers or correctors. The list is quite long.

Here is an example of an ander:

> 'And, where did you go on your last holiday?'
>
> 'Spain.'
>
> 'And, how did you get there?'
>
> 'I flew.'
>
> 'And, who was that with?'
>
> 'Ryanair.'
>
> 'And, when did you go?'
>
> 'February.'

Or an echoer:

> 'Where did you go on your last holiday?'
>
> 'Spain.'
>
> 'Spain. How did you get there?'
>
> 'I flew.
>
> 'You flew. Who was that with?'
>
> 'Ryanair.'
>
> 'Ryanair. When did you go?'
>
> 'February.'
>
> 'February.'

Or a thanker:

> 'Where did you go on your last holiday?'
>
> 'Spain.'
>
> 'Thank you. How did you get there?'
>
> 'I flew.'
>
> 'Thank you. Who was that with?'
>
> 'Ryanair.'
>
> 'Thank you. When did you go?'
>
> 'February.'
>
> 'Thank you.'

A very senior judge once told me that an advocate in his court began every question with the words, 'Now let me ask you this ...'.

The judge said that after a short time it was so annoying that he found himself unable to hear the evidence.

I call them gremlins because as soon as you get rid of one another is likely to bob up.

As human beings we learn to react to what a person is saying to us by nodding or smiling or repeating what they have said from time to time. In court, you are not having a conversation with the witness. You are facilitating so that the witness will give her evidence to the decision-maker.

Once you know you have a gremlin you should eradicate it by pausing or taking a small imperceptible breath after the witness answers.

14 END STRONGLY

Your last question should draw out an answer that makes an impact and is memorable for the right reasons.

For example, this is one way to end.

Advocate:	'What did you see?'
Witness:	'I saw the defendant throwing a punch at me.'
Advocate:	'What did you do?'
Witness:	'I thought, steady on old man. That's a bit out of order.'
Advocate:	'No further questions.'

It doesn't have much of an impact. You are not ending on a high.

What about this?

Advocate:	'What did you see?'
Witness:	'I saw the defendant throwing a punch at me.'
Advocate:	'Describe the punch.'
Witness:	'It was a left hook which shattered the right-hand side of my jaw.'
Advocate:	'No further questions.'

Of course, you may not wish to stop there. There may be questions about the aftermath. But the last answer is strong and memorable.

Whatever you do, make sure the last question complies with the rules. If you ask a leading question, you will probably get an objection from your opponent. The power of the last answer will disappear.

Chapter 11
Cross-Examination

In popular imagination, cross-examination is the most glamorous part of advocacy. This is because the destruction of a dishonest witness evokes in the audience the feeling that justice has been done. But it is also because the systematic and clever dismantling of the evidence of a witness is a dramatic spectacle.

It is even more exciting if it is gladiatorial and the protagonists are evenly matched. The drama is heightened when the stakes are increased. People love a fair fight and will applaud whoever wins.

The trouble with the popular conception of cross-examination is that it is generally wrong. People think that it is arguing with the witness until he says, 'I am the murderer.' That's TV. Or arguing with the witness until the judge says, 'No! I am the murderer.' That's American TV. Or saying to the witness, 'You can't handle the truth.' That's Hollywood.

But I want to show you that real cross-examination is none of these things. It is a method of using your opponent's witness to highlight the good facts of your client's case and the bad facts of theirs. It is also used to show the omissions in your opponent's case.

It is all about control. I have heard it said that the cross-examiner is really telling her client's story, fact by fact, through the mouth of her opponent's witness.

Some judges are not happy with this definition. They say it is the witness who is here to give evidence, not the advocate. But unless you have special reasons (which we come to later) you do not want the witness taking control or talking too much.

Let's face it, your opponent's witnesses do not want to help your client and it is more likely they want to cause damage; so why let them?

Another popular misconception is that the cross-examiner should shout or sound affronted by the witness's answers. That might make good TV, but it is not effective in court or before an arbitration panel.

Sir Garfield Barwick QC was very frank about his approach to cross-examination:

> 'Cross-examination is an art I do not think I ever fully mastered, certainly not to the degree attained by others. Some were successful in attacking a witness in an endeavour to destroy his credibility and thus eliminate his evidence from the case. I developed no such talent.'[1]

As Lord Millett put it, 'Let the witness believe that you are accepting his evidence, gain his confidence and lead him gently to agree when you ask the crucial question.'[2]

This is not as easy as it sounds. Even a person as distinguished as Lord Millett, whose stellar career as an advocate and a judge led him to the pinnacle at the House of Lords, said that in the 25 years he practised at the Bar he doubted he had 'more than three successful cross-examinations'.[3]

1 THE PURPOSE OF CROSS-EXAMINATION

The first purpose of cross-examination is to strengthen your client's case by eliciting helpful facts from your opponent's witness.

Look at the statement of the witness. Compare it to your case analysis. Can this witness confirm any facts which appear in the 'Good' column of your case analysis?

---

1 Garfield Barwick, *A Radical Tory* (Federation Press, Sydney, 1995) 23.

2 Peter Millett, *As in Memory Long* (Wildy, Simmonds & Hill Publishing, London, 2015).

3 Ibid, 94.

It does not have to be direct confirmation. Can the witness agree with something that shows it to be more likely than not that the fact is true?

Some people say, 'Why do you have to do this, if your witness has already given evidence of the fact or is due to?'

Well, because corroboration or support from another witness or piece of evidence (such as Monica Lewinsky's dress), particularly a witness called by your opponent, makes it much more reliable and persuasive.

The second purpose of cross-examination is to undermine or discredit your opponent's case by showing the witness is unreliable or, more specifically, that the witness's evidence is unreliable.

If you think about it, most if not all of the laws of evidence are designed to ensure that what a court bases its decision on is reliable. So speculation, conjecture and theories of lay witnesses are excluded by law.

In order to show that evidence is unreliable, you don't need to jump to the conclusion that the witness is lying. The vast majority of witnesses are honest or believe they are being honest. It does not help to attack these people for lying. It smacks of bullying and is not persuasive.

The best definition of cross-examination came from Sir Edward Clarke, who was the Solicitor General from 1886 to 1892 and leader of the Bar in England for many years. He also represented Oscar Wilde in the case against the Marquess of Queensberry. He was unsuccessful, but that was because his client, the celebrated playwright, assured him he was telling the truth.

Clarke's definition appeared in an unfinished treatise. Speaking of the three best cross-examiners of his youth, William Ballantine, Henry Hawkins and John Coleridge, Sir Edward said:

> '[They] were very different in style, but the secret of success with each of them was this, that he always tried to interest the jury, was never tedious, and never forgot that *the object of*

> *cross-examination was not the collection of a complete series of facts, but the placing [of] selected facts in such a light as to lead to a particular conclusion.*'[4]

I would add only the words 'or omissions' after the words 'selected facts'.

The word 'object' is interesting. Cross-examination is inextricably linked with the closing speech. The arrangement of facts or omissions is done to achieve an objective. The objective is what the advocate intends to argue in the closing submission or speech. In other words, it is the advocate's explanation to the decision-maker of what the arrangement of facts or omissions means. Sometimes, the meaning will be obvious.

Clarke's definition raises the vexed issue of how one should put one's case, but I come to that subject in due course.

Sir Edward Clarke put it this way:

> 'The most skilful and effective cross-examination is that which interests the [decision-makers] and sets them thinking what the answer to the [claimant's] case ... can possibly be, and by the selection and arrangement of the facts referred to, suggests the [respondent's] case instead of stating it.'[5]

Let us look at an example of a factually arranged cross-examination.

Let's say the witness has just said that she saw John Pearce coming out of a bar at 2:50 am. It is crucial evidence because Mark Johnston was killed in the bar and no one else had been in there.

Here is the cross-examination of the witness. Note the selection and arrangement of the facts:

---

4 Printed in EW Fordham, *Notable Cross-examinations* (Constable & Co London 1952) Appendix 193 (emphasis added).

5 Sir Edward Clarke KC, 'Unfinished Treatise', reproduced in ibid, Appendix 193.

'The person you saw was 30 yards away?'

'Yes.'

'In a group of other people?'

'Yes.'

'With their backs to you?'

'Yes.'

'It was 2:50 am?'

'Yes.'

'And raining?'

'Yes.'

'The person was wearing a dark coat?'

'Yes.'

'And a dark hood?'

'Yes.'

'I have no further questions.'

1 What is the cross-examiner's objective?

To be able to argue in closing that the witness could not have been able to identify John Smith.

2 Did the cross-examiner need to state boldly, 'You could not identify him?' or 'You would not have been able to?'

No.

3 What is the source of the witness's evidence that the cross-examiner is seeking to undermine or weaken?

Her eyesight.

4 Was there any need for the cross-examiner to go any further?

No.

This little illustration pre-supposes that the cross-examiner knows what the answers are going to be. But that point aside, it is also a neat illustration of selected and arranged facts.

Here is an example of a cross-examination (often seen in court) that selects all the facts:

> 'The person you saw was 30 yards away?'
>
> 'Yes.'
>
> 'Adjacent to a building with a neon sign?'
>
> 'Yes.'
>
> 'Which was a big golden M?'
>
> 'Yes.'
>
> 'Because it was McDonald's?'
>
> 'Yes.'
>
> 'And they had chicken burgers on special that day?'
>
> 'Yes.'
>
> 'For £1.69?'

And so it goes on, relating all the facts, relevant or otherwise.

Here is an example of a cross-examination where the facts are badly arranged:

> 'The person you saw had a dark hood on?'
>
> 'Yes.'
>
> 'And it was raining?'
>
> 'Yes.'
>
> 'And it was 2:50 am?'
>
> 'Yes.'
>
> 'The person was wearing a dark coat?'
>
> 'Yes.'
>
> 'You couldn't see his face?'
>
> 'No.'
>
> 'He had a dark coat on?'
>
> 'Yes.'

'In a group of other people.'

'Yes.'

'And you were 30 yards away?'

Now, this cross-examination is not as smooth as the first. It is clunky. It troubles the mind's eye. And it also introduces an unwanted word – the word 'he' – which is not helpful to the cross-examiner's case because it tends to identify the witness.

Cross-examination may also be used to arrange the witness's omissions – things that the witness could have done but did not.

Let's say the witness has just given evidence that someone made an important admission to her over the telephone. Now that virtually everyone has a mobile phone this example may be obsolescent, but it illustrates the point about 'omissions':

'You took the call at 3 pm?'

'Yes.'

'In your kitchen?'

'Yes.'

'Where there is a phone?'

'Yes.'

'Fixed to the wall?'

'Yes.'

'And underneath the phone is a bench?'

'Yes.'

'On that bench was a pad of paper?'

'Yes.'

'And next to that pad was a pen?'

'Yes.'

'Yet you didn't write down what the caller said?'

'No, I didn't.'

'You didn't write it down after the call?'

'No, I didn't.'

'You didn't write it down an hour later?'

'No.'

'Or a week later?'

'No, I didn't.'

'And here we are in court one year later and you still haven't written it down, have you?'

'No.'

'We are relying entirely on your memory?'

Now, my students sometimes remark 'What if the witness says they have written it down?' Then your next question will also be a closed question, 'You haven't disclosed that note, have you?'

It could be argued that the question 'We are relying entirely on your memory?' is unnecessary and therefore risky. The question is a conclusion which really belongs in the closing speech.

You will note how the cross-examiner built the case brick by brick or fact by fact then omission by omission.

A poor cross-examiner would have started by saying, 'We can't rely on your memory because you didn't write it down.'

Think how a witness would have dealt with that question. She would have chosen which part of the question to argue with or given a non-responsive answer such as, 'I have a very good memory, thank you.'

2 SHOWING EVIDENCE TO BE UNRELIABLE

Showing that the evidence of a witness is unreliable does not mean showing they are making the evidence up or being dishonest.

Here are a few categories of unreliability. They make good objectives to argue in your closing speech.

2.1 Mistaken, lazy or unprepared

An example of a witness being shown to be mistaken is the cross-examination above of the woman claiming to be able to identify a person who was 30 yards away and wearing a dark coat and dark hood.

2.2 Incompetent

This is an attack on the ability of the witness – not so much a full-frontal assault as a series of facts suggesting in total that the witness was unable to come to the conclusion which she did:

'You decided to fire Mr James?'

'Yes.'

'Because you believed he sent the email?'

'Yes.'

'You consulted your IT department?'

'Yes.'

'They told you the email had been sent?'

'Yes.'

'From the computer of Mr James?'

'Yes.'

'You didn't ask them who else had access to that computer?'

'No, I didn't.'

'Access on the day the email was sent?'

'No.'

'Nor did you ask Mr James about the email?'

'I didn't need to.'

'You assumed he sent it?'

'He did.'

'You didn't speak to his colleagues did you?'

'No. Why should I?'

'You didn't know he was not at work that day?'

The cross-examiner will argue in his closing speech that Mr Jones's boss was not only incompetent but unfair.

2.3 Negligent

This is the classic area where you can put omissions to a witness: the things they should have done but did not do:

'You drove your car.'

'Yes.'

'Up Chancery Lane?'

'Yes.'

'The speed limit is 30 miles per hour?'

'Yes.'

'You drove at 45 miles per hour?'

'Yes.'

'You were looking for a CD to play?'

'Yes.'

'And not at the road?'

'That's right.'

The cross-examiner has not mentioned the words 'speeding' or 'not paying attention' or 'distracted'. Crucially, the cross-examiner has not used the word 'negligent'.

As the cross-examination unfolded the judge would have been drawing those conclusions herself.

2.4 Lacking authority

'You are a Police Community Service Officer?'

'Yes.'

'You have been so for 3 months?'

'Yes.'

'You work as part of a neighbourhood policing team?'

'Yes.'

'Supporting police officers?'

'Yes.'

'And front-line policing?'

'Yes.'

'You don't carry handcuffs?'

'No, I don't.'

'Or a baton?'

'No.'

'You are not allowed to?'

'No, I'm not.'

'You have no power of arrest?'

'No, I don't.'

'You spoke to my client?'

'Yes.'

'On Scarcroft Green?'

'Yes.'

'He was alone?'

'Yes.'

'You were with Police Community Service Officer Jones?'

'Yes.'

'You handcuffed my client?'

'Yes.'

'And put him in the back of your car?'

'Yes.'

'Then took him to the police station?'

'Yes.'

2.5 Unqualified

This can be done in a number of ways: for example, by undermining the qualifications of a masseur who claims to be a physiotherapist; or simply by showing your opponent's witness is not as qualified as yours. (See Chapter 13, 'Expert Witnesses'.)

2.6 Speculating or exaggerating

'You were six feet away from the men?'

'Yes.'

'There were over 50 customers in the restaurant?'

'Yes.'

'Ten waiters?'

'Yes.'

'Taking orders?'

'Yes.'

'Pouring drinks?'

'Yes.'

'Serving food?'

'Yes.'

'People were talking?'

'Yes.'

'Some were louder than others?'

'I suppose so.'

'You believed the men were talking about money laundering?'

'Yes.'

'You didn't hear the word "money"?'

'No, I didn't.'

'Or "laundering"?'

'No.'

'Or "cash"?'

'No.'

'Or "proceeds"?'

'No.'

'Or "bank accounts"?'

'No.'

'Or "carousel fraud"?'

'No.'

'Or "VAT"?'

'No.'

2.7 Biased or defensive

'You were Mr Johnson's line manager?'

'Yes.'

'On the 4th April?'

'Yes.'

'You told him you were unhappy with his timekeeping?'

'Yes.'

'He complained to your boss?'

'He did.'

'Your boss told you to leave him alone?'

'He did.'

'Your boss told you there had been a mistake?'

'Yes.'

'You didn't agree with that?'

'I did not.'

'Your boss told you to bring any further problems to him?'

'Yes.'

'And not to confront Mr Johnson?'

'Yes.'

'On the 5th April you confronted Mr Johnson?'

'I did.'

'You raised your voice?'

'I was angry. Johnson tells lies.'

2.8 Hiding something

Sometimes a witness may be protecting someone or reluctant to reveal information which may be damaging to the case.

There is a famous story about Clarence Darrow, the fabled US attorney who appeared in a medical case in Hawaii.

The doctor called by his opponent had a reputation for withholding vital pieces of evidence during his direct examination so he could spring them on the unsuspecting cross-examiner.

This was Darrow's cross-examination:[6]

'Doctor, have you been paid for giving your evidence today?'

'Yes I have.'

'And have you enjoyed your trip to Honolulu?'

'Yes.'

'No further questions.'

2.9 A combination of the above objectives

The case may require the cross-examiner to put a combination of facts which lead to more than one conclusion. Be careful not to put too many or you run the risk of diluting your argument.

---

6 Cross-examination of Dr Paul E Bowers, *Territory of Hawaii v Ahakuelo, et al* (1931) *Territory of Hawaii v Grace Fortescue, et al* (1932).

2.10 Previous behaviour in any of the above

The witness may be unreliable because he has been biased or lacking authority in the past or has given evidence which was specifically rejected by a court. Be careful, though: ethical rules in some jurisdictions preclude a cross-examination based on a previous court's rejection of a witness's evidence, as it does not prove the witness is necessarily wrong this time.

3 PREPARING TO CROSS-EXAMINE

Once you have a settled case theory and have extracted sub-sets of the case theory in the form of closing speech objectives or points to argue, you can begin to plan your cross-examination.

Put simply, you should study the statement of the witness you are to question, extract facts from that statement and arrange the facts in an attractive order.

The selection of facts (or omissions) and their arrangement is crucial to the success of the cross-examination.

It will enable you to argue in the closing speech that your objectives have been achieved.

It is important that you avoid formulating too many objectives. It depends, of course, on how long the cross-examination will take.

But you don't want your main point or points to become lost in a mass of material.

Each fact or omission will become a short, closed question.

Returning to the *Cavendish v Downham* case study in Appendix 1, here is a cross-examination of Mr Cavendish. Note the arrangement of the short, closed questions:

> 'Mr Cavendish, Mrs Downham called you?'
>
> 'Yes.'
>
> 'On the morning of the last Tuesday in November?'
>
> 'Yes.'

'She told you that you were welcome to see the carving?'

'Yes.'

'At any time?'

'Yes.'

'You went to Downham Gallery?'

'Yes.'

'The next morning?'

'Yes.'

'You looked at the relief?'

'Yes.'

'Thought it was damaged?'

'Yes.'

'You were not impressed?'

'Yes.'

'The stone appeared to be a little too yellow?'

Note, the cross-examiner is using Cavendish's exact words.

'You looked at the sculpture?'

'Yes.'

'With Mrs Downham?'

'Yes.'

'She told you the asking price was £850,000?'

'She did.'

'But that you could have it for £820,000?'

'Yes.'

'You thought it was a reasonable price?'

'I did.'

'You made her an offer?'

'Yes.'

'No one accompanied you that day?'

'No.'

'You didn't bring an expert with you?'

'I didn't.'

'You didn't ask if you could have the sculpture examined?'

'No.'

'Mrs Downham didn't stop you from getting a second opinion?'

'No she didn't.'

'You made your offer then and there?'

'I did.'

'Of £820,000?'

'Yes.'

The cross-examiner proceeds slowly: step by step or bite by bite. She doesn't rush to make her point. The questions are all closed and attractively arranged. The cross-examiner will be able to argue in the closing speech that Mr Cavendish satisfied himself about the authenticity of the carving before buying it for the large sum of £820,000.

4 TAKING FACTS FROM OTHER WITNESS STATEMENTS

It is tempting to say to a witness that another witness disagrees with them or to put a proposition to a witness drawn from another witness and ask them to comment on it.

But both methods of cross-examination are unethical. The first is implicitly inviting the witness to comment on the disagreement and the second is openly doing so.[7]

---

7 Justice Stephen Estcourt, 'Ethical Advocacy', www.supremecourt.tas.gov.au/publications/speeches-articles/ethical-advocacy, para 22, quoted at page 45 of this book.

The decision-maker will decide which version she prefers. It is not up to the witness to say which version should be preferred.

However, a witness may be challenged on his version using facts from another witness statement.

1 The unethical method:

 'Mrs Smith says that you took Johnson's car?'

2 The appropriate method:

 'You took Johnson's car?'

With question 1, the cross-examiner is by implication inviting the witness to comment.

There might be a number of possible answers to question 1:

> 'Mrs Smith doesn't know what she is talking about'; or
>
> 'Mrs Smith wasn't there'; or
>
> 'Mrs Smith hates me'; or
>
> 'Mrs Smith is wrong.'

None of these possible answers helps the court on the issue of whether the witness took Johnson's car. A couple of them might imply that the witness did not take the car, but the focus of the question is upon Mrs Smith and not who took the car.

This is especially important when the cross-examiner is putting the case to the witness – a separate subject. Bear with me, for it is coming.

In a nutshell, don't tell the witness where you are getting your evidence from (e.g. whose witness statement). Just put the fact or omission.

5 IS THE CROSS-EXAMINATION NECESSARY?

Ask yourself whether there is anything to be gained or defended by conducting a cross-examination. Clearly, if you are obliged with a particular witness to challenge his evidence or put facts you will later rely upon, then you must cross-examine.

But sometimes you might conclude that there is nothing or very little to be gained by cross-examination. The witness may not have touched your case at all. By opening up subjects, you run a risk that the witness will damage you. Two stories, and the first may be apocryphal, show the value of a short cross-examination.

Sir Edward Carson, the famous advocate who was the leader of the Bar in Ireland, then England, wanted to be rid of a red-nosed witness quickly. Carson could not hope to dispel the damaging evidence of the witness, but he did not want to leave the jury with a favourable impression of him:

Carson:	'I believe y'er a heavy drinker?'
Witness:	'That's my business.'
Carson:	'And have y'er any other business?'[8]

The second example is more recent. The actor William Roache is known for his role as Ken Barlow, the longest-running character in the British soap opera *Coronation Street.*

Roache was charged with sexual offences allegedly committed in the mid-1960s.

He called as a witness his on-screen wife, Deirdre Barlow, who was played by the late Anne Kirkbride. Their on-screen marriage took place in 1981 and received higher audience figures than the wedding of Prince Charles and Lady Diana Spencer.

Kirkbride gave evidence for Roache. She said he had always been helpful and supportive to her, adding that he was 'the perfect gentleman'.

---

8 Recounted in *The Autobiography of Sir Patrick Hastings* (Heinemann, London, 1950) 85–86.

Roache's lawyer asked her to describe him in one word and she replied 'lovely'.

The prosecutor, Anne Whyte KC, asked one question in cross-examination:

Whyte:	'In 1965 you would have been about 9?'
Kirkbride:	'That's about right.'[9]

6 PUTTING YOUR CASE

This is an obligation in common law countries. Where your client's case differs from the version being offered by the witness *on a material issue*, you must challenge that version in cross-examination.

For example, in a case involving the sale and delivery of goods, imagine the main witness for the defence says in evidence that the goods arrived on time. It is your client's case that the goods arrived 20 days late. You must challenge the witness on that point.

How do you do it? This is the obvious way:

> 'The goods arrived 20 days late?'
>
> 'No.'

Here is a more subtle way:

> 'The goods were to arrive on the 1st July?'
>
> 'Yes. And they did.'
>
> 'In fact, they arrived on the 21st July?'
>
> 'That's not right.'

It is obvious that the answers have not been helpful but it is your painful duty to challenge that version.

---

[9] 'Roache "is sticking to his script"', *Belfast Telegraph*, 30 January 2014.

It's all because of a misunderstood decision of the House of Lords in a case from 1898 called *Browne v Dunn*.[10] It is a case which centres on the British notion of fair play. It is not fair to make an allegation or challenge someone or their story if you haven't given them an opportunity to answer it.

It is put much more eloquently in the Canadian case of *R v Pasqua*:[11]

> 'There is a general duty on counsel to put a matter directly to a witness if counsel is going to later adduce evidence to impeach the witness's credibility or present contradictory evidence.'

The rule is much vexed because so many lawyers have so many different interpretations of it.

The UK Supreme Court gave some helpful clarification to the rule in 2023. Lord Hodge stated:

> '(i) The general rule in civil cases … is that a party is required to challenge by cross-examination the evidence of any witness of the opposing party on a material point which he or she wishes to submit to the court should not be accepted. That rule extends to both witnesses as to fact and expert witnesses.
>
> (ii) In an adversarial system of justice, the purpose of the rule is to make sure that the trial is fair.
>
> …
>
> (vi) Cross-examination gives the witness the opportunity to explain or clarify his or her evidence. That opportunity is particularly important when the opposing party intends to accuse the witness of dishonesty, but there is no principled basis for confining the rule to cases of dishonesty.
>
> (vii) The rule should not be applied rigidly. It is not an inflexible rule … Its application depends upon the

---

10 (1893) 6 R 67.

11 [2009] AJ No 702, 2009 ABCA 247.

> circumstances of the case as the criterion is the overall fairness of the trial.'[12]

Lord Hodge identified a number of exceptions to the rule. This included insignificant matters; obvious mistakes by the witness; testimony which is patently absurd; or circumstances where a witness has been given sufficient opportunity elsewhere to respond to criticism.[13]

The rule is anathema to American trial lawyers. 'Why give a witness the opportunity to deny something or disagree with you?'

It also breaches Irving Younger's 10th commandment of cross-examination, 'Save the ultimate point for your closing argument.'[14]

The other problem is that putting your case also involves putting a conclusion and conclusions are open invitations to the witness to take control.

Some lawyers belabour the point. Others say that your obligation is simply to show you have joined issue with the witness's version then move on. Some judges think putting the case is the most important thing in cross-examination. I disagree.

Some advocates use the dreaded phrase, 'I put it to you.'

This is not good advocacy for a couple of reasons. First, it is a signal to the witness that they are going to get a question they can disagree with. Second, a lawyer who says 'I put it to you' is distancing himself from his client's case. 'The goods arrived 20 days late?' is an assertion of fact and much more powerful than the rather lame 'I put it to you that the goods arrived 20 days late.'

---

12 *Griffiths v TUI UK Limited* [2023] UKSC 48, 70.

13 Ibid, 61–68.

14 Irving Younger, 'Ten Commandments of Cross-Examination' taken from *The Advocate's Deskbook: The Essentials of Trying a Case* (Prentice Hall, London, 1988).

I saw one dreadful example of client-ditching where the barrister said 'Now I'm obliged by law to do this so I put it to you ...'.

But if your witness intends to rely on facts, say a conversation, which differ from that given by the person you are cross-examining you must put that version to the witness.

You must also put your client's instructions but remember there should be a good reason. You are solely responsible for the presentation of your case.

The consequence of not putting the case can be pretty severe, depending upon the attitude of the judge.

First, the cross-examiner may be labelled as being unfair. Second, an allegation which is not put to an opponent and said for the first time in evidence-in-chief might be seen by the judge as having been recently invented. But lastly, and worst of all, a failure to join issue might amount to an acceptance of the witness's versions, which could be sudden death for the cross-examiner and his case.

I think that too much is made of the rule in *Browne v Dunn*.[15] If witness statements have the allegation or the challenge within them, then I think both parties have behaved fairly. I think it is more apposite in criminal cases where new information might crop up in the course of a trial.

But civil trials and arbitration hearings should not be trials by ambush. All the evidence should be made available to each party before the hearing.

In Canada, Chief Justice McEachern in *R v Khuc*[16] made a sensible observation, 'the rule does not go so far as to require counsel to risk contradictory questions about straight forward matters of fact on which the witness had already given evidence that he or she is very unlikely to change.'

---

15 (1893) 6 R 67.

16 [2000] BCCA 20, 142 CCC (3d) 276.

It depends upon the attitude of the judge and what the court is likely to do if the rule is breached. If the judge is a stickler for the rules, make sure you put your case plainly.

Above all, do not be unfair.

The next question is *when* you should put your case. Skilful cross-examiners such as Sir Patrick Hastings KC typically put the case at the start:[17]

> 'You stabbed him?'
>
> 'No I didn't.'

Then he would put a series of facts to the witness which showed that he had stabbed the victim. Hastings was probably hoping that the witness's denial would fade in the memory of the jury. Here is an invented example of the sort of thing Hastings did:

> 'You stabbed him?'
>
> 'No, I didn't.'
>
> 'You were in the kitchen?'
>
> 'Yes.'
>
> 'With him?'
>
> 'Yes.'
>
> 'No one else was there?'
>
> 'No.'
>
> 'It was 2 am?'
>
> 'Yes.'
>
> 'You had a knife in your hand?'
>
> 'Yes.'
>
> 'He didn't stab himself?'
>
> 'No he didn't.'

---

[17] John H Munkman, *The Technique of Advocacy* (Butterworths, London, 1991) 86.

'You were arguing?'

'Yes.'

'At 2:05 am he had a knife wound?'

Other cross-examiners bury the question in the middle of the cross-examination, in effect, to hide the denial or give it less weight.

The bad cross-examiner puts it at the end. I saw it happen once. After a cross-examination lasting over a day the lawyer finished like this:

'I put it to you, that you killed Mr Jones.'

'No I didn't.'

'No further questions.'

The air in the courtroom hung heavily with that weakness for several seconds after counsel sat down.

Let's take an example of putting the case in the wrong way from the *Cavendish v Downham* case study in Appendix 1:

'I put it to you Mr Cavendish that you relied upon your own judgement when you bought the sculpture.'

'No, I relied upon what Mrs Downham told me.'

'No you didn't?'

'Yes I did. She talked me into it.'

'No she didn't.'

You see how the cross-examiner has lost control. The witness is doing most of the talking and the repeated denials are solidifying his version.

This is how it should be done:

'Mr Cavendish, when you bought the sculpture you relied on your own judgement?'

'No, I relied on what Mrs Downham told me.'

'You went to Downham Gallery?'

'Yes.'

'You saw the sculpture?'

'Yes.'

'Thought it was damaged?'

'Yes.'

'You were not impressed?'

'I wasn't.'

'Thought it to be a little yellow?'

'I did.'

'No one accompanied you that day?'

'No.'

'You didn't bring an expert with you?'

'No. I didn't.'

'You didn't ask if you could have the sculpture examined?'

'No.'

'You didn't ask if you could get a second opinion?'

'No.'

'Mrs Downham didn't stop you from getting a second opinion?'

'No. She didn't.'

'You made your offer then and there?'

'Yes.'

'Of £820,000?'

'I did.'

In this example, the case was put as the first question. There is no need to put it again. The facts or omissions speak for themselves.

In summary, if you wish to rely upon a version of the facts which differs from your opponent's, you must put your version question by question to the relevant opposing witness. You are likely to get an answer you do not want.

If in doubt, put your case, but don't overdo it.

7 DELIVERY

The first thing to remember is that cross-examination is your show – the spotlight should be on you and not on the witness. Your questions should all be short, closed and leading. Unless you are putting your case, the answers should all be 'yes' or 'no'.

You are stating the good facts of your client's case and the bad facts of your opponent's case one by one and brick by brick.

In a sense, it doesn't matter what the witness says. Go slowly so that the decision-maker can write your questions down.

'Did you go to the shop?' may not cause you too much damage but it is an open question and the witness could reply, 'Yes but I also had lunch in a restaurant.'

A much better question is, 'You went to the shop?' because it is closed and the witness cannot move very far.

Another example is, 'Didn't you call the police?', which is open. A better question is the bald assertion achieved by swapping two words, 'You didn't call the police?'

Watch the witness and the decision-maker. Look for the slightest reaction or trace of discomfort. If you have planned your cross-examination carefully and crafted short, closed questions, the witness will feel as if he is in a straitjacket.

For many years my training business hired actors to play witnesses in assessments for the Higher Rights of Audience qualification. I remember a rather nice but theatrical fellow who used to believe he was the witness he was playing. One day he ventured to tell me that he didn't think I was a very good teacher. It wasn't a clever move since I was hiring him, but I didn't mind because I was intrigued.

When I asked why he said 'Because the students don't let me *be* Mr Christie! All they make me say is yes or no.'

He didn't get the point.

I warned the candidates in the training sessions: 'Keep your questions short and tight.' For the most part they did, but if they asked the actor an open question or put a conclusion or theory to him, he would be away like a runaway train. The straitjacket was off and the look of panic on the face of the candidate who struggled to control the witness was a sight to behold.

8 KNOW THE ANSWER OR BE SURE IT WON'T HURT YOU

If you prepare your case thoroughly, nothing should take you by surprise. Effective advocates have a pretty good idea of what the witness is going to say. That is usually because they will have prepared the case from the witness statements and documents. A witness will not be able to move very far in cross-examination if you put facts to them from their statement because usually they have signed the statement as being true.

However, sometimes the really good advocate will take a risk. I do not recommend beginners taking risks. When I was a young lawyer, we were called upon to cross-examine police officers who were professional, trained witnesses. We were not allowed to see their statements, so we didn't know exactly what they were going to say. A lot of our preparation was based on what our client or his witnesses had told us.

The rest was a combination of guesswork, common sense and experience. Sometimes we found ourselves fishing for information and often it was not helpful. You learned to tread carefully and to make sure that whatever the answer, it wouldn't hurt your client's case.

Sir Patrick Hastings KC prepared his cross-examinations thoroughly:

> 'I wrote little or nothing, and my case was carried in my head ... For weeks before a trial I cross-examined my prospective opponents to myself; mentally I prepared myself for every difficulty. I assumed they would find means of escape from any pitfall, and I searched for a method with which to block their exit.'[18]

---

18 *The Autobiography of Sir Patrick Hastings* (Heinemann, London, 1950) 137.

When the witness began his evidence-in-chief, Hastings was not taking a note. He was looking at the witness, assessing his demeanour and gauging the sort of person he was about to cross-examine.

A lot of young advocates develop interesting theories about the case and try to get the witness to agree with them. They sound less like Norman Birkett and more like a third-rate detective. Of course, the witness rarely agrees with them.

The worse offence is when an advocate puts questions to which he clearly does not know the answer and gets a response which badly damages his case.

Simon Brown KC recalls competitions in Chambers among the barristers:

> 'The introduction of witness statements made it easier to prepare cross-examinations in advance. I would highlight perhaps 8 statements and then draw up a list of questions to get points for my final speech. We had competitions to see how few questions we needed to get there. The late Sir James Hunt[19] was a master. It meant you had almost full control of the answers.'

Brown remembers a criminal barrister who saw cross-examination in reckless terms, like going over the top in the battle of the Somme:

> 'He was petrified that the wrong answer would come out and the jury would notice it. He was ill-prepared and liked the sound of his own voice. He invariably lost.'

9 ASSERT; DON'T ASK

Along much the same lines is the idea that you should be telling the witness what the facts or the omissions are. A cross-examination should be nothing but leading questions.

---

19 'James Hunt (judge)', *Wikipedia*, https://en.wikipedia.org/wiki/James_Hunt_(judge).

There is no Evidence Act in the world that says that questions in cross-examination should be open.

Sometimes the judge will intervene and say, 'Is that a question?' Sometimes witnesses do it themselves, which I think is a good thing because it doesn't create a good impression.

If a judge insists upon you framing your assertions as a question, then every now and again you may add the words either before or after the question 'Isn't that right?' or 'Is it correct?' Personally, I don't like these words. They are called tag-ons. They are, in fact, another question entirely. And they make it sound as though you are not sure.

The problem is compounded if you ask questions in the Australian style of speaking, which is known as 'rising terminals' or going up at the end of your sentences. I call it the *Home and Away* cross-examination, based on the way the characters speak in the Australian soap opera.

Imagine the voice going up at the end of the question:

> 'You're 33 years of age?'
>
> 'Yes.'
>
> 'You live in Bristol?'
>
> 'Yes.'
>
> 'You're a schoolteacher?'
>
> 'Yes I am.'
>
> Now add the tag-ons
>
> 'You're 33 years of age? Isn't that right?'
>
> 'Yes.'
>
> 'You live in Bristol? Isn't that correct?'
>
> 'Yes.'
>
> 'You're a schoolteacher? Is that right?'
>
> 'Yes.'

Question with rising terminal = not sure of the answer.

Question with tag-on = not sure of the answer.

Rising terminal + tag-on = twice as unsure.

10 ONE FACT PER QUESTION

If you put more than one fact in your question, from a purely practical point of view, the witness can choose which fact he wishes to respond to. It is not a good technique, nor does it assist the decision-maker. And what if the witness just says 'Yes'?

Looking at the *Cavendish v Downham* case study in Appendix 1, here is an example:

> 'You went to Mrs Downham's gallery and the sculpture was delivered to yours?'
>
> 'Yes.'

Which fact is the witness agreeing with?

Or the witness might choose the part of the question that suits them and make a speech:

> 'Yes I remember going to Mrs Downham's gallery. It was the day after she called me. She told me I was welcome to see the sculpture at any time.'

These questions are called compound questions. They are not only examples of bad technique, they are, according to some countries, unethical:

> 'A compound question simultaneously poses more than one inquiry and calls for more than one answer. Such a question presents two problems. First, the question may be ambiguous because of its multiple facets and complexity. Second, an answer may be confusing because of uncertainty as to

> which part of the compound question the witness intended to address.'[20]

The compound question, according to Mr Justice Heydon in the High Court of Australia, has additional vices including the fact that:

> 'Even though the answers desired by a cross-examiner to a compound question may all be affirmative or all negative, the witness may wish to answer to some affirmatively and some negatively. To place witnesses in the position of having to reformulate a compound question and answer its component parts bit by bit is unfair to them in the sense that it prevents them doing justice to themselves.'[21]

There are positive reasons for delivering questions one fact at a time.

Sir Patrick Hastings KC was cross-examining a Mr Sievier, who was charged with murdering his wife. He established that she had divorced him in 1886:

Hastings:	'For desertion?'
Sievier:	'Yes.'
Hastings:	'And adultery?'
Sievier:	'Yes.'
Hastings:	'And cruelty?'
Sievier:	'I know nothing about cruelty.'
Hastings:	'I have her petition here …'[22]

---

20 Charles Wright and Victor Gold, *Federal Practice and Procedure: Evidence* (West Publishing Co, St Paul, 1997) 354, approved in *State of Hawaii v Sanchez* 923f 2d 934 (1996), 948 [25].

21 *Libke v The Queen* [2007] HCA 30, 127.

22 Cited in Richard DuCann, *The Art of the Advocate* (Penguin, London, 1993) 156–157.

By framing the questions one fact at a time, Hastings allows the case to be built up against Sievier like hammer blows. It would not have had anywhere near the impact if the question had been:

> 'She divorced you for desertion, adultery and cruelty?'

11 DON'T ARGUE WITH THE WITNESS

Every lawyer dreams of destroying a witness's credibility by pointing out some devastating inconsistency or by getting the witness to agree with a question that holes them below the waterline.

Yet this rarely happens.

There are so many times that I have seen very clever young lawyers take the approach of arguing with the witness in the hope they can trip him up and win a crushing victory.

An opponent's witness is generally not there to help you or your client. In addition, we have already seen the problems of putting conclusions, theories or arguments to the witness: it simply empowers him. The straitjacket comes off.

As cross-examiner, you have two unique advantages over the witness.

First, generally speaking, the witness must answer your question. At best, an unresponsive answer looks bad for him and bodes well for you. Why diminish that power by getting into an argument with the witness?

Second, the witness does not know what your question will be. You control the topics, the selection of facts or omissions and the order in which they will be delivered. Why cede that power by getting into the arena with the witness? If you do, you will be on his territory and that is where he wants you. He will also know what your question is likely to be.

Argumentative cross-examinations don't help the decision-maker either. They may look good on TV or in a Hollywood movie, but they don't advance your case or undermine your opponent's case.

I concede that sometimes you can make an argumentative witness look bad, but it is better if you do not react to what the witness says. Remain above the fray and do your job properly.

An American advocacy teacher, who is a trial lawyer from the southern states, says, 'Arguing with a witness is like wrestling with a pig. Both of you get dirty. But only one of you likes it.'

In the case of *R v Philpott*,[23] a husband and wife were charged with setting fire to their home, killing their six children. Counsel for the wife cross-examined the husband. According to the news report by Emma Sword[24] the following questions were asked:

1 'You regarded her as your property, didn't you? Your slave. That's what she was, wasn't she?'

2 'She did everything in that house, didn't she, even when you were having a relationship with another woman?'

3 'Mairead wasn't leaving, Mairead wasn't going anywhere. You think you own her, don't you?'

Shaking his head, Philpott replied, 'No.'

This is taken from a newspaper report and one must be wary, but there seems to be only one occasion when the witness replied and that was at the end.

But have a look at the questions. If reported correctly, they contain more than one proposition, a number of conclusions and theories and don't seem to be advancing much more of a case theory from the wife than the husband told her to help him.

It was a particularly unpleasant case and counsel had a difficult job, but the questions are bordering on the argumentative.

---

23 Nottingham Crown Court, 14 February 2013.

24 *The Scotsman*, 15 March 2013.

In *R v Baldwin*,[25] Lord Hewart CJ made the following remarks:

> 'One often hears questions put to witnesses by counsel which are really in the nature of an invitation to argument. One hears, for instance, such questions as this: "I suggest to you that ..." or "Is your evidence to be taken as suggesting that?" If the witness were a prudent person he would say, with the highest degree of politeness: "What you suggest is no business of mine. I am not here to make suggestions at all. I am here only to answer relevant questions. What the conclusions to be drawn from my answers are is not for me, and as for suggestions, I venture to leave those to others."
>
> An answer of that kind, no doubt, requires a good deal of sense and self-restraint and experience, and the mischief of it is, if made, it might very well prejudice the witness with the jury, because the jury, not being aware of the consequences to which such questions might lead, might easily come to the conclusion (and it might be true) that the witness had something to conceal.
>
> It is right to remember in all such cases that the witness in the box is an amateur and the counsel who is asking questions is, as a rule, a professional conductor of argument, and it is not right that the wits of one should be pitted against the wits of the other in the field of suggestion and controversy. *What is wanted from the witness is answers to questions of fact.*'

It is clear that in Australia and England, at least, argumentative questions (unless you are putting your case and that should be one or two questions only) are forbidden.

And remember, European arbitration panels do not like watching aggressive cross-examination.

---

25 (1925) 18 Cr App R 175, 178–179 (cited by Heydon J in *Libke v The Queen* [2007] HCA 30) (emphasis added).

12 MAKING COMMENTS IS WRONG

A student at a very famous law firm once told me he had been taught on an advocacy training course to comment on a witness's answer and before the witness had been given time to react, to ask his next question.

Clearly, that trainer had been watching too much TV:

> 'Statements of counsel's personal opinion have no place in a cross-examination.'[26]

The time to make comments and observations and to draw conclusions or theories is in the closing speech. Obviously, they must be reasonably open to be made based on the evidence.[27]

13 CUTTING OFF ANSWERS

You often see a cross-examination where counsel doesn't like the answer or feels the witness is being unresponsive, so they interrupt with 'That's not the question I asked you' or 'Just answer the question yes or no' or the very curt 'Yes or no?'

As Heydon J observed:

> 'The cutting off of an answer by a further question, though always to be avoided as far as possible, can happen innocently when a questioner is pursuing a witness vigorously and the witness pauses in such a fashion as to suggest that the answer is complete; it can happen legitimately if a witness's answer is non-responsive ...
>
> ... The rule against the cutting off of a witness's answer follows from the encouragement which the law gives to short, precise and single questions. It is not fair to ask 2 questions which are disparaging or otherwise damaging to a witness and to cut off an answer which the cross-examiner does not like.

---

[26] *R v R (AJ)* (1994) 94 CCC (3a) 168, 178.

[27] See *Randall v The Queen* [2002] UKPC 19, [2002] 1 WLR 2237.

> The right of a cross-examiner to control a witness does not entail a power to prevent the witness from giving any evidence other than that which favours the cross-examiner's client.'[28]

The cross-examiner who does not permit the witness to answer can do damage to his own client's case. He may appear rude, fearful of the full answer, self-important or may look like he has simply lost control.

In para 19, 'Getting the answer you want', I deal with how to handle an unresponsive witness.

14 QUESTIONS BASED ON CONTROVERSIAL ASSUMPTIONS

It is impermissible to put a leading question to a witness in cross-examination that assumes the existence of a fact in issue or that the witness has said something that he didn't say. This is obviously unfair.

Experts may be cross-examined on assumed facts even though they are controversial because the expert is not being invited to accept the truth of the fact, but merely to give an opinion based on that fact.

15 QUESTIONS ON STEREOTYPES

In Australia it is unlawful, i.e. in breach of the Evidence Acts, to preface your question on a stereotype.

Even if it is lawful to do so in the jurisdiction where you appear, it is not good practice because it gives the witness a chance to seize control. Such a question usually begins like this:

> 'Would you agree with me that accountants are very careful people?'; or
>
> 'An engineer is generally someone who likes to know how things work?'; or
>
> 'Is it fair to say that police officers are trained to be observant?'

---

[28] *Libke v The Queen* [2007] HCA 30, 128.

These questions might receive affirmative answers but they invite the witness to comment and they are really of no use to the decision-maker. They also signal to the witness that the cross-examiner wants to trip them up or make a telling point.

They should be avoided.

16 VULNERABLE WITNESSES

You should take extra care to be fair to children or other vulnerable witnesses. Shouting at them or getting frustrated is as wrong with vulnerable witnesses as it is with strong witnesses. It will not come across well to the decision-maker and may reinforce sympathy with the witness.

In England, you should consult the Equal Treatment Bench Book[29] when you prepare the cross-examination. It will be used by the judge and contains invaluable advice.

You must be firm but polite, soften your voice, keep your questions short and simple, and avoid confusing the witness.

Don't use tag-ons, especially with children. It may be difficult for them to understand what you are asking them. For instance, 'He didn't touch you, did he?' confronts the witness with two questions: one negative and the other positive.

The Court of Appeal expressly warned advocates in *Barker v The Queen*[30] about using such questions to children.

But always remember, if it is a trial or a hearing, you are representing your client. You are not working for the other side. You are a lawyer, not a social worker.

---

29 Published by the Judicial College. The latest version is available at www.judiciary.uk/about-the-judiciary/diversity/equal-treatment-bench-book/.

30 (1983) 153 CLR 338.

17 CONTROLLING THE WITNESS

'A cross-examiner', wrote Heydon J:

> 'is entitled to ask quite confined questions, and to insist, at the peril of matters being taken further in re-examination which is outside the cross-examiner's control, not only that there be an answer fully responding to each question but also that there be no more than an answer.'

His Honour observed that 'a cross-examiner is given considerable power to limit the witness's answers and to control the witness in many other ways.'[31]

On TV, the script writers have counsel saying firmly, 'Just answer the question yes or no?' or more sarcastically 'A simple "yes" will suffice.'

The trouble is that it looks like bullying. Yet as counsel you don't want the witness taking control and running away with the evidence.

There are three things to bear in mind:

1 Did you cause the witness to take control? If so, what went wrong and how can you avoid it in future?

2 How serious is the witness's offence? Does it matter?

3 If so, which weapon in your arsenal can you use to fix the situation, always bearing in mind that your punishment of the witness must fit the crime?

I now examine how to deal with each of these questions.

18 CAUSING THE PROBLEM

There is no point in insisting on a 'Yes' or 'No' answer if the question you asked has caused the witness to talk. You should ask leading questions. But if you ask an open question, e.g. 'Where did you go?' or 'What did the man say to you?', the witness will usually see it

---

[31] *Libke v The Queen* [2007] HCA 30, 119.

as an opportunity to speak. We have already seen that principle in Chapter 10, 'Examination-in-Chief or Direct Examination'.

A compound question will enable the witness to choose which part of the question he wants to answer:

> Question: 'You shouted at your boyfriend because he had not made you any lunch?'
>
> Answer: 'I didn't shout'; or 'He never makes lunch.'

Giving the witness wrong facts will cause an answer you do not want:

> Question: 'You made your statement two days later?'
>
> Answer: 'Actually it was a week later.'

This sort of question just gives the impression to the witness and to the court that you don't know your case.

Sometimes, you might put your own spin on the witness's words:

> Question: 'The weather was pleasant?'
>
> Answer: 'It was a sunny day.'

Fair enough. This is what the witness said in the statement. Use the witness's own words back at her, then she can't wiggle.

If you sound unsure, such as letting your voice go up at the end of the question or by starting or ending your question with a tag-on, such as 'Isn't it right?' or 'Correct?', the witness may well take control.

Another problem is if your question is long. Usually, long questions breed long answers.

Starting your question with a word like 'so' or 'yet' or 'therefore' signals to the witness that you are about to state a conclusion or, in other words, give something to them to argue with.

The final way, and this list is not exhaustive, that you might lose control, is to put a tag-on at the start of your question which reveals the source of your information. It happens regularly in cross-examination and in arbitration has become almost habitual:

> 'You say in your witness statement that you examined the sculpture for 2 hours and 47 minutes?'

Let us look at that question. First, it is two questions: (1) that he examined the sculpture for two hours and 47 minutes; and (2) that he mentioned the fact in his witness statement.

Part (2) is unnecessary. If the witness agrees that he examined the sculpture for two hours and 47 minutes, your job is done.

In truth, it is a compound question and the witness could choose that part of the question which doesn't help you. For example:

> 'Did I say that in my witness statement? I said a lot of things in my witness statement.'

The fact that the witness said it in his witness statement only becomes important if he forgets or denies the fact that he examined the sculpture for two hours and 47 minutes. (In paras 19 to 21 I deal with how you handle that problem.)

The other problem with the question is that the decision-maker might have to keep looking for the part in the witness statement that you are referring to. It is distracting to say the least. The witness statement is evidence of the fact you are seeking to establish or emphasise. It is not the fact itself.

Similar questions are those such as, 'You testified that you examined the sculpture for 2 hours and 47 minutes?' or 'You said in direct examination etc ...'.

So be careful that it is not your question which has caused you to lose control. Keep the question tight.

19 GETTING THE ANSWER YOU WANT

We readily assume that if a witness is being unresponsive, it is a deliberate act. But sometimes a witness may simply have misheard or been mistaken about the question:

Question:	'You are an artisan?'
Answer	'I have never painted anything in my life.'

I suppose the only comeback could be 'But you are a decorator?' In England, a decorator is an artisan and as we know from Hilaire Belloc, 'It is the business of the wealthy man to give employment to the artisan.'[32]

There may be other reasons, such as the witness has forgotten, he is nervous or he doesn't understand your question.

Of course, there are uncooperative or argumentative witnesses. The best witness of all to cross-examine is the dishonest witness, particularly one who isn't too bright.

As the cross-examiner, you have to decide how serious the offence is that has been committed by the witness.

For example:

Question:	'It was a Sunday?'
Answer:	'I think it was definitely on a weekend.'

Does that answer advance your case theory or damage it? Or is the answer so vague that it does neither? It is correct but not exactly responsive.

If it is important to you that the witness agrees that it was a Sunday, there are various tools at your disposal for regaining control of the witness and getting a responsive answer. It is crucial that you remain calm and polite. Don't change your demeanour. Whatever you do,

---

32 Hilaire Belloc, *Cautionary Tales* (Folio Society, London, 1997) 86.

don't nod or smile at the witness. He will think to himself that he can do it again and be unresponsive:

1 Don't interrupt the answer.
2 Put the question again, word for word, but this time more slowly and deliberately. Don't raise your voice. If anything, lower your voice, just like your father used to do when you got into trouble as a kid.
3 If the answer is still unresponsive, put the question one more time, just as slowly and deliberately. If after a third time the witness is still unresponsive, you might consider that it is best to leave the subject. Remember, the witness will not have created a good impression.
4 If the answer is important to you and the fact is contained (as it should be) in the witness's statement, you could direct the witness and thereby the decision-maker to the relevant line in the statement.

There will be times when the unresponsive answer is so trivial or weak that you might choose to ignore it. But sometimes a witness might be empowered by your failure to deal with his unresponsive answer. He may contrive to pepper you with unresponsive answers.

My late friend Daniel Simons, who was American, as you will see, believed it was important to discipline the witness as soon as he committed an offence. He used to say to bemused English audiences, 'You gotta potty-train the witness.'

20 MORE SERIOUS OFFENCES

What if the point you want to make with the witness is more important than just 'It was a Sunday?'

Say you are cross-examining Mr Cavendish (from the *Cavendish v Downham* case study in Appendix 1) and he gives you an affirmative answer but tries to lessen its impact with a long explanation. It is important that you get a short answer to make your point. You could repeat the question twice (as we have just seen) but you could also do this:

'Mr Cavendish, Assyrian antiques are becoming increasingly sought after?'

'Yes.'

'Partly due to their rarity?'

'Yes.'

'But also because of modern-day conflicts in Iraq?'

'Yes.'

'And the Middle-East?'

'Yes.'

'These have reignited awareness in the West?'

'Yes.'

'Of the region's importance to art history?'

'Yes.'

'People have particular interest in Assyrian tableaux of this type?'

'Yes.'

'Because they demonstrate the development of the written form?'

'Yes, but you have to remember that my main interest lies in the Babylonian cities of Nippur, Larsa and Ur.'

'My question was these tableaux demonstrate the development of the written form?'

'Yes but the region is famous for its enormous bas-reliefs and clay tablets.'

'The answer to my question is yes?'

'Yes.'

It is clear from the behaviour of Mr Cavendish in this passage that he does not like being tied down to answering short questions with a 'yes'. So he resorts, much like a politician, to answering his own question.

You will see that the effect of the cross-examiner saying, 'The answer to my question is yes?' is a little stronger than merely repeating the question and, after the third time, moving on.

As one goes up the punishment scale the cross-examiner can try different techniques, some of which border on sarcasm, but the punishment must fit the crime or else it will look like bullying.

The next level is to reverse the question, especially if the answer does not begin with a 'yes':

> 'Because they demonstrate the development of the written form?'
>
> 'You have to remember that my main interest lies in the Babylonian cities of Nippur, Larsa and Ur.'
>
> 'Are you saying they don't demonstrate the development of the written form?' [a reversal of the question]
>
> 'No I'm not. They do.'

There is no reason for counsel to make this assumption from the answer given but it is a handy way of showing the witness who is in control.

There are other variations which may be used depending upon the severity of the witness's offence but be very careful. Ask yourself, 'Am I going to lose the sympathy of my listener?'

For example:

> 'Please answer my question?'; or
>
> 'Perhaps I wasn't clear. My question was ...'

An American attorney I know favours turning his back on an evasive witness. I advise strongly against doing this in Commonwealth or European courts and I don't think a lot of US judges would condone the practice either.

21 REFRESHING A WITNESS'S MEMORY IN CROSS-EXAMINATION

Whether a witness has forgotten what is in his statement or is being wilfully obstructive or is just plain lying, the following technique is the best method of handling the witness. It should not be used for trivial matters. But it should be carried out fairly, slowly and deliberately:

> 'Mr Cavendish these tableaux demonstrate the development of the written form?'
>
> 'That's wrong'; or 'I disagree with you.'
>
> Stop and look at the witness. Take your time:
>
> 'Mr Cavendish, do you have your statement in front of you?'
>
> 'Yes I do.'
>
> 'Would you please turn to paragraph 4?'
>
> 'Yes.'
>
> 'Would you please read the last four lines of paragraph 4 quietly to yourself?'
>
> 'Yes.'
>
> 'Have you read it?'
>
> 'Yes.'
>
> 'Now, I will put the question again. These tableaux demonstrate the development of the written form?'
>
> 'Yes. They do.'

Most witnesses would realise early and admit their mistake as soon as they looked at paragraph 4. You wouldn't need to ask the last two questions.

As a method it has certain advantages:

1 You don't embarrass a witness who simply may have forgotten.

2 You have complete control over the process.

3 The witness and the court are aware that you know more about the witness's evidence than the witness himself.

4 The witness is unlikely to play the 'unresponsive' game again.

My students ask me why we don't just force the witness to read the passage out loud like they do on TV. Well, it is humiliating. You are rubbing the witness's nose in it. And anyway, the witness may take control and read out the wrong passage or read out the right passage in an unabsorbable manner, too quickly or too quietly to be heard.

22 IMPEACHMENT

Impeachment is when a witness is confronted with evidence that proves he is lying. It is similar to para 21, 'Refreshing a witness's memory in cross-examination', but more confrontational.

It should be reserved for a major point, otherwise it looks like a case of using a sledgehammer to crack a nut.

If the version being given in the witness box is different from the one the witness gave previously, say, at the scene of the crime or the traffic accident, impeachment may still be used but you might consider one of the gentler methods set out earlier. You may still achieve the same result: a retraction or an admission from the witness.

You must have the evidence, either in a witness statement or a document, to prove it.

The substance of the method is to give credit to the evidence you wish to rely upon and then confront the witness with it.

For example, let us say the witness has given evidence in a traffic case that when she went through the traffic light it was green. This is contrary to what she said to the police at the time and that statement is in evidence:

> 'Mrs Sullivan, the traffic light was red?'
>
> 'It was green.'
>
> 'You made a statement to the police just after the accident?'
>
> 'I did.'

'The events were fresh in your memory?'

'Yes. It had just happened.'

'And you told the police the truth?'

'I did.'

'Let's turn to that truthful statement.'

Make sure the judge is reading it and have the page and line reference to hand.

'Mrs Sullivan, you told the police that the light was red?'

Some witnesses may capitulate before you get to the last question.

The temptation to call for an explanation in your moment of triumph is sometimes too hard to resist but you risk undoing all your good work and again, it looks like bullying.

If you ask for an explanation you might get one you don't like, e.g. 'I was very upset at the time and made a mistake.'

Don't gloat or look triumphant or rub the witness's nose in it. After a suitable pause to let it sink in, move on.

It is crucial that you practise this method so that it becomes a mantra:

1 Put your version, 'The light was red.'
2 Get the witness to give the evidence of your version its proper weight: made to police at the time and truthful.
3 Confront the witness with it.
4 Don't ask for an explanation.
5 Save it for the big points.

Don't deviate from it and do not let the witness get a chink of light so that she can take control. It is there for all to see in red and green: two inconsistent statements. With luck, both will be on oath (as in a deposition) or affirmed to be true.

When I teach in the United States, the students seize upon the impeachment method and use it at the first opportunity.

I recall training in Indiana. One student was performing a simple red light/green light drill similar to the example above. This is how it went:

> 'The light was red?'
>
> 'Well ...'
>
> 'This isn't the first time you've been asked about this?'

I had to intervene. 'If you're going into a full-scale impeachment, at least wait for the witness to deny it!'

Impeachment is intended to discredit the witness as a reliable source of information. It should not be attempted unless a witness statement or other evidence is reasonably available to complete the impeachment.

The impeachment method is a nuclear weapon. It should only be used on a big point when the witness is lying and your chances of success are extremely high.

Perform the ritual then leave it. Save your comments for the closing speech.

23 THE TALKATIVE WITNESS

Sometimes, whatever method you use, the witness will still talk. You have to make a judgement as to whether the witness's talking is helping you or hurting you. Don't react to it. Don't show frustration or annoyance. Remember, if it is frustrating or annoying you, it will probably be having the same effect on the court.

I love what Sir Patrick Hastings KC said to Professor Harold Laski, a witness who was constitutionally incapable of a brief answer.

During another interminable reply Hastings moved to sit down and remarked, 'I'm afraid you must go on by yourself Mr Laski. I cannot go on.'[33]

24 WHEN TO ASK OPEN QUESTIONS

Open questions may be necessary when a witness is lying or giving an implausible account, but you should prepare a response for every possible answer and take your time.

Open questions are a signal to the witness to give information. I know an advocate who has reached the rank of King's Counsel. He loves open questions. He says they are good for detecting lying witnesses. He is from the school of 'give them enough rope and they will hang themselves'.

I say unless you are on a winner, don't risk your money. If you do ask an open question, just make sure the information won't hurt you. Better still, don't ask one at all.

But sometimes open questions are necessary. Simon Brown KC told me of his former Head of Chambers, Sir Roy Beldam, who was a master of the art. He said he would cross-examine like this: Closed question. Closed question. Closed question. Closed question. Then 'Why did you do that?'

Sir Roy was closing all the avenues of escape then throwing in an open question, the answer to which could only damage the witness.

Let us go back to the cross-examination of Mr Cavendish in the *Cavendish v Downham* case study in Appendix 1 and look at the risks:

> 'Mr Cavendish, you looked at the sculpture yourself?'
>
> 'Yes.'

---

33 *Laski v Newark Advertiser Co Ltd & Parlby* (1947), cited in Richard DuCann, *The Art of the Advocate* (Penguin, London, 1993) 167.

'You didn't ask if you could take it away for inspection?'

'No, I didn't.'

'Or get a second opinion?'

'No.'

'Mrs Downham didn't stop you from getting a second opinion?'

'No, she didn't.'

'You made up your mind to buy it?'

'Yes, I did.'

'Why?'

'Because if it hadn't been for her eloquence and obvious knowledge of the sculpture and her firm assurance that it was genuine, I would never have bought it.'

The last question, an open question, is unnecessary and the answer is damaging. The lesson is that inexperienced advocates should avoid open questions.

Here is an example of a devastating cross-examination by Edward Carson.

Cadbury, the famous chocolate makers, sued the *Evening Standard* for libel, when the paper accused the company of profiting from slave labour. The *Evening Standard* was defended by Carson, who cross-examined the white-haired and venerable head of the company, William Cadbury.

The defence was that the libel was true. The cross-examination is worth reading in full, but for the present purposes, it is useful to see the mixture of closed and open questions that Carson employed.

The last question, though open, is a killer:

Carson:	'The men who were producing the cocoa you were buying procured it by atrocious methods of slavery?'
Cadbury:	'Yes.'

Carson:	'Men, and not only men, but women and children were taken forcibly away from their homes against their will?'
Cadbury:	'Yes.'
Carson:	'Were they marched on the road like cattle?'
Cadbury:	'I cannot answer that question. They were marched in forced marches down to the coast.'
Carson:	'How far had they to march?'
Cadbury:	'Various distances: some came from more than a thousand miles, some from quite near the coast.'
Carson:	'Never to return again?'
Cadbury:	'Never to return again.'

You will note that Carson is prepared to ask open questions but knows not only that the answer will not harm him, but, like the second last question, the answer will actually help his case:

Carson:	'From the information you procured did they go down [to the coast] in shackles?'
Cadbury:	'It is the usual custom, I believe, to shackle them at night on the march.'
Carson:	'Those who could not keep up with the march were murdered?'
Cadbury:	'I have seen statements to that effect.'
Carson:	'You do not doubt it?'

This is skilful. Cadbury's answer was evasive and Carson pins him down:

Cadbury:	'I do not doubt that it has been so in some cases.'
Carson:	'The men, women and children are freely bought and sold?'

Cadbury: 'I do not believe, as far as I know, that there has been anything that corresponds to the open-slave markets of 50 years ago. It is done more by subtle trickery and arrangements of that kind.'

Carson: 'You do not suggest it is better because it is done by subtle trickery?'

An average cross-examiner might tackle Cadbury's evasive last answer with an open question such as 'How do you know that?' Such a question would have given Cadbury control. But you see how Carson nails the evasion and presses home the advantage with his question:

Carson: 'Knowing it [the slavery] was atrocious, you took for eight years the main portion of your supply of cocoa for the profit of your business from the islands conducted under this system?'

This could have been broken down but hey, it's Carson:

Cadbury: 'Yes, for a period of some years.'

Carson: 'You do not look on that as anything immoral?'

Cadbury: 'Not under the circumstances.'

Let us skip to the end. It's an open question but it is brutal:

Carson: 'Now I have come to the end, and I ask you only this question. From 1901 down to 1908, when you ceased trading, was there anything effective you did at all?'

Cadbury: 'I think so myself. I admit that my efforts resulted in a good deal less than I should have liked but I do not admit that I did nothing at all.'

Carson: 'Have you formed any estimate of the number of slaves who lost their lives in preparing your cocoa from 1901 to 1908?'

Cadbury: 'No, no, no.'

The jury found that Cadbury's had been libelled. But Carson had achieved his purpose. The sum of damages awarded was a farthing.[34]

25 THE RISKS OF OPEN QUESTIONS, ARGUMENTS AND CONCLUSIONS

Mr Justice Robert Jackson was a distinguished Supreme Court judge of the United States. He stood down from the Bench to lead the prosecution of the Nazi war criminals at Nuremberg. He considered it to be his duty.

It is clear that the leading witness for the Nazis, Herman Goering, soon got the better of Justice Jackson. James Owen, in his book *Nuremberg* remarked that 'From the beginning Jackson's line of questioning was too vague and too passive, seemingly seeking to engage Goering in elevated moral debate rather than to pin down his involvement in specific crimes.'[35]

You will see that the questions are open and replete with conclusions, and this is how Goering handles them:

Jackson: 'You are perhaps aware that you are the only living man who can expound to us the true purposes of the Nazi party and the inner workings of its leadership?'

Goering: 'I am perfectly aware of that.'

---

34 Edward Marjoribanks, *The Life of Lord Carson* (Victor Gollancz, London, 1932) 395–397.

35 James Owen, *Nuremberg: Evil on Trial* (Headline, London, 2006) 132.

Jackson: 'You, from the very beginning, together with those who were associated with you, intended to overthrow, and later did overthrow, the Weimar Republic?'

Goering: 'That was, as far as I am concerned, my firm intention.'

Jackson: 'And, upon coming to power, you immediately abolished parliamentary government in Germany?'

Goering: 'We found it to be no longer necessary. Also I should like to emphasise the fact that we were moreover the strongest parliamentary party, and had the majority. But you are correct, when you say that parliamentary procedure was done away with, because the various parties were disbanded and forbidden.'

Jackson lets this damaging fact go and proceeds to debate with the witness:

Jackson: 'You established the Leadership Principle, which you have described as a system in which authority existed only at the top, and is passed downwards and is imposed upon the people below; is that correct?'

Goering: 'In order to avoid any misunderstandings, I should once more like to explain the idea briefly, as I understand it. In German parliamentary procedure in the past responsibility rested with the highest officials, who were responsible for carrying out the anonymous wishes of the majorities, and it was they who exercised the authority. In the Leadership Principle we sought to reverse the direction, that is, the authority existed at the top and passed downwards, while the responsibility began at the bottom and passed upwards.'

Jackson:	'In other words, you did not believe in and did not permit government, as we call it, by consent of the governed, in which the people, through their representatives, were the source of power and authority?'
Goering:	'That is not entirely correct ...'

You get the gist. Goering's answers were long and self-justifying but Jackson was causing them by asking such vague questions.

After some time, Jackson lost his cool and said to the tribunal:

> 'Well, I respectfully submit to the Tribunal that this witness is not being responsive, and has not been in his examination ... It is perfectly futile to spend our time if we cannot have responsive answers to our questions.'[36]

The next day, the President of the Tribunal ruled:

> '... the only rule which the Tribunal can lay down is the rule – already laid down – that the witness must answer if possible "yes" or "no", and that he may make such explanations as may be necessary after answering questions directly in that way, and that such explanations must be brief, and not be speeches.'

The President was Lord Justice Lawrence. His alternate judge, who many believe wrote most of the Nuremberg judgment, was Sir Norman Birkett KC.

Birkett had been the most celebrated advocate in England. He kept a private diary of the trial and it was scathing. He wrote:

> 'The true art of cross-examination is something in a different plane [from merely putting incriminating documents to the witness] altogether; and it has not been yet seen at Nuremberg in any shape or form.'[37]
>
> ...

---

36 Ibid, 145.

37 Ibid, 123.

> 'Jackson has no real knowledge of the art of cross-examination. Almost the chief quality of a cross-examiner is to have a complete mastery of the case he proposes to make, so that he may attack the witness whenever a weak place appears, with the knowledge he carries in his head. If he is unsure of his case or his facts, so he stumbles or delays, the richest opportunity of the cross-examiner is lost. This is one of the first and main weaknesses of Jackson ...'[38]

Birkett's major criticism of Jackson was his lack of ability as a cross-examiner. But Birkett was fair. Earlier in his diary, he had written of Jackson's masterly addresses to the tribunal.[39]

The concept of mastering the brief and seizing opportunities in cross-examination was reinforced by Jonathan Sumption QC, in a short question and answer session he gave for the BBC.

Sumption, who was later elevated to the UK Supreme Court, was asked, 'What is the key to a good cross-examination?' He replied, 'Know your material backwards, preferably better than the witness; spot your opportunities when they arise and know exactly what it is you are trying to prove.'[40]

It echoes the exhortation of the Victorian barrister Henry Hawkins, who said, 'Know your brief and examine from your head.'[41]

My favourite cross-examination is by Norman Birkett. The case was not momentous like Nuremberg or salacious like one of his celebrated murder trials.

---

38 Ibid, 224.

39 H Montgomery Hyde, *Norman Birkett: The Life of Lord Birkett of Ulverston* (Hamish Hamilton, London, 1965) 509.

40 'Five Minutes With: Jonathan Sumption QC' (YouTube) www.youtube.com/watch?v=I8DlcexQiPw.

41 Advice given to Sir Edward Clarke by Hawkins (later Lord Brampton). Cited in EW Fordham, *Notable Cross-examinations* (Constable, London, 1951) Appendix 196.

He acted for the plaintiff in a claim against the General Motor Cab Company. His client had been very badly injured while being driven in a taxi between Waterloo Station and King's Cross.

Apparently, the road was greasy after a sprinkling of rain. The cabbie said he had been travelling slowly and that what happened had been an accident.

This cross-examination is a deft selection and arrangement of the facts. The last question is a comment, but who could resist it? Above all, the examination is calm, polite and definitely not cross:

Birkett:	'You say you were travelling quite slowly.'
	'Yes.'
Birkett:	'Not fast at all but quite slowly?'
	'That's right.'
Birkett:	'And you drew out to pass another vehicle?'
	'Correct.'
Birkett:	'Still not going fast?'
	'Yes.'
Birkett:	'Let's just see. You skidded slightly?'
	'Yes.'
Birkett:	'Mounted the pavement?'
	'Yes.'
Birkett:	'Hit a plate-glass window and smashed that?'
	'Right.'
Birkett:	'Knocked over two or three stalls loaded with fruit and vegetables outside a shop?'
	'Correct.'
Birkett:	'Knocked down one policeman and two pedestrians?'
	'I'm afraid I did.'

Birkett: 'And finally knocked down a lamp-post?'

'Yes.'

Birkett: [Pause] 'Well now, I wonder if you would like to estimate how much more damage you might have done if you had been going fast?'[42]

Look at the style. No aggression, no righteousness and a gentle leading of the witness to the conclusion he wanted.

An average advocate would have approached it differently:

'You were speeding?'

'You were a danger on the roads?'

'You shouldn't have been driving so fast in the greasy conditions?'

But Birkett just chose the facts, arranged them well and let them speak for themselves – except for the irresistible final comment.

Some of my students ask, 'Did he put the case? He should have put the case!'[43]

But he did put the case through a subtle and clever arrangement of the facts.

26 DON'T BE POMPOUS

Michael Meacher, a British Labour MP, sued Alan Watkins, a distinguished political journalist, for calling him middle class.

Meacher liked to describe himself as a farmer's son when in fact, his dad had been trained as an accountant.

---

42 Cited in AE Bowker, *Behind the Bar* (Staples Press, London, 1947) 95.

43 See the rule in *Browne v Dunn* (1893) 6 R 67 and para 6, 'Putting your Case'.

The case lasted three weeks in the High Court. At one point, under cross-examination from Meacher's counsel, Watkins smirked.

'Are you not aware', said the barrister, 'that this is a very serious matter?'

Watkins laughed incredulously, 'No it isn't!'[44]

Meacher lost the case.

27 THE 'DID YOU?' QUESTION

The 'Did you?' question is used to considerable effect by skilful barristers but is something which is best avoided by the junior advocate.

Examples of these questions are:

> 'Did you think of telling someone what happened?'
>
> 'Do you know his voice well?'
>
> 'Did it occur to you at the time that it was not like his voice?'

The 'did you?' question has numerous variations:

> 'Did you not think …?'
>
> 'Could you explain why?'
>
> 'Can you tell the court your full name?'

I asked this last question in court once. My client who had been briefed to answer the questions honestly and directly simply replied, 'Yes.'

There are two obvious problems with these questions. The first is that if they start with a verb, such as did, can or could, they are invariably leading:

ı Leith, *You Talkin' to Me?* (Profile Books, London, 2011).

'Can you say why you shouted?'

'No, I can't.'

Second, they are open questions. They give a degree of control to the witness. It's better if you re-arrange the words in them and close them down. For example, rather than asking:

'Did you think you should tell your husband?'

Change it to:

'You didn't think to tell your husband?'

Or even better:

'You didn't tell your husband?'

The closed questions, assuming you know the answer, will cause the witness to say, 'No I didn't.'

Look at what could happen if you were to ask the question in an open form:

'Did you tell your husband?'

'Yes I did and I told my children Mark and Jane and they told all their friends.'

The witness has taken control and may just be giving facts that you do not want.

It is noticeable that advocates who start their questions with the words 'Did you?' are likely to start most of their questions with those words. My American colleagues call it catching the disease of 'Didyouitis'.

Careful advocates use the open question commencing with a verb (Do you?) but only in circumstances where they know the answer and have complete control.

Sir Charles Russell cross-examined a stable owner called Sir George Chetwynd.

Chetwynd had sued Russell's client for libel. The client said Chetwynd ran his stables dishonestly because he continued to employ a man called Wood whom he knew pulled horses so that they would not win:[45]

Russell:	'Did you hear that Walton had paid large sums to Wood for information about his mounts?'
Chetwynd:	'No.'
Russell:	'Did you say that you never heard that Walton had paid large sums to Wood?'
Chetwynd:	'Well, I heard something mentioned about a race in which Wood rode.'
Russell:	'Do you say that you never heard that Walton had paid large sums to Wood?'
Chetwynd:	'I only heard of one instance.'

Russell is persistent and always in control.

Of course, there is the masterly final question by Carson in the Cadbury case which starts with a verb and is open.

> 'Have you formed any estimate of the number of slaves who lost their lives in preparing your cocoa from 1901 to 1908?'

But my advice is that unless you are approaching the experience and skill of Sir Charles Russell or Sir Edward Carson, keep the questions closed and short.

28 COLLATERAL QUESTIONS

Collateral questions are questions that do not go to the issues that the court must decide. They run alongside the issues and are typically questions that go to the credibility of the witness.

---

and Durham Turf Libel Case (1889), cited in Richard DuCann, *The* *ocate* (Penguin, London, 1993) 118.

The general rule is that the cross-examiner is bound by the answers of the witness on these questions.

The reason for the rule is that it prevents the trial becoming bogged down or lengthened while the court assesses a multitude of side issues.

A good example was shown in the case of *Harris v Tippett*.[46]

The defendant's witness was cross-examined on whether he had tried to deter one of the plaintiff's witnesses from giving evidence. He denied doing so, but the court ruled that the plaintiff could not recall the witness to prove he had been influenced.

Mr Justice Lawrence said the question was permissible but:

> 'when these questions are irrelevant to the issue on the record, you cannot call other witnesses to contradict the answer he gives. No witness can be prepared to support his character as to particular facts, and such collateral inquiries would lead to endless confusion.'

It seems like a rule which might cause injustice, but I suppose the law is saying 'We have to draw the line somewhere.'

Lord Chief Baron Pollock said:

> 'The test whether a matter is collateral is this: if the answer of a witness is a matter which you would be allowed on your own part to prove in evidence – if it has such a connection with the issues, that you would be allowed to give it in evidence – then it is a matter on which you may contradict him.'[47]

There are exceptions to the rules. The party calling the witness can call another one on a matter which but for the cross-examination would not have arisen. Most relate to criminal cases.

---

46 (1811) 2 Camp 637, 170 ER 1277.

47 *Attorney-General v Hitchcock* (1847) 1 Exch 91 and 99.

In short, on collateral matters or side issues, ask the question and if you get a denial, move on. You are bound by the answer. The court will hear or have heard your witness's version at some stage and decide which it prefers.

29 CROSS-EXAMINATION ON DOCUMENTS

As we have seen, a document such as a letter is evidence of the facts contained within it. Nowadays, electronic correspondence is vastly more prevalent than letters.

Emails have the advantage of being contemporaneous and a good indication of the creator's state of mind at the time. Metadata is available to show when and by whom the document was made.

In some countries, a document may be used to refresh a witness's memory, but only for that purpose.

If it is for any other purpose, the cross-examiner's opponent may call upon the cross-examiner to tender the entire document.

There could be some unfortunate passages within the entire document which don't help the cross-examiner's case. Tread carefully.

The safest technique is to say:

> 'Please have a look at this. Don't say what it is. Now read the fifth line to yourself. Have you read it?
>
> Now, I'll put my question again.'

In arbitration cases or civil trials or when the parties have stipulated the exhibits prior to the hearing there should be no problem because the evidence is in.

30 HOW THE CROSS-EXAMINATION FITS INTO CLOSING

In the end, you are cross-examining to be able to make an effective closing speech which you hope that the decision-maker will agree with.

Try not to steal the judge's thunder. As far as you can, let the decision-maker think he has worked it out for himself.

Sir Garfield Barwick QC said:

> 'My method was to try to elicit from the witness answers which would qualify the evidence already given, minimise its effect and if possible find contradictions within it.
>
> I also sought answers which would provide material for my final address to the tribunal whether judge or jury, according to a logical plan I had already formed.'

But he sounded a warning:

> 'I did not seek to publicise that plan when cross-examining. Often, I think, the delay in expressing it weakened its impact. Perhaps a contrary impression had thus been allowed to be formed by the tribunal.'[48]

31 HOW TO FINISH

'How to finish' should more correctly be entitled 'when to finish'. When you have put all the facts and the failures to the witness and you believe you can argue an inference from them in your closing speech, in other words you have earned the right to argue a conclusion, you should sit down. It takes finesse, judgement and timing on the part of the cross-examiner to know when to sit down.

The temptation, sometimes overwhelming, is to put the conclusion to the witness in triumph. For example:

> 'And finally you forged the will didn't you?'
>
> 'No I didn't!'
>
> 'No further questions.'

---

[48] Barwick, *A Radical Tory* (fn 1) 23–24.

It's terribly lame. No witness, unless you are very lucky, is going to agree with the case against them. So leave it alone.

Obviously, you have an obligation to put your case but that should have been done at the start or buried in the middle; not left until the end. Unless, of course, you judge that in the face of overwhelming facts and omissions a denial at the end from the witness will look ridiculous. But those situations are uncommon.

The tendency of counsel to finish with a flourish is often called 'one question too many' – the one point that should have been saved for the closing speech.

The best example I know is of a barrister who became a High Court Judge, and who used to tell this story against himself.

As a young barrister, he was called upon to cross-examine a police officer who had witnessed his two clients breaking into a jewellery shop in the early hours of the morning. From a distance of 12 feet, in a totally empty village square he had seen the two men picking the lock.

The barrister's objective was to show it would have been impossible for any person, let alone the police officer, to have come so close without anyone noticing.

The questions were short and well informed – all neatly ordered facts:

> 'Sergeant, would you be kind enough to tell us how tall you are?'
>
> 'Six foot, three, sir.'
>
> 'Would you mind telling us your weight?'
>
> 'Tip the scales at just under 23 stones, sir.'
>
> 'That night – wearing uniform were you?'
>
> 'Yes, sir.'
>
> 'Helmet?'

'Yes, sir.'

'Great coat?'

'Tunic actually, sir.'

'Boots?'

'Yes, sir.'

'Regulation issue boots, sergeant?'

'Yes, sir.'

'What size were they?'

'Size 12, sir.'

'Yes I see. Size 12 boots. Studded with hobnails like the normal regulation issue?'

(Pause) 'Yes, sir.'

'They have a kind of small horseshoe of metal on each heel?'

'Err, yes, sir.'

'And you say you approached to within 12 feet of these men without their seeming to notice your arrival, sergeant?'

(Pause) 'Yes, sir.'

'In a totally empty square at two in the morning?'

(Pause) 'Yes, sir.'

'Nobody else around was there?'

'No, sir.'

'Normal flagged pavements were there?'

'Yes, sir.'

'I mean, you didn't approach over a lawn or grass of some kind, did you?'

'No, sir.'

Counsel has done a good job so far. But he cannot resist another question and it is an open question:

'Well really, sergeant, can you suggest to the magistrates how you could possibly have got as close as you say you did without being heard by the defendants?'

'On my bicycle, sir.'[49]

32 CROSS-EXAMINATION: CHECKLIST

32.1 Preparation

- Formulate objectives: what you wish to argue in closing.
- Arrange facts or omissions to achieve those objectives.
- Use the witness's own words.
- One fact per question.
- Be ethical.
- Plan the putting of your case (or the challenge) for the start or put it in the middle.
- If you wish to rely on your client's version of the facts in evidence or in closing, make sure you put it to the opponent's witness.
- Avoid conclusions, theories or speeches.
- Save them for closing.

32.2 Delivery

- Closed short questions keep control (sometimes you might ask 'why?'); but
- Know the answer or be sure it won't hurt you.
- Assert, don't ask – 'You did', not 'Did you?'
- One fact per question: keeps control and has a particular effect of making the evidence appear to mount up.
- You may put omissions: things that the witness failed to do. 'You didn't write it down?'

---

49 Keith Evans, *Advocacy at the Bar – A Beginners Guide* (New Edition, Blackstone Press Ltd, London, 1992).

- Don't argue with the witness.
- Most courts do not like aggressive cross-examination.
- Don't put conclusions, theories or speeches to the witness.
- Is the answer good enough? Get the answer you want but try only three times.
- Long questions breed long answers.
- Avoid one question too many.
- Unless you are putting your case, leave the court to draw the conclusion.[50]

32.3 Style

- Avoid notes – know your brief and cross-examine from your head.
- Avoid gremlins.
- Be polite.

[50] See Sir Edward Clarke KC, 'Unfinished Treatise' (fn 5), quoted on page 158 of this book.

Chapter 12
Re-Examination

Re-examination, or re-direct as it is called in arbitrations and in the United States, is when you get to ask questions of your witness when the cross-examination is finished.

The purpose of re-examination is to remove any uncertainties or ambiguities caused by the cross-examination. In addition, you may re-examine if you think your witness is able to give an explanation which you know will assist and which the witness was prevented from giving by the cross-examiner. In some jurisdictions you may have the good fortune of being allowed to consult your witness first.

It is not, as is mistakenly thought, an opportunity for your witness to repeat what was in the evidence-in-chief (direct) or the witness statement. Nor is it an opportunity to open new ground. You do not get a second bite of the cherry.

Your questions must arise from the cross-examination. They must not be leading and you had better know what the answer is. More importantly, the witness had better know the answer. In a sense, you and your witness have to be telepathic.

The first decision you must make is:

1 Is this something which is important? Has the court been given the wrong impression? Was the witness's answer not in proper perspective?

The second decision is:

2 Can I fix it? Will I run the risk of making it worse? Will the witness know what I want him to say?

Lord Justice Phillimore said, 'If the witness has been discredited in cross-examination there is not much you can do about it. If not, leave well alone.'

Most seasoned counsel say that re-examination should be done sparingly. If the cross-examination takes 20 minutes and the re-examination takes 30 minutes, then, as Judge Mark Drummond says, it tells you something.

The point is that you don't want to be giving the court the impression that your witness was damaged by the cross-examination.

Sir John Simon once said to his witness, who had been cross-examined all day, 'You are a witness that does not need re-examination, thank you.'[1]

You will re-examine if the wrong impression has been given by the witness's answers.

There is a good example provided by Richard DuCann. A witness had admitted in cross-examination that he had been convicted of a felony:

Counsel:	'When were you convicted?'
Witness:	'29 years ago.'
Judge:	'You were only a boy?'
Witness:	'Yes, My Lord.'[2]

Note that counsel's question is open, non-leading and short.

The most effective technique to re-examine is to take the witness to the point you want to ask about. If it is a document, then make sure the court is looking at it too. Take your time. Your first question, as a means of orienting the witness and the court, may be leading but the next question may not.

---

1 Cited in Richard DuCann, *The Art of the Advocate* (Penguin, London, 1993) 180.

2 Ibid.

For example, returning to the *Cavendish v Downham* case study in Appendix 1:

Question:	'Mr Cavendish it was put to you in cross-examination that you relied solely on your own judgement?'
Answer:	'It was.'
Question:	'And you replied "that's not correct"?'
Answer:	'I did.'
Question:	'Why did you say that?'
Answer:	'Because I relied solely on what Mrs Downham told me about the sculpture.'

Lastly, if the court asks its own questions of a witness, it will usually allow counsel to ask any questions arising from the answers.

1 RE-EXAMINATION: CHECKLIST

The MADRAS method:

MUST arise from cross-examination.

AIM to rehabilitate or let the witness explain.

DIRECT the witness to the point you want to ask about.

RE-RUNS of the direct examination are forbidden.

ASK open, non-leading questions.

SPARINGLY – do it sparingly.

Chapter 13
Expert Witnesses

It has been said that one needs at least 10 years in an area of knowledge or practice before one can truly be considered to be an expert. I don't think Mozart would agree. But remember what the expert is there for: to help the court to make a decision based on technical issues which are outside the ordinary knowledge of the judge.

The best expert is a teacher. In other words, an expert will be of far more assistance to the judge if she teaches the judge about the problem, its extent and its solution. It's not much different, on its face, to the role played by a good advocate.

However, the expert who strays into advocacy, or into arguing his side's case, will not assist the judge. He will most probably annoy the court.

The role of teacher carries with it a number of techniques. The expert must begin at the level of the judge's knowledge of the subject. You don't want the judge thinking, to paraphrase Lord Denning, 'Well that's very impressive, he obviously knows a great deal about the subject, but I'm afraid it all went over my head.'[1]

A good teacher begins at the level of the student and, step by step, shows the way, until the student can walk unaided.

---

1 Lord Denning, *The Closing Chapter* (Butterworths, London, 1983) 60.

The primary duty of the expert is to assist the court, and he will do that by helping the decision-maker understand a subject of special skill whether technical, scientific or otherwise.

The best way to do that is to be credible or believable. To that end the expert must be well dressed (in a business suit or equivalent), well prepared and positive.

He must sit or stand with a good upright posture, he must speak directly with just the right amount of eye contact and he must be conversational. He should use analogies and illustrations and vary his tone of voice. Above all, he must be interesting and inject just the right amount of passion into what he says.

He must be prepared to make concessions where appropriate and show the decision-maker that he is fair.

What he must not do is ramble; hesitate or talk down to the court. He must think before answering the questions. He must not be arrogant or immovable or use technical words which the listeners do not understand. He must not exaggerate or over-sell his position.

1 DIRECT EXAMINATION OF THE EXPERT

The basic skills are the same: you must think of short, open questions which are not leading and which comprise simple words.

In preparing for the direct examination you must think about how best your expert will be able to teach the decision-maker.

Most expert testimony is based upon facts. That is why it is important to conduct a proper case analysis, which necessarily includes a persuasive distillation of the facts.

Once you have received the expert's report, you will have to think of the best way that this expert can teach the decision-maker. Will it be by oral evidence, charts, maps, photographs, videos or physical demonstrations? Or a combination of some or all of them?

If you want your expert to demonstrate something in court, make sure it's not the first time he does it. The performance should be rehearsed (it should not look rehearsed) and polished.

In some countries you must not coach or rehearse the witness if you are going to be the advocate. See Chapter 9, 'Preparing Witnesses'.

Remember to appeal to as many of the listener's senses as you can.

A judge in Indiana told me of a nuisance case she tried. Neighbours complained about the sound and smell of the chicken farm next door. Their lawyers produced a container of chicken poo and invited the jury to smell it. Not an attractive story, but the tactic worked.

Many good lawyers try to get the expert in front of the flip chart or the white board as soon as possible, carrying out calculations or drawing diagrams.

These days they might use a PowerPoint presentation or show a diagram on a screen. You should ensure the equipment will work properly. How many times have you been to an event where there is a glitch with the PowerPoint presentation or the projector?

1.1 Introduction and qualifications

You might want to organise the expert's evidence into topics. But before you do anything you must establish the expert's credibility. Why is the expert here? What qualifies him to give evidence to the court or tribunal?

This is the first stage, and it is crucial. You first must introduce your expert to the court. Look happy and proud but not smug. This is one of the stars of your show, if not the star. Your demeanour should suggest to the decision-maker that you really think this witness is going to help.

The adoption of this attitude is not easy. There are so many other distractions and things you will be thinking about.

If your expert has a title, you must use it in the introduction. Let us return to the *Cavendish v Downham* case study in Appendix 1:

Question:	'You are Professor Christophe Fournier?'
Answer:	'I am.'
Question:	'You live at ...'

A good practice is to get the decision-maker interested in why the witness is here. The Americans called it a 'teaser' or 'foreshadowing' the witness's evidence. It's a leading question but it rarely receives an objection:

Question:	'Professor Fournier. Are you here today to give your opinion as to the genuineness of the sculpture "A Soldier and Two Horses"?'
Answer:	'Yes I am.'

The next step is to qualify the witness. If you are not careful, this section can become repetitive and boring. You do not want your expert's qualifications to be boring.

Where is the best place to start?

Well it would be good if you could arrange for your opponent to agree the expert's qualifications, then you can ask a series of leading questions.

But if that is not forthcoming, you will have to think of the most interesting way of arranging the questions. Do you begin at the very beginning?

> 'Where did you go to school?'

That's a better question than the type lawyers often ask:

> 'Where did your education take place?'; or
>
> 'What was your first contact with the educational system?'

But what about starting at the end?

> 'How long have you been the Curator at the Athénée Museum?'

Or even better:

> 'What qualifies you to give an expert opinion in this case?'

As in everything in life, it all depends on the context. It also helps if you ask the following sort of question after a witness has stated one of his qualifications.

> 'What is it about your PhD that will enable you to assist the court in this case?'; or
>
> 'What is it about your PhD that helped you form your opinions in this case?'

It's not just his qualifications – it's also his experience. What are the memorable things that your expert has done? Has he achieved eminence in his field or won awards or written seminal texts?

How should you present these achievements? It's no use burying them in the middle of his qualifications. Make an impact. Ask him about them early on. Of course, you don't want him to appear boastful, but he shouldn't hide his light under a bushel.

1.2 Method

Once the decision-maker is satisfied that the expert is qualified to help, you must ask a series of questions about how the expert reached his conclusion.

What materials was he given? Which facts were presented to him? What were his instructions? Who hired him? What was he told?

This is very important because if his opinion was based on faulty information, it too will be flawed.

The next topic is the method he used.

These are critical questions. You are closing off the avenues of attack your opponent might use.

Your expert's method must be competent, rigorous and fair. Any departure from these three styles will mean an open goal for the opposing lawyer. Let's look at Worthington and Fournier from the *Cavendish v Downham* case study once more.

In short, Worthington is less qualified than Fournier, but he saw the sculpture and examined it. Fournier is the world authority, but he only looked at photographs.

If you are calling Fournier, you have a problem. How do you present that weakness in methodology in its best possible light?

Do you begin with it?

Question:	'Professor Fournier, what method did you use in forming your opinion about this sculpture?'
Answer:	'I looked at 10 digital photographs.'
Question:	'Why?'
Answer:	'Because it had been destroyed.'
Question:	'What were you able to see when you looked at the photos?'
Answer:	'I could clearly see that they were photographs of a bas-relief from the lost Palace of Sennacherib.'

In this way you will get the weakest part of Fournier's evidence out of the way early. You can then spend more time on questions which will strengthen his credibility.

Your primary objective is to help the decision-maker to conclude that the sculpture is genuine – or at least that it is more likely than not that the sculpture is a bas-relief from the Palace of Sennacherib.

Your questions about the expert's method should be short and simple, and you must sound like you are interested in the answers – as if you are hearing them for the first time.

If the expert uses a technical term or bundles a lot of thoughts into one or two words, don't be afraid to ask, 'What do you mean by that?'

Take your time. Allow the expert's answers to sink in. Watch the judge, jury or tribunal carefully. Did they appear to understand what the witness just said? If you didn't understand it, there's a fair chance that the decision-maker didn't understand it either.

Use every tool at your disposal to make the decision-maker's job easier.

Ask your expert before he testifies what things would help explain his methodology to an intelligent layman.

Does he have an analogy? Is there a way of illustrating what he did using a story? Does he have diagrams or illustrations?

In your preparation time the expert should be educating you. Do you understand what the expert is saying? Can it be made clearer? The expert must be seen to be independent and fair and therefore reliable. He must be prepared to make appropriate concessions or admit weaknesses where necessary, as long as such admissions do not undermine your whole case.

But if the expert shows the court that he is being fair and reasonable and that the methods he used were sound, it is more likely his evidence will be relied upon. The parallel with the role of the advocate is clear. In Fournier's case, it would be a good idea now and again to tie in his qualifications to his method:

> 'What has your experience of Austen Henry Layard taught you about identifying Assyrian sculpture?'

What makes this question so effective is that the opposing expert, Edward Worthington, never mentions Layard and may not even have heard of him. It's significant because Layard was the leading archaeologist of the relevant Assyrian period.

If you want your expert to demonstrate something, make sure he practises it beforehand. It has to look seamless and it has to look professional. Make sure everyone in the room can see what the expert is doing and take it slowly enough so that everyone will follow it. In short, the expert must be seen, heard and understood.

1.3 Opinion

When your expert has explained which method he used and why it helped him to come to his opinion then it is time to ask him what his opinion is. There are various ways you can do this:

> 'Professor Fournier, after examining the photographs what did you conclude?'
>
> 'What can you tell the court about the sculpture you saw in the photographs?'
>
> 'When, in your opinion, was this sculpture created?'

Make sure your question is plain and direct and that it doesn't overshadow in length or complexity what the witness's answer is.

When you have the answer to the 'opinion' question, it is time to ask a one-word question: 'Why?'

In other words, you must establish the basis of the opinion in the mind of the decision-maker. You might go further and try to undermine your opponent's case:

> 'What do you say to the proposition that this sculpture is a 19th-century reproduction?'

Make sure you finish strongly. Don't ask a leading question or any question which may form the basis of an objection from your opponent. The expert must not appear pompous or absolutely certain or even triumphant – just believable and reliable.

In short, the direct examination of the expert should be mapped out along the following lines:

1 Why are you here?

2 What are your qualifications?

3 What is your experience?

4 What did you do?

5 What did you look at?

6 Why?

7 How did you do it?

8 Do other experts do that?

9 What is your opinion?

10 Why is it right?

2 CROSS-EXAMINATION

'What is the co-efficient of the expansion of brass?' is often mentioned as being the most devastating opening question of an expert witness in trial history.

Yet it breaks many of the rules about cross-examination that I have been at pains to point out to you in this book.

It is an open question, which we know will invite the witness to speak at length. Second, it gives the witness an opportunity to take control of the cross-examination and demonstrate his superiority over the questioner.

But the third problem is that the cross-examiner did not know whether the witness knew the answer. It was a stab in the dark and the advocate really ought to have come unstuck.

But he did not, for this was no ordinary violinist – this was Norman Birkett, the courtroom virtuoso.

Two young men discovered a car blazing by the side of the road. They had seen a stranger walking past and were later able to identify him to the police.

The car belonged to Alfred Arthur Rouse, who was the stranger identified by the men. Inside the car were the charred remains of a man who could not be identified.

Rouse was charged with murder. It was the prosecution case led by Birkett that the deceased had been saturated in petrol from a can and that Rouse had deliberately loosened the union at the carburettor end of the petrol pump.

The body had been found face downwards in the driver's seat. The loosening of the union would have caused petrol to flow from the car's tank on to the floor next to the deceased's feet.

A man from Cricklewood called Arthur Isaacs was a motor engineer who read of the case in the newspaper. He volunteered to give expert evidence in Rouse's defence as to whether the union joint had been loosened accidentally or on purpose.

Isaacs was emphatic in his examination by Rouse's counsel: a fire in the car invariably loosened this particular joint. He said the loosening was caused by the contraction and distortion of the metal threads cooling down after the fire. The evidence that the movement of the joint was not deliberate appeared to drive a hole into Birkett's case.

The star advocate rose to cross-examine:[2]

Birkett:	'What is the co-efficient of the expansion of brass?'
Witness:	'The what?'
Birkett:	'The co-efficient of the expansion of brass?' [See how Birkett doesn't change his question at all.]
Witness:	'I am afraid I cannot answer.'
Birkett:	'Do you know what the question means?'
Witness:	'Well, if you put it that way, I don't.'

2 *R v AA Rouse* [1931], cited in H Montgomery Hyde, *Norman Birkett: The Life of Lord Birkett of Ulverston* (Hamish Hamilton, London, 1965) 307.

Birkett:	'But aren't you an engineer? You are not a doctor or crime investigator, or an amateur detective. Do you know what the co-efficient of [the expansion of] brass is?'
Witness:	'No.'
Birkett:	'But your company deals with the heat treatment of metal. What do you make?'
Witness:	'Springs.'

The witness went on to say that in the last year he had investigated 15 to 20 car fires, mostly by the roadside:

Birkett:	'What is the melting point of brass?'
Witness:	(After some hesitation) 'Ah! Brass! Oh! About 1,800 degrees Fahrenheit.'
Birkett:	'If you took half an inch of brass and heated it to 1,800 degrees Fahrenheit, what expansion would you get?'
Witness:	'I would not like to say.'
Birkett:	'Do help me about it. Surely, Mr Isaacs, you have been giving evidence about the effect of intense heat upon the brass nut. Do you now tell the jury that you have no idea what effect 1,800 degrees of heat would have on a half-inch of brass?'
Witness:	'I do not know. I have no need to know.'

Rouse, because of this and other factors such as his terrible performance in the witness box, was eventually convicted and executed.[3]

The Birkett style of cross-examination should not be attempted until you have thoroughly mastered the basic techniques; here they are.

---

3 Ibid, 297–308.

2.1 Preparation

You must have a case theory. What do I want to prove through this expert? What can I prove through this expert?

From that case theory will spring your objective: What do I want to say in my closing address?

Thorough preparation is essential. You must know as much about the subject as you can. You have the crucial advantage of the internet search engine that wasn't available to Norman Birkett. Be careful, for a lot of internet data can prove to be unreliable. But it is a good place to start and may lead you to some fruitful lines of enquiry.

In addition, there are learned texts and treatises.

Lastly, there is your own expert. What can she teach you? How can she teach you to help the court? What does she say about the other expert's evidence? Why is he less credible? Why is he wrong? How did he fall into error? What is his reputation in the industry? What does his evidence mean?

Good advocates approach the cross-examination of an expert in one of three ways:

1 Is there something wrong with the expert?

2 Is there something wrong with the process or his methodology?

3 Is there something wrong with the result?

Be careful about the third factor. My late friend Daniel Simons, who was an excellent advocacy teacher, said that cross-examining an expert was like chopping down a tree. He would draw a rudimentary tree on the board and write 'Qualifications' and 'Experience' at the base, 'Methodology' on the trunk and 'Opinion' on the branches and leaves. He would then ask the class 'If you want to chop down the tree do you go for the opinion?'

I expect Norman Birkett would have ring-barked the tree in the dead of the night.

Let us deal with your preparation of the first line of attack: is there something wrong with the expert?

2.2 Your opponent's expert

Find out as much as you can about your opponent's expert. The first question is whether the expert is entitled to give an opinion. Ask yourself: Where did she go to school? Did she go to university? Was it an Institute of Technology? What were her results? What is the reputation of her place of learning? How does her area of study qualify her to give an opinion on the subject before the court? Can the court rely upon the expert?

On the same theme you must find out about her experience. Do your research thoroughly. Perhaps the expert is highly qualified in one particular area but not the specific area before the court. For example, a lawyer may be an expert on the law, but is it employment law or the law of mergers and acquisitions?

Mr Worthington is a trade specialist. Professor Fournier is the world authority on Assyrian sculpture, but Worthington had the advantage of physically examining the piece; not relying on photographs.

Do some digging on the possible bias, interest or motive of the expert. Is the expert impartial or does she bring baggage to court? Is the expert regularly asked to testify for claimants? Does she have a connection with the party calling her? Is she employed by the party or does she or any of her family have a financial interest (stocks or shares) in the party calling her? Does this expert have an interest in the outcome of the case? Is there prestige in being asked to give evidence in this case?

What are her professional associations? Is she affiliated to a group which takes a certain stance about general issues in the case? Is she truly impartial?

What has she said in the past? Has she written text books or articles? Has her opinion changed from what she has written or said before? Why? Are there any inconsistencies which you can highlight?

Does the leading authority or text book in the area take a different view to the expert?

Find out whether she has been criticised or discredited by other experts or professional bodies. Has a court made adverse findings about her methods or her credibility?

2.3 The opposing expert's method

In preparing to cross-examine your opponent's expert you should look at a number of areas which relate to her method.

Upon which facts did the expert base her opinion? Have they been proved? It will be like a house of cards if one or more of the facts are wrong.

What assumptions did the expert make? For instance, did the expert assume that the price of iron ore will increase over the next two years? Is this a reasonable assumption to make? On what was it based? Would a professional expert make this assumption?

It is often the case that the expert will have a basic theory and then fit the facts and assumptions to support that theory.

This happened in the famous Australian case of *Chamberlain v The Queen*,[4] which American readers may know was made into a movie starring Meryl Streep: *A Cry in the Dark*. Most people will remember the Australian accent which Streep employed to say, 'A dingo's taken my baby.'

The case gripped the nation. A mother was convicted by a jury (and almost a majority of the public) of cutting her baby's throat in a car at a campsite near Uluru, or Ayers Rock as it used to be known.

Mrs Chamberlain said the baby had been killed and spirited away by a wild Australian dog-like animal called a dingo.

---

4 *Chamberlain v The Queen (No 2)* [1984] HCA 7, (1984) 153 CLR 521.

The prosecution believed otherwise and charged her with murder.

The prosecution had an impressive array of forensic experts including the late Joy Kuhl.

Mrs Kuhl did a number of extensive tests on a substance found in the car and concluded that it contained foetal haemoglobin.

This opinion, along with the odd behaviour of the defendant and her husband, led to a conviction. Mrs Chamberlain was later released from prison when a Royal Commission cleared her. But this was after a number of courts, including the highest court in the land, had ruled that her conviction was safe.

In reading the Royal Commission's findings, one cannot help but be struck by the way the prosecution's interpretation of the facts fitted its case theory.

The most damning conclusion of the Royal Commissioner was that the substance Mrs Kuhl found to contain foetal blood was in fact paint and soundproofing material. One of the problems which the Royal Commissioner exposed was the practice of Mrs Kuhl's forensic team of destroying the gels and materials used after each test was concluded. This meant that no other expert could test what the Crown's forensic experts had done.

The next thing you should look at is whether your opponent's expert carried out her investigations in an unusual way or at least in a different way from other experts. You must ask yourself whether there were things the expert did not do and whether she ought to have done them.

Could she have been assisted with other information which was not available at the time of her examination? Have new techniques come to light since then?

Has the opposing expert depended too much on guesswork or inference?

Look at the opposing expert's calculations. Do they stand up? This is where your own expert can help you.

Lastly, if your opponent's expert has produced the first report in the case and you want the materials examined by a potential expert of your own, do not tell your opponent who that expert is. Make sure you deliver the material to your expert yourself.

Otherwise, if your potential expert agrees with the findings of the opposing expert, and you decide it would not be right to call him, your opponent might put two and two together and grab your erstwhile expert.

2.4 The cross-examination itself

Now you are on your feet and the opposing expert has finished his direct examination. You have a lot of ammunition. But don't go in all guns blazing. Start in a kindly and moderate manner.

Is there any information you can glean from the witness which will help your client's case? Are there any areas where the witness can agree with your expert?

Next you may wish to neutralise the expert's testimony. On the basis that the most reasonable experts can disagree, you might be able to take the sting out of his evidence.

So start pleasantly and professionally, getting as many favourable or neutral concessions as you can.

As part of your strategy you will know the weaknesses you can exploit. Choose the best ones and try to avoid more than three. What are the three points you want to argue that this expert's testimony means in your closing address?

Any more than three and you tend to dilute your argument. Ten weaknesses and the decision-maker may get lost and forget some or worse, miss the most important ones. You must choose the most important ones in advance and lay them out simply, clearly and memorably.

The decision-maker must know which points you consider most important and remember them.

So, do you go for the witness's qualifications or experience or his methodology?

Make sure the decision-maker is following you. A senior judge told me once that a rather self-important barrister was cross-examining a physician about the make-up of the human brain. To the judge it appeared as a cosy, little esoteric chat between counsel and the witness. He recalled, 'I didn't have a clue what they were talking about. I had to intervene.'

The barrister looked down his nose at the judge and said to the witness, 'His Honour doesn't understand. Let's go back to the beginning. Can you tell His Honour what penicillin is?'

It was atrocious advocacy and the judge never forgot it.

The techniques you should use in cross-examining an expert witness are not very much different from those you would employ to question a lay witness.

You must remain in control using short, closed questions. You must not concede control by asking open questions or by arguing with the witness. Naturally, this being an expert, you might need to put propositions or theories to the expert. Be prepared for what he will say. Have a follow-up question or two ready, and above all have an escape route.

In the organisation of your cross-examination, use headlines – or announcements to the expert and the decision-maker – that you are about to change the subject. A well-organised cross-examination will be easier to note down and of more assistance than one which shoots all over the place.

It is not just things that the expert did; the things he did not do or forgot about may also be crucial.

Lastly, on the subject of escape routes, Norman Birkett was asked many years later what he would have done if the witness had known what the co-efficient of the expansion of brass was (apparently, it is 0.0000189).

He replied that he would have gone on to copper, then aluminium and other metals before leaving the subject as if it were of no particular importance.

Without doubt, he would not have been fazed by the witness's answers.

Don't argue with the expert. He will want to get you onto his home turf. It is a mistake to go there with him and relinquish your position of strength as a cross-examiner.

If you are going to ask an open question, make sure you know the answer or be certain it will not harm you.

Avoid asking one question too many. David Ross QC tells a chilling story which was related to him by Don Campbell QC.

Campbell was cross-examining the plaintiff's doctor in an Australian personal injury case:

Question:	'How would you describe the pain?'
Answer:	'Like a red-hot iron placed on the sole of the foot.'
Question:	'What would you know about a hot iron placed on the sole of the foot?'
Answer:	'I was a prisoner of war in Changi.'

It is commendable that Mr Campbell was able to tell this story against himself, but what makes it egregious is that the doctor was Edward 'Weary' Dunlop, the most famous prisoner of war in the Japanese camp in Singapore.[5]

2.5 Case study: cross-examination of the claimant's expert

Let us return to the *Cavendish v Downham* case study in Appendix 1.

In preparing the cross-examination of the claimant's expert, Mr Worthington, you must think first about your case theory.

---

5 David Ross QC, *Advocacy* (Cambridge University Press, Cambridge, 2007) 59. Reproduced with permission of the licensor through PLS Clear.

The defendant's case theory is that the sculpture is genuine and if it is not, then the claimant did not rely on what the defendant told her. He made up his own mind.

The only part of the case theory that relates to Mr Worthington is the genuineness or otherwise of the sculpture.

What are your objectives for the cross-examination? These will be subsets of the case theory. In other words, what do you want to argue in closing?

Study Worthington's report carefully to see if he agrees with your expert on anything. Unless you have a very good reason not to, the questions seeking helpful answers (facts or omissions which support your case and with which the witness will agree or not dispute) should be put first.

One of your objectives should be to show that Worthington is not well qualified to give an opinion on Assyrian antiquities. At least, he does not have the academic qualifications and depth of knowledge about the area that your expert, Professor Fournier, has.

What you should not do is put Fournier's qualifications to Worthington one by one and say, 'You don't have that qualification do you?' It is not subtle and will allow Worthington to argue.

The time for making comments about the significant difference in qualifications is in the closing speech.

I suggest you put the number of the relevant paragraph and line from his witness statement next to each question in case he forgets or denies it.

Don't forget to put your case:

Question:	'Mr Worthington. The bas-relief was Assyrian?'
Answer:	'I strongly disagree.'
Question:	'Mr Worthington, you are trade specialist?'
Answer:	'Yes.'

Question: 'You run a dealership in Middle Eastern artefacts?'

Answer: 'Yes.'

Question: 'And you have been the consultant to the antiques department at Harling's Auctioneers for the last 10 years?'

Answer: 'Yes.'

Question: 'Mr Worthington, you examined the sculpture didn't you?'

Answer: 'Yes.'

Question: 'Your examination took two hours and 47 minutes?'

Answer: 'That's correct.'

Question: 'You carried out a chemical analysis of the sculpture?'

Answer: 'Yes. I did.'

Question: 'You have a Bachelor of Arts from Cambridge?'

Answer: 'Yes.'

Question: 'And a Master of Arts?'

Answer: 'Yes.'

Arts degrees are in subjects such as History, English and Philosophy but you have no information about the subjects Worthington did. It is a risky area because you do not want him saying 'I majored in the History of Art, in particular Assyrian antiquities.' However, you would think that if he had, it would be in his witness statement. Just leave it and let the judge speculate.

Question: 'You do not have a science degree?'

Answer: 'No, I don't.'

Question: 'Or a qualification in chemistry?'

Answer: 'I don't.'

Question: 'Or chemical analysis?'

Answer: 'I have experience in carrying out chemical analyses.'

Question: 'You don't say that in your report?'

Answer: 'I don't.'

Question: 'Or what analysis you carried out on this occasion?'

Answer: 'It was a chemical analysis.'

Question: 'You don't say which tools you used.'

Answer: 'I used the proper equipment.'

Question: 'You don't say which tools you used.'

Answer: 'No I didn't in my report. I didn't think it was necessary.'

Question: 'You don't think it might have helped the court?'

Answer: 'In hindsight, maybe it would have.'

Question: 'You don't say which chemicals you used?'

Answer: 'No I don't.'

Question: 'You didn't compare the sculpture to photographs of similar sculptures?'

Answer: 'I did not.'

Question: 'Or drawings?'

Answer: 'No. I knew what I was doing.'

Question: 'Or sketches?'

Answer: 'No.'

Question: 'By Austen Henry Layard?'

Answer: 'No, I didn't think it was necessary.'

Question: 'You don't mention Layard in your report?'

Answer: 'Why should I?'

Question: 'You didn't compare the bas-relief to sculptures of the same period?'

Answer: 'No.'

Question: 'During the examination, you had no similar sculptures in the room?'

Answer: 'No. There weren't any.'

Question: 'You didn't take the sculpture away?'

Answer: 'No.'

Question: 'To check you were right?'

Answer: 'I didn't need to.'

Question: 'To compare with other sculptures?'

Answer: 'No.'

Question: 'Or to check with another expert?'

Answer: 'No.'

Question: 'You say that the stone is significantly harder than that found close to the Tigris River in northern Iraq?'

Answer: 'Yes.'

Question: 'During your examination, you did not have stone from the Tigris River?'

Answer: 'I did not.'

Of course, there are a number of other areas where you could attack Worthington, such as his reliance on the information in the auction catalogue or his brief opinion on the date of the cuneiform script. But the purpose of this exercise is to illustrate a technique for cross-examining Worthington on his qualifications.

2.6 Case study: cross-examination of the defendant's expert

The defendant's expert, Professor Christophe Fournier, is eminently well qualified but never saw the sculpture. You must leave his qualifications alone and attack his method.

Your case theory is that the sculpture is a Victorian copy.

The objective should become clear as the cross-examination unfolds:

Question: 'Professor Fournier, the sculpture is not Assyrian?'

Answer: 'It most assuredly is.'

Question: 'You were sent 10 digital photographs of the carving?'

Answer: 'I was.'

Question: 'By Mrs Downham?'

Answer: 'Yes.'

Question: 'You concluded that you had no need to examine the carving itself?'

Answer: 'That's correct, but by then it had been destroyed.'

Question: 'You were not told who took the photographs?'

Answer: 'I was not.'

Question: 'You do not know where they were taken?'

Answer: 'I assume in Mrs Downham's shop.'

Question: 'You do not know what the lighting conditions were?'

Answer: 'I don't.'

Question: 'Or the temperature of the room?'

Answer: 'What has that got to do with it?'

Question: 'You do not know the distance the camera was from the sculpture?'

Answer: 'No.'

Question: 'Whether or not a zoom lens was used?'

Answer: 'I didn't need to as I used the zoom on my computer.'

Question: 'Whether or not a zoom lens was used?'

Answer: 'No.'

Question: 'When you were looking at the photograph you couldn't measure the depths of the indentations?'

Answer: 'I didn't need to. I could see them clearly.'

Question: 'You could not measure the depth of the indentations?'

Answer: 'I formed a view.'

Question: 'You couldn't tell the hardness of the stone?'

Answer: 'No.'

Question: 'Or its temperature?'

Answer: 'No.'

Question: 'Or what it was made of?'

Answer: 'No.'

Question: 'Or whether it would crumble under pressure?'

Answer: 'That would be vandalism.'

Question: 'Or whether it would crumble under pressure?'

Answer: 'No. I did not need to. It was Assyrian.'

You get the gist. These are short, closed questions with which he has to agree and which leave him little room to argue. But there is a killer

Norman Birkett-style question lurking in the wings. You should leave it right to the end. It is open, but who cares?

> 'Professor Fournier, if you had been given the choice between looking at photographs of the sculpture or the sculpture itself, which one would you have chosen?'

3 RE-EXAMINATION

The same rules apply. Re-examination must arise from the cross-examination and the questions must not be leading.

The problem with expert evidence is that it revolves around two competing opinions, which is fertile ground for an argument. As you know, lawyers love an argument.

Remember that re-examination is for the purpose of rehabilitating a witness or allowing the witness to explain something which was clouded by the cross-examination.

If the court has already heard the witness's opinion, it's not right to seek it again. If you spend a lot of time rehabilitating a witness it will look bad.

Do it sparingly, if at all, and hope your witness is telepathic and knows what you are driving at.

If you do re-examine, make sure your last question elicits a good answer.

Chapter 14
Addresses

I have called this chapter 'Addresses' to cover a number of terms used in different jurisdictions to describe what advocates say about the evidence. So I include in the term 'addresses', speeches and statements.

There are different opinions from country to country about the importance of addresses. Some jurisdictions dispense with them altogether, some allow a closing address but not an opening address and some have different rules depending upon whether it is a civil or criminal trial.

I want to draw some common threads from all the learning in the area to offer some practical advice.

You may be appearing in a hearing where, say, the arbitration panel does not want you to talk about the evidence but merely wants to know how the law applies to the facts. I will deal with Submissions of Law in the next chapter.

1 STRIKING THE RIGHT NOTE

In a list of distinguished advocates, no one but her staff would put Her Majesty Queen Elizabeth II in the top drawer.

But her performance in relation to the then Prince Charles succeeding as Head of the Commonwealth was outstanding.

For months prior to the Commonwealth Heads of Government Meeting in April 2018 there were stories in the media to the effect that Charles was not the right person to take over. In fact, it seemed that his popularity amongst the hard-bitten politicians who were attending the meeting was inversely proportionate to that of his mother.

Speaking to the leaders in the grand setting of the Buckingham Palace Ballroom, the late Queen said:

> 'It is my sincere wish that the Commonwealth will continue to offer stability and continuity for future generations and will decide that one day the Prince of Wales should carry on the important work started by my father in 1949.'[1]

It is not a command. It is not a plea. There is no suggestion of anything so demeaning as begging.

On the other hand, there is nothing about Charles's qualities or suitability for the job.

In addition, the late Queen, whose reign had by then lasted 66 years, makes no reference to herself. The mention of King George VI and his three years in the role is enough to highlight what she has done.

Her unmentioned theme is tradition.

Accompanied by all the pomp and circumstance, it was impossible for the Heads of Government to refuse her. At Windsor Castle a couple of days later, her sincere wish was granted.

2 THE OPENING ADDRESS

If you are required to deliver an opening speech, it is important that you make the most of the opportunity.

An American trial lawyer I know says that the opening is the most crucial part of the trial. He says that first impressions linger and if you can capture the jury in your opening statement you are as good as home.

---

1 'A Speech given by Her Majesty The Queen, Head of the Commonwealth, at the Formal Opening of CHOGM', www.royal.uk/speech-given-her-majesty-queen-head-commonwealth-formal-opening-chogm.

That is with a jury. Some judges say they are no different from juries but at the very least a judge will be greatly assisted by a well-made opening address.

First of all, check to see if there are any special rules in the jurisdiction you are appearing in.

If it is a criminal trial, and you appear for the prosecutor, you will be under a special obligation to be fair.

Some years ago, a motorist was accused of causing the Selby train disaster in England by dozing off at the wheel. Ten people died and 82 suffered serious injuries. He was exhausted after a five-hour night-time chat with a woman he met through an internet dating agency.

The prosecutor James Goss QC was not emotional; nor did he plead for a conviction. He said:

> 'He knew at the time that he was deprived of sleep. We say he must have been aware of his sleepiness and fought it for some time before succumbing, falling asleep and drifting off the road.
>
> Although the circumstances are highly unusual and exceptional in their magnitude, any driver who sleeps is a danger to others.'[2]

The last sentence is eminently fair. The motorist was convicted.

There are two main reasons why an advocate delivers an opening address:

1 to tell the court or tribunal what the case is and how it will be proved; and

2 to persuade the court or tribunal to give you the award or judgment that you want.

---

2 Reported in the *Daily Mail*, 28 November 2001.

The mark of success of a good opening speech is that when the advocate sits down, the judge should be thinking, 'If they prove that, they will win.'

In America, an opening address should not contain argument. In England and Australia, it is permissible, but it should be more of a story – it is not the time for theatrics or emotion.[3]

Abraham Lincoln's real skill as a trial lawyer was to make the jury feel as if they were working out the case with him:

> 'Mr. Lincoln's speeches to the jury were most effective specimens of forensic oratory. He talked the vocabulary of the people, and the jury understood every point he made and every thought he uttered.
>
> He never made display for mere display, but his imagination was simple and pure in the richest gems of true eloquence. He constructed short sentences of small words, and never wearied the mind with mazes of elaboration.'[4]

A good opening address sets out the facts so that the issues to be decided are clear. It begins with a case theory.

Ian Barker QC in the *Chamberlain* case delivered an opening speech for the prosecution which lasted for a day.[5]

He began with clarity:

> 'A baby was killed at Ayer's Rock on 17 August 1980, during the evening, between eight and nine o'clock. It was a Sunday. The child was then just under ten weeks old, having been born on 11 June.

---

3 John H Munkman, *The Technique of Advocacy* (Butterworths, London, 1991) 150.

4 Mark E Steiner, *An Honest Calling: The Law Practice of Abraham Lincoln* (Northern Illinois University Press, DeKalb, 2006).

5 *Chamberlain v The Queen (No 2)* [1984] HCA 7, (1984) 153 CLR 521.

> She was called Azaria Chamberlain, and was the daughter of the accused, Michael Leigh Chamberlain and Alice Lynne Chamberlain.
>
> The body of the child was never found but, having heard the evidence concerning the baby's disappearance, you will have no difficulty determining that she is dead, and that she died on the night she disappeared.
>
> As to the manner and the cause of death, one cannot be precise because the body was never found.
>
> However, what will be proved, largely upon scientific evidence of the baby's clothes, is that the child lost a great deal of blood, in all probability from injury to major vessels of her neck.
>
> She died very quickly because someone had cut her throat.'

Mr Barker certainly grabs your attention, but his words are simple and he sets out the facts in an interesting way.

Then he comes to the Crown's case theory:

> 'The Crown does not venture to suggest any reason or motive for the killing. It is not part of our case that Mrs Chamberlain had previously shown any ill-will towards the child, nor do we assert that the child was other than a normal healthy baby. The Crown does not, therefore, attempt to prove motive, nor does it invite speculation as to motive. We simply say to you that the evidence to be put before you will prove beyond reasonable doubt that, for whatever reason, the baby was murdered by her mother.' [6]

The last seven words are striking. You can imagine the jurors thinking 'What sort of mother could murder her baby in this way?'

---

6 See 'The Trial Transcript in Crown v Lindy and Michael Chamberlain ("The Dingo Trial"): Selected Excerpts', www.famous-trials.com/dingo/462-transcript. Also cited in John Bryson, *Evil Angels* (Penguin Books, London, 1988) 347.

The case is not overstated. It is better to present the facts conservatively. If you overstate something or cannot prove it, you will be subjected to justifiable criticism from your opponent.

Another reason for a moderate opening address is to insure yourself in case any of your witnesses do not come up to proof.

It is crucial that you speak in simple words. As Justice Heydon said, 'The more simply and clearly something is stated, the more both its virtues and fallacies emerge.'

You should not spend too much time dealing with your case's weaknesses. It looks defensive. Well-known US trial lawyer, Mike Roake, puts it more starkly, 'I would rather open my veins than talk about the other side's case in opening.'

Sometimes the weakness in your case is obvious, like a spot on the end of your nose; but if you ignore it, it will not go away. Think of something to say, but make sure it is judicious.

All your presentation skills should be on hand in case they need to be deployed. Don't read. It is not persuasive. Think about your stance, your voice, your eye contact and your changes in tone for emphasis. Pausing when you make an important point is crucial.

Make sure the structure is attractive and easy to follow.

Try to come up with a theme. In the Oscar Wilde trial, Sir Edward Carson was defending Lord Queensberry, a most unattractive individual, in front of an all-male jury. Wilde unwisely sued Queensberry for criminal defamation after he left a card addressed 'To Oscar Wilde, posing as a somdomite [sic]'.

Carson's theme – 'it is what any father would do' – is apparent early in his opening address:

> 'May it please your Lordship, gentlemen of the jury, appearing in this case for Lord Queensberry, I cannot but feel that a very

> grave responsibility rests upon me in putting this case before you as best I can.
>
> So far as Lord Queensberry is concerned, as to any act he has done, as to any letter he has written, or as to any card which has put him in his present position, he withdraws nothing.
>
> He has done what he did premeditatedly and he was determined, at all risks and hazards, to try and save his son.'[7]

The irony of Carson using this theme is that Queensberry's son hated his father and was the main instigator of the legal action.

One of the best opening speeches is the address of the Attorney-General, FE Smith, in the treason trial of Sir Roger Casement.[8] It bears reading in full, but is too long to reproduce here in its entirety.

Casement was knighted by the King in 1911. By 1914, according to the Crown, he was visiting German gaols to drum up support from Irish prisoners against the British.

This is how Smith finished:

> 'What occurred between 1911 and 1914 to affect and corrupt the prisoner's mind, I cannot tell you, for I do not know. I only know of one difference. The sovereign of this country to whom his humble duty was sent in 1911 was, in that year, the ruler of a great and wealthy nation, living in peace, unassailed, and it almost seemed unassailable.
>
> In 1914 this same nation was struggling for its possessions, for its honour, for its very life, in the most prodigious war that has ever tested human fortitude.
>
> To the sovereign of that country, in the hour of its unchallenged greatness, he sends his humble duty. It will be my task to acquaint you with the manner in which he carried out his

---

7 Merlin Holland, *Irish Peacock and Scarlet Marquess* (Fourth Estate, London, 2003) 249.

8 *The King v Casement* [1917] 1 KB 98.

> humble duty in times dark enough to test the value of the unsolicited professions he was so forward in making.'

Then the Attorney-General comes to the peroration. No wonder he was regarded as one of the finest speakers of his day:

> '... Such is the case which the Crown guarantees to prove, and upon which, the Crown relies.
>
> I have, I hope, outlined the facts without heat of feeling. Neither in my position would be proper, and fortunately, neither is necessary.
>
> The prisoner, blinded by hatred to this country, as malignant in character as it was sudden in origin, has played a desperate hazard. He has played it, and he has lost it. Today the forfeit is claimed.'[9]

On a lighter note, FE Smith may not always have been prepared and told this story against himself:

> 'Mr Justice Darling said to one counsel: "I would rather hear FE Smith open a complicated case before me than any counsel at the Bar". Gratified, perhaps, rather than surprised by this tribute, I asked:
>
> "Did the judge say why?"
>
> "Yes", replied my friend. "He said it was so interesting to discover which of two fresh minds would grasp the facts first."'[10]

A suggested structure for an effective opening speech is:

1 Introduction.

2 A statement of the issues (this is your case theory).

3 Proof: the narrative (what happened and how we will prove it).

---

9 Second Earl of Birkenhead, *FE: The Life of FE Smith, First Earl of Birkenhead* (Eyre & Spottiswoode, London, 1965) 292–293, 295.

10 First Lord Birkenhead, *Contemporary Personalities* (Cassell, London, 1924) 254.

4 Peroration: what we want and why.[11]

At the very least, use the statements of case or points of claim as a guide.

3 THE CLOSING ADDRESS

It is often said that advocates should write the closing speech before they do any trial preparation and work backwards. But I think you need to begin with a case theory.

Nevertheless, there is a lot to be said for writing the closing speech early. Much of what is written on submissions of law in the next chapter applies to this section, particularly if you are appearing in front of a judge sitting alone or an arbitration panel.

This is where it all comes together – where you tell the decision-maker everything relevant. This is where you proudly display all the objectives you aimed for in cross-examination and when you tell the court what it can infer from the evidence it has heard. This is when you say why you should win.

The Supreme Court of Canada approved this statement of what a closing address should be:

> 'A closing address is an exercise in advocacy. It is the culmination of a hard-fought adversarial proceeding. Crown counsel, like any other advocate is entitled to advance his or her position forcefully and effectively.
>
> Juries expect that both counsel will present their positions in that manner and no doubt expect and accept a degree of rhetorical passion in that presentation.'[12]

As a practical matter, you should review the pleadings: the statements of case or points of claim, the defences and counterclaims, and check what has been covered or missed.

---

11 John H Munkman, *The Technique of Advocacy* (Butterworths, London, 1991) 144.

12 *R v Rose* [1998] 3 SCR 262.

Of course, you will need to tone down the 'rhetorical passion' if you are closing in front of an arbitration panel or a judge sitting alone. But you should still speak with conviction and try to appeal to the decision-maker's common sense.

A sharp analogy is often decisive. When Camelot and Richard Branson were vying to run the National Lottery in Britain, the Lottery Commission chose to end talks with Camelot and speak solely to Branson.

In the court hearing that followed, David Pannick QC for Camelot said, 'It's like getting to the end of the World Cup final with the score 0–0 and the referee allowing only one side to take penalties in the shoot-out.'[13]

In closing, you should be slightly passionate but never theatrical. You should not repeat the facts at length. You should avoid giving what US attorneys call a 'civics lecture'. For example, don't talk about the burden and standard of proof.

Don't repeat the facts just for the sake of it. The court wants to hear what you say the facts mean.

Don't mis-state the facts or draw inferences that are not sustainable on the facts.

Don't say things in closing, such as versions of what happened or challenges to their evidence, that were not put to the witnesses in cross-examination.

Write the decision for the judge. Make her job easier.

A checklist covering addresses and submissions of law is at the end of Chapter 15, 'Submissions of Law'.

---

[13] *R v National Lottery Commission, ex parte Camelot Group plc* [2001] EMLR 3.

Chapter 15
Submissions of Law

A submission of law is the advocate's opportunity to invite a decision-maker to apply the law to the facts in a way which will suit the advocate's client.

Sometimes a submission of law will form part of an address. At other times counsel may wish to make a submission of law or be invited to do so when a problem arises.

Rarely is there a submission of pure law, because courts are reluctant to hand down advisory opinions. A judgment or ruling is usually rooted in the particular facts of the case or the problem at issue.

A court or tribunal will be assisted by an advocate who has considered the problem thoroughly, sorted out the good points from the bad and comprehensively read and understood all the relevant decisions and legislation.

A decision-maker is paid to make the right decision. That cannot always be possible but in making a decision of any kind the court or tribunal is entitled to rely on the advocate's assistance. Submissions of law have the unique ethical characteristic that the advocate is obliged to inform the court of all relevant authorities and legislation even if on their face they go against his client's case.

1 PREPARATION

1.1 Know the court and its powers

There is no point in asking a court to do something which it is not empowered to do. A thorough knowledge of the hierarchy of the courts and the doctrine of precedent is fundamental. You cannot ask a court to ignore a decision which is binding upon it. You may ask the court to distinguish the facts, but it is futile and stupid to ask a judge to do something which a higher court has specifically forbidden her from doing.

It is equally wrong to submit that an appeal court is bound to follow the approach of the single judge below.

So when you are preparing your submissions, begin by asking yourself what court you will be appearing in and what its powers are.

1.2 Know the facts

You should master the facts of the case. You should know both sides, what has been agreed between the parties, what has been proved and the findings that were made.

The irony is that the higher you climb in the court hierarchy, the more important the facts become. Appeal Court judges are proficient in the law. They have probably encountered that provision or that principle before. They want to know what it is about your facts that makes your case so special.

You must be deadly accurate about the facts. Don't mis-state them or it will colour your whole submission. Make sure your opponent also states the facts correctly.

1.3 Know the law

Obviously, because you are making submissions of law you must give the court confidence that you know of which you speak.

This involves a thorough review of legislation and its history and the way, if any, other courts have interpreted it.

Become very familiar with the permissible forms of statutory interpretation in your jurisdiction.

If it is important, consult a dictionary about the meaning of contentious words.

Read every relevant case thoroughly, including any dissenting judgments. Study how judges in other jurisdictions have approached the problem. But most of all, take care to see what the judge or judges you are appearing before have said on the subject in the past.

1.4 Cite authorities properly

Find out how cases are referred to in your jurisdiction. In some countries, it jars when counsel refers to *Smith v Jones* and pronounces the 'v' or says 'versus' instead of 'and'.

It grates when the advocate submits that a single judgment from the court below is binding or, for no good reason other than that it helps counsel's case, the advocate refers to a dissenting judgment at length.

You must know where the court you are addressing stands in the hierarchy and what powers it has.

You must also be aware of what the Official Law Reports are (e.g. in England: AC, QB, Ch, Fam) and in what circumstances you may refer to an unreported judgment.[1]

When on your feet you should refer to 'Appeal Cases', 'the Weekly Law Reports' or 'Mr Justice Bell', rather than using abbreviations such as 'AC', 'WLR' or 'Bell J'.

Make sure the court and your opponent have a full and legible copy of the cases and legislation to which you will refer.

Stick to what is relevant and that which will assist the court. Don't dismay the decision-maker with a large slab of vaguely relevant authorities. Clear the path for the court and make the judge's job easier.[2]

---

1 See Lord Chief Justice of England and Wales, 'Practice Direction: Citation of Authorities (2012)', www.judiciary.uk/wp-content/uploads/JCO/Documents/Practice+Directions/lcj-pract-dir-citation-authorities-2012.pdf.

2 For written submissions you will be assisted by OSCOLA (Oxford University Standard for the Citation of Legal Authorities), www.law.ox.ac.uk/oscola.

1.5 Know where your documents are

Be well organised. Make sure you have identified and have within easy reach every document or authority to which you will refer or about which the court might ask.

Finding it quickly makes the judge feel you are on top of things and gives the court confidence in you.

The best advocates are also the most organised.

1.6 Anticipate your opponent's arguments

In preparing for the submission ask yourself two questions:

1 What is your opponent likely to say?

2 What would you say if you were in your opponent's shoes?

Unless it is obvious that your opponent must submit something which you intend to counter, don't make your opponent's submission for him, for he might not have thought of it, and you will be tipping him off.

1.7 Anticipate what the court might ask

Look at the problem carefully. What would you ask if you were the judge? What areas would trouble you? What would you be reluctant to do? By the same token, what would make you comfortable? What would help you do what counsel is asking you to do?

If there is more than one judge or arbitrator on the panel, your problem as the advocate may be compounded. There could be a disagreement. The main point is that you should anticipate any questions and have a reasonable and sensible answer ready.

2 STRUCTURE

Courts are assisted by an attractive and persuasive structure. But submissions of law should not be constructed like a thriller novel.

Judges don't want your answer skilfully disguised and only to be revealed at the end.

Look at the rules for skeleton arguments. Most courts these days like or even demand a skeleton argument. Use them effectively.[3]

Remember that three points are better than five, and one point is better than three. As Sir Patrick Hastings KC pointed out, most cases revolve around one main point. It's up to you to find it.

3 ARGUMENT DILUTION

This is a fascinating concept which is counter-intuitive. As human beings we think that the more points we have in favour of our argument, the more it is strengthened.

Let's say, someone has upset you. You'll be in the shower and you'll think. 'That's another thing she's done. That's 17 things she's done wrong!' And then you will confront her with all of them at once. It never works out well.

In fact, the more points you have in favour of your argument, the more you dilute it.

Good advocates stick to one, two or three points. They don't come up with 17. It undermines their credibility if they do.

Murray Gleeson QC, who became Chief Justice of the High Court of Australia, said, 'Never be afraid to give away a bad argument. I don't believe in trying to run every possible argument. It detracts from the strength of your good points.'[4]

I remember appearing with an advocate who insisted on coming up with, on average, 20 grounds of appeal. When he did win, there was only one successful ground.

---

3 See Chapter 8, 'Skeleton Arguments'.

4 Michael Pelly, *Murray Gleeson – The Smiler* (Federation Press, Sydney, 2014).

As he began, the judges would say to him, 'But surely, grounds two to 20 have nothing in them?'

'On the contrary', he would always reply. It was not good advocacy. It seriously undermined his credibility.

I am not saying you should only have one ground, because sometimes cases are won on the unsuspected ground which appeals to the judges. Just make sure that the grounds you submit are properly arguable.

As Philip Larkin wrote in *Dockery and Son*:

> 'Why did he think adding meant increase?'
>
> 'To me it was dilution.'[5]

4 KNOW WHAT ORDER THE COURT SHOULD MAKE

You should always aim to find a reasonable solution to the problem. The court is never going to be persuaded to do something unreasonable, unjust or wrong in law. Your submissions should steer the court to making the right order which, hopefully for you, should win it for your client.

Have a draft order ready. It's not presumptuous. It's good advocacy.

It follows that you should know how to achieve the result you want. Make the task easy for the decision-maker.

5 METHOD

5.1 The psychology of a judge

The Hon William Rehnquist, former Chief Justice of the Supreme Court of the United States, was a plain-speaking man. He said the advocates who annoyed him most were those who thought he knew more than they did. To him, the advocate had been working on the

---

5 Philip Larkin, *Whitsun Weddings* (Faber & Faber, London, 1964) 37.

case for a long time to get it to the Supreme Court. He should know it backwards.

In effect, Justice Rehnquist was saying, 'I have six cases in my list today and I'm not excited about any of them. You've got to get me excited about yours.'[6]

As Justice Laskin[7] argued in his paper, the judge is thinking of two things when you get to your feet:

1 Can you help me?; and

2 How fast?

He put it another way, 'Are you someone we think can find a sensible, workable solution to the real-life problem we must resolve?'

5.2 Point-first advocacy

The decision-maker is paying most attention to what you say in the first 30 seconds that you say it. Make the most of that time. Don't waste it.

There is much to be said for a pithy and apt analogy or a memorable illustration.

In 1948, the distinguished English advocate Cyril Radcliffe opened for the Australian banks in a crucial constitutional case.

The Chifley government had legislated to nationalise all the banks. The legislation had been challenged all the way to the Privy Council.

Radcliffe was dealing with the compulsory purchase of the property of the banks, which had to be on just terms. He pointed out that one section of the legislation empowered the government to acquire the

---

6 William H Rehnquist, *The Supreme Court* (Vintage Books, New York, 2001) 250.

7 The Hon Justice John I Laskin, 'What Persuades (or, What's Going On Inside the Judge's Mind)' (2004) 23(1) *The Advocates' Society Journal*, 4–9, http://ellynlaw.com/PDFs/Justice%20Laskin%20-%20What%20Persuades%20(2).pdf.

business of a bank; and another allowed the Treasurer, on notice, to stop a bank from doing business at all.

He said, 'My Lords, remarkably like your money or your life; of course a well-recognised form of acquisition of property but hitherto not thought to be on just terms.'[8]

The judge is looking for a solution. You must be candid. Sir Owen Dixon, who was a superb advocate before becoming the most esteemed judge in Australian history, said:

> 'Candour is not merely an obligation, but in advocacy it is a weapon.
>
> It is not the case law which determines the result. It is a clear and definite solution, if one can be found, of the difficulty the case presents – a solution worked out in advance by an apparently sound reconciliation of fact and law.
>
> But the difficulty which has to be solved must be felt by the Bench before the proper solution can exert its full powers of attraction.'[9]

The approach of showing the court the extent of the problem it faces before suggesting a just solution has much to commend it, but it is also clever psychology. Obviously, to work, the court must trust the advocate. Some advocates steer the court to a point where it can decide for the advocate without him telling the court what to do. In other words, the court feels as if it has reached the decision itself.

Before his elevation to the UK Supreme Court, Jonathan Sumption QC was asked, 'Have you ever been unable to solve a legal problem?' He answered, 'No. At the end of the day the judge has got to have something to say so you've got to work out what you think he's going to find appealing.'[10]

---

8 Garfield Barwick, *A Radical Tory* (Federation Press, Sydney, 1995) 76.

9 Sir Owen Dixon, *Jesting Pilate* (The Law Book Company Ltd, Melbourne, 1965) 250.

10 'Five Minutes With: Jonathan Sumption QC' (YouTube) www.youtube.com/watch?v=I8DlcexQiPw.

A judge once told me that Sumption would say things along the lines of 'This is the problem. This might be how you arrive at the solution. But there is another way.'

Of course, the judges would be eating out of his hands.

Other counsel have their wiles. The eminent judge Sir Wilfred Greene became Master of the Rolls, the most senior civil judge in England. He had been a distinguished classical scholar, a superb judge of law on appeal and an excellent lawyer who wrote judgments which dozens of years later are still cited.

Lord Hailsham, the former Lord Chancellor, tells of a dinner he had with Greene when Hailsham was a pupil at the Bar. Greene suddenly asked him a question.

'Supposing', he said, 'you were instructed in a case where you had two points to argue, both of them bad but one worse than the other; which would you argue first?'

Hailsham replied, 'I suppose I would argue the less bad of the two.'

'Quite wrong', said Wilfred Greene:

> 'You must argue the worse, and put your very best work into it. Eventually they [the court] will drive you into a corner, and you will have to admit defeat. You will then say, "My Lords, there is another point which I am instructed to argue. But I am not quite sure how to put it." And then you will put the better of the two arguments, but not quite as well as it could or should be put.
>
> After a little while, one of the old gentlemen will interrupt you. He will say: "But surely Mr Greene, you might put it this way." And he will put it exactly as you really ought to have put it in the first place. At that stage you will lay your papers on the desk before you. You will raise your eyes to the ceiling. And in an awestruck voice, you will say: "Oh my Lord, I do believe ..." And then you will be at least half way to winning your case.'[11]

---

[11] Lord Hailsham, *A Sparrow's Flight* (Collins, London, 1990) 86–87.

5.3 Say why you should win; not why the other side should lose

There is a curious phenomenon prevalent among young advocates who set out their opponent's case in some detail before making an attempt to demolish it, point by point.

The result is that the first thing the judge hears is your opponent's case. If the court has already heard your opponent, it will be hearing it for the second time and repetition is a powerful persuasive tool.

Don't dwell on your opponent's case. Don't give it the oxygen it doesn't deserve. By all means, respond to the best points, but concentrate on your own case, and why you should win.

5.4 Pick only the best points to argue

This is similar to argument dilution, but Justice Laskin argues that judges absorb information much better when they know it is important.

The former Chief Justice of the High Court of Australia, Murray Gleeson, was, in his time, the pre-eminent advocate at the Bar. His colleague, Justice Heydon said this about his style:

> 'He endeavoured to refine the issues to some narrow point or points on which he was likeliest to win. He also structured his argument so as to form the basis of the court's judgment. He certainly tried to occupy any vacuum left by his opponent. He would present his position as the only one that ought to be accepted. He would say, "My friend contends for proposition A. But proposition B follows from proposition A. And proposition B is absurd. So proposition A must fail."'[12]

5.5 Don't read

Most decision-makers, unless there are cogent reasons, will resent you reading to them. Apart from not being persuasive, it is patronising and

---

12 Pelly, *Murray Gleeson* (fn 4) 133.

boring. You are being paid to summarise or explain the principle you are placing before them.
Imagine you want to ask someone out for dinner. Put the request in writing. Read it to them. I guarantee you will be dining alone.

5.6 Keep to the point

It is sometimes difficult, especially when there is more than one decision-maker (e.g. a panel) to prevent one of the members going off on a tangent or pursuing a particular hobby horse.

It is important that you do not cause the discussion to veer off the subject. You should always try, as politely as possible, to bring a wayward panel member back to the path that you want them all to follow.

It has been said that appeal judges are sometimes trying to persuade each other during the argument. Sometimes they use the advocate to do it.

I remember appearing before three judges on an appeal. Two of them were men in their mid-60s who had disliked each other since university. One would say things like 'Wouldn't you agree that the point just made by my colleague is wrong?'

If I did agree that the point made by the colleague was wrong, it was a diplomatic achievement to say so without empowering one judge and offending the other. Yet it had to be done.

6 ANSWERING QUESTIONS

When preparing, put yourself in the position of the judge and try to guess what questions the judge will ask. What are the weaknesses in your case? How would you deal with them?

6.1 Answer questions directly

When someone on the bench or panel asks you a question, it is fairly obvious that she wants an answer. Don't put her off. Don't say 'Would you bear with me please? I'll come to that on Thursday.'

She wants to know now because it is exercising her mind now. It may be a chance for you to kick a goal or make a point that helps you. So answer it then and there.

6.2 How to answer

Answering a court's questions is an art.

Listen carefully to the question. If you don't understand it or didn't hear it properly, say so.

When the judge has finished asking the question, pause and think.

Whatever you do, don't start speaking immediately because you will say what is on your mind. You will think out loud.

Judges don't mind you pausing. It is not an episode of *University Challenge*. Judges like it if they can see you are thinking. In a way it is a compliment to the question.

While you think, imagine how you can advance your case theory when you answer.

6.3 The purpose of the question

What sort of question is it? Is it designed to get further information? Is the judge looking for clarification or an affirmation that her understanding of the case is correct?

Is the question highlighting a flaw in your argument? If so, can you answer it directly and turn it to your advantage?

Sometimes, the judge may ask you a question which appears to contain a criticism of your case. Don't assume the question is hostile. Sometimes the bench is testing your case. The judge may be looking for re-assurance. Or she might be intending to go with you but wants to make the case watertight or plug the holes.

Don't become defensive. Remember the judge wants you to help.

There will be occasions when a question does not appear to be helpful, but the judge is throwing you a lifeline. Don't hurl it back.

Australian lawyer Michael Hodgman QC won many criminal cases from impossible positions. Justice Peter Heerey, formerly of the Federal Court of Australia, told a story about Hodgman appearing in the High Court of Australia in a real property case:

> 'The case concerned indefeasibility of pre-existing easements under Torrens system legislation.
>
> Michael's greatest admirers, amongst whom I would include myself, would concede that this was not his usual line of country. Things were not going all that well, when all of a sudden Justice Deane intervened in a most helpful way:
>
> > "Mr Hodgman, it could be said that if A B C were the case, it would follow that D E F and thus X Y Z and you would win."
>
> Michael took one step back and said:
>
> > "Your Honour, that's why you're up there and I'm down here."'

At other times, the question will point out the weakness in your position. You must be prepared to make reasonable concessions and acknowledge problems but don't back down at the first sound of gunfire.

Never forget the fate of Gabriel Wendler SC who was appearing in the High Court of Australia. The Chief Justice, Sir Anthony Mason, was testing his submission. Wendler said 'I believe Your Honour may have me on the ropes.'

Mason replied, 'I have you on the canvas Mr Wendler and you're not getting up.'

Whatever you do, be polite. Don't lose your cool. Remember that the judge has to make a decision which is fair.

Lastly, if the judge says, 'I don't need to hear from you', then that is code for saying 'You have won'. It is not another way of saying, 'I don't *want* to hear from you'. So sit down.

6.4 If you don't know the answer

If you do not know the answer you must say so – firmly and clearly – but your job is not done.

You must, if the situation demands it, say that that you will research the point in a break, in the lunch hour or overnight.

A famous US attorney who practised in England in the last few years of his life was called David Shapiro. He told me that when he was in his early 20s he got a case that went all the way to the US Supreme Court. With the confidence of youth, he decided that he would argue the case himself.

He and his team booked into a nearby hotel to practise. They rehearsed for days. His colleagues threw him nearly every question that the judges of the Supreme Court were likely to ask him.

He arrived on the big day and sat proudly but nervously at the Bar and waited for the distinguished judges to file in.

Then in horror, he heard his father's voice say, 'That's our David up there.' The embarrassment was compounded when the court usher brought his parents up to sit right behind him.

The hearing began. The Chief Justice was Earl Warren.

Shapiro was called upon. He said he was fantastic:

> 'I answered every question those judges asked: William Brennan; Harlan; Douglas; Hugo Black. I was terrific.
>
> Then Frankfurter asked a question. I didn't know the answer. He asked again. I tried my best. He kept pressing. I didn't know the answer. All of a sudden came my mother's voice. "Who's that little weasel upsetting our David?"'

Years later, Shapiro met Justice Frankfurter at a cocktail party. He reminded him of the incident and how uncomfortable it felt. He asked him what the answer to the question was. The judge shrugged his shoulders and said, 'How would I know? I've been asking the same question for 30 years.'[13]

7 YOUR STYLE – IMPACT

The internationally famous linguist Dr Albert Mehrabian says that if your total message is 100%, the visual clues you give, such as gestures and facial expressions, will account for 55%; your vocal inflection will be worth 38%; and the words you use will have 7% impact.

You only have to look up Dr Mehrabian or the 55–38–7 rule on the internet to know that the study is used and misinterpreted around the world.

As an advocate you are not there for impact or to entertain the court. You are there to assist the decision-maker in resolving a real-life problem. If you make an impact (in the best sense) or entertain the court with good changes of tone and effective gestures it may make your message easier to absorb.

Generally speaking, an over-the-top presentation will not be well received. Excessive gestures and changes of tone will be distracting and counter-productive.

---

13 Told by Shapiro to the author 50 years later in a coffee break.

The former Chief Justice of the High Court of Australia, Robert French, watched Murray Gleeson QC at a Special Leave hearing (which are short and timed) and said this:

> 'I thought he was presenting his argument with a kind of dry, authoritative legalism – a method which is consistent with his later explanations of his approach to the judicial function. There wasn't an element of purple prose in it – none of the sort of distracting rhetoric that some people think is helpful to their argument.
>
> He just showed a glimpse of moral steel – a hint of the underlying morality of his argument – not putting it upfront, because if overdone it becomes unpersuasive.
>
> I thought the way he combined those two elements in advocacy was very impressive. I hadn't seen it done as well as that anywhere before.'[14]

By the same token, a flat, motionless delivery may well put the tribunal to sleep. As always in life, moderation is best.

8 SKILFUL ADVOCATES MAKE IT SIMPLE

When Jonathan Sumption QC was asked, 'How do you persuade someone of a difficult argument?', he replied, 'You reduce it to its simplest dimensions. Ultimately, the law is just common sense with knobs on.'[15]

The advocate must concentrate on the facts and legal issues and narrow them down. In other words, all the hard work must be done before the hearing. The advocate must test and try all the points before he presents his submission.

In *Ashmore v Corporation of Lloyd's*, Lord Templeman said that:

> 'The parties and particularly their legal advisers in any litigation are under a duty to co-operate with the court by

---

14 Pelly, *Murray Gleeson* (fn 4) 134.

15 Emma Brockes, 'The Importance of Being Learned', *The Guardian*, 1 November 1999.

> chronological, brief and consistent pleadings which define the issues and leave the judge to draw his own conclusions about the merits when he hears the case.
>
> *It is the duty of counsel to assist the judge by simplification and concentration and not to advance a multitude of ingenious arguments in the hope that out of 10 bad points the judge will be capable of fashioning a winner.*
>
> In nearly all cases the correct procedure works perfectly well. But there has been a tendency in some cases for legal advisers, pressed by their clients, to make every point conceivable and inconceivable without judgment or discrimination.' [16]

All members of the House of Lords who sat in this case agreed with Lord Templeman's speech, but Lord Roskill returned to what Lord Templeman said about the duties of practitioners:

> 'In the Commercial Court and indeed in any trial court it is the trial judge who has control of the proceedings.
>
> *It is part of his duty to identify the crucial issues and to see they are tried as expeditiously and as inexpensively as possible. It is the duty of the advisers of the parties to assist the trial judge in carrying out his duty. Litigants are not entitled to the uncontrolled use of a trial judge's time.*
>
> Other litigants await their turn. Litigants are only entitled to so much of the trial judge's time as is necessary for the proper determination of the relevant issues.'[17]

It is not an easy task to be succinct.

The French mathematician and philosopher Blaise Pascal said in the year 1657:

> 'Je n'ai fait celle-ci plus longue que parce que je n'ai pas eu le loisir de la faire plus courte.'

---

16 [1992] 2 All ER 486, 493 (emphasis added).

17 Ibid, 488 (emphasis added).

> ('I have made this longer than usual because I have not had time to make it shorter.')

President Woodrow Wilson was asked about the amount of time he spent preparing speeches:

> 'That depends on the length of the speech.
>
> If it is a ten-minute speech it takes me all of two weeks to prepare it; if it is a half-hour speech it takes me a week; if I can talk as long as I want to it requires no preparation at all. I am ready now.'[18]

Then the task is to make the propositions as simple as possible. As Justice Heydon said, the simpler the proposition is expressed the sooner its attractions and fallacies will emerge.

You may hope that your judge is not like Lord Justice Lawton, who once said to counsel in the Court of Appeal:

> 'We have read your Notice of Appeal. It raises 7 points does it not?'
>
> 'Yes, my Lord.'
>
> 'We think that point number 4 is your best point. Do you agree?'
>
> 'Er ... Yes, my Lord.'
>
> 'Well, we don't think much of it.'[19]

It was said by a judge of Sir Garfield Barwick QC, who was one of Australia's finest advocates, that he could make the binomial theorem sound like the alphabet.[20]

---

18 Josephus Daniels, *The Wilson Era: Years of War and After 1917–1923* (The University of North Carolina Press, Chapel Hill, 1946) 624.

19 Peter Millett, *As in Memory Long* (Wildy, Simmonds & Hill Publishing, London, 2015) 68.

20 David Marr, *Barwick* (Allen & Unwin, Sydney, 2005) 36–37.

Binomial theorem: it is possible to expand the power $(x + y)^n$ into a sum involving terms of the form ax^by^c where the exponents b and c are non-negative integers with $b + c = n$ and the co-efficient a of each term is a specific positive integer depending upon n and b:

$$(x + y)^4 = x^4 + 4x^3y + bx^2y^2 + 4xy^3 + y^4$$

The judge who made this observation, the Hon George Amsberg, went on to say of Barwick:

> 'He could make the dullest judge understand. It was always lightly done. Once, when he argued before me, he made a submission which switched me right round. I don't know what it was, but he suddenly showed me the way as plain as blazing daylight.'

9 CREDIBILITY

In Justice Laskin's paper,[21] His Honour reduces advocacy to some mathematical equations. He begins with the concept of credibility which is a crucial quality in a good advocate.

First impressions are usually very important. As soon as you stand up the judge is forming a view about you. How are you dressed? How do you stand? Are you organised? Or are you slouching; not looking at me; rifling through papers; mumbling or hesitant?

According to Justice Laskin, credibility = trust + expertise.

Trust means the advocate:

1 is prepared;

2 does not oversell (understatement works far better); and

3 makes concessions or acknowledges weaknesses.

---

21 Laskin, 'What persuades … ' (fn 7).

There is nobody less credible than the advocate who overstates his case and is inflexible.

If you persist with 10 points, nine of which are hopeless, it will undermine the effectiveness of your single good point.

A judge of the Court of Appeal once made the following observation to me:

> 'We sit there and look at counsel. We think, "Oh dear it's Mr Jones. He is never prepared. He is disorganised. He mis-states the facts. He gets the law wrong. We are going to have to work. We are going to have to check everything he says. He may well lead us into error."'

The last two sentences said it all.

'Alternatively', the judge said, 'we might have Miss Smith before us' (reader, please note the deft change of gender):

> 'We can relax. She will be prepared and organised. She will be accurate and fair. We can trust her.'

Justice Laskin also wrote of something he called the 'persuasive burden' – the task facing the advocate. Judges do not want to make radical decisions. They are usually conservative and most are bound by precedent or assisted by the deliberation and approach of previous courts.

To Laskin, the persuasive burden = distance x resistance.

In other words, it is for the advocate to minimise the legal distance that the court or panel must travel to agree with you. Then minimise their resistance to being moved.

His Honour concludes his article with a telling observation: the best advocates are the best story tellers.

10 WHEN TO REPLY

You should reply if it is necessary. It is necessary if your opponent needs correction on a significant point or you have something to say which will hole his case below the waterline and help the judge find for you.

As I said earlier, do not reply just because you can. Don't reply and repeat your original submissions. And remember, the more time you spend replying, the more it looks like your case has been damaged.

A former Chief Justice of the High Court of Australia, Sir Gerard Brennan, described Murray Gleeson QC as being devastating in reply:

> 'He would do the analysis of the response to his argument and have his response ready as clearly and precisely as possible, and he would just deliver it, bang, bang, bang.
>
> There are some advocates who have a high reputation who are not very precise and groan on and on.
>
> Murray never did that. He thought analytically and logically and he was able to present things in that way, and once you do that in front of a bench, you've given them the building blocks for a judgment.
>
> Once you've got a counsel who can see what the main issue is, the rest falls into place.'[22]

11 DOES ORAL ADVOCACY MAKE A DIFFERENCE?

There are a number of views on whether a judge changes her mind after hearing an advocate.

Nowadays, decision-makers are relying more and more on written submissions. In my opinion, this is as disturbing as the current trend

---

[22] Pelly, *Murray Gleeson* (fn 4) 132.

amongst young people of texting messages to each other while they sit together.

I prefer the view of the late Chief Justice Rehnquist of the United States Supreme Court.

He was the clerk to Justice Robert Jackson for 18 months from 1952. He was an Associate Justice of the Supreme Court between 1972 and 1986 and then Chief Justice from 1986 until his death in 2005.

He wrote:

> 'In a significant minority of cases in which I have heard oral argument, I have left the bench feeling differently about a case than I did when I came on the bench. The change is seldom a full 180 degrees and I find it is most likely to occur in cases involving areas of law with which I am least familiar.'[23]

One can bet there were few of those. But the remark is telling. Oral advocacy does matter.

12 CONCLUSION

Always bear in mind that whatever style of advocacy you adopt, it must comply with the rules and customs of the court or tribunal in which you are practising. As an advocate, you must be adaptable.

But you must build your knowledge and skill every day. Senior practitioners have developed a style of their own. Watch them carefully. Ask yourself what works and what does not. Keep a notebook and record everything you learn.

This book was intended to teach you the violin. It cannot turn you into a virtuoso – that is for you.

---

23 William H Rehnquist, *The Supreme Court* (Vintage Books, New York, 2001) 243–244.

Lastly, an Australian judge told me of a young prosecutor who appeared before him. He had prosecuted a man who had committed a vicious assault on his girlfriend. Her face was badly cut and bruised.

The defendant said she had slipped and hit her face on the floor. It had been an accident and he was not to blame.

The young prosecutor's closing speech comprised six words.

He stood in front of the jury and held up a photograph of the young woman's face. He paused and then he spoke very slowly and deliberately, 'Does this look like an accident?'

He paused again, still holding the photo. Then he sat down.

The jury convicted in 10 minutes.

'Now', said the judge, 'that was advocacy'.

13 ADDRESSES AND SUBMISSIONS OF LAW: CHECKLIST

13.1 Nerves

- Prepare thoroughly and practise.
- Learn the first three sentences off by heart.
- Go to bed early and get up early.
- Practise again.
- Get to the court or venue at least 15 minutes before show time.
- Take charge of your case and make sure everyone knows you are in charge.
- Avoid tea and coffee.
- Take a deep but not obvious breath or two when you stand up.
- Breathe deeply again when you feel scared or your heart is racing.
- Remember, the judge wants you to help.

13.2 Structure

- Use a skeleton argument as often as you can.
- Five points are better than 10.
- Three points are better than five.
- Start with your best point.
- Make sure the structure is logical.
- Give headings to each main point.
- Cite case law in accordance with the rules.
- Start well and end well.

13.3 Notes

- Help the court to write its decision.
- Make sure everything (exhibits, documents or submissions) is organised into neat files or has Post-its attached.
- Reduce your notes to very large bullet points in block letters.
- Don't read your submissions word for word.
- Reading makes you speak quickly.
- If you have to read, slow right down.
- Remember, judges were taught to read for themselves at a young age.

13.4 Stance and gestures

- When you stand to speak, make sure you are centred.
- Your core should be about three inches below your belly button and inside you.
- Your feet should be flat on the floor and your ankles should be parallel with your shoulders.
- If you are required to sit, make sure you are at the front of the chair and your feet are tucked under the chair to keep your balance. Your back must be straight and your shoulders level.

- Don't cross your legs because you will squash your voice and look smaller.
- Don't slouch.
- If you like to play with objects such as pens, keys or glasses, put them right out of reach.
- Don't flap around among your papers.
- Get someone to film you and you will instantly see if you have any annoying mannerisms.
- Remember, the judge is forming an impression of you.
- Imagine a box in front of you which is six inches wider than your body at either side and about 18 inches in front of you.
- Keep your gestures within that area.
- When not using gestures, return your hands to the centre of your stomach and rest one openly over the other without gripping (actor neutral).
- Otherwise, put your hands on either side of the lectern or podium but don't grip it.

13.5 Delivery

- Try to use words of one syllable because they are easier to absorb.
- Don't use complicated words or jargon unless you are sure that the listener understands them.
- Reading slabs of judgments or texts is never persuasive.
- Try to use picture words.
- Don't use words that drain an image of its colour.
- Don't be too colourful or you will lose credibility.
- Arrange the facts in the most persuasive or attractive order.
- Tell a story, but remember it is not a murder mystery novel. Don't save the punch line until the end.
- Vary your tone of voice.

- Stress the right word in each phrase.
- Deliver your speech in small bite-sized portions or chunks.
- Pause after each chunk to let the information sink in.
- Watch your audience or the judge for a sign that the phrase has been digested.
- Signs include a blink, a nod, a smile, words such as 'yes' or 'I see' or the judge finishes writing.
- Watch the judge or the audience like a hawk.

Appendix 1
Case Study

Robert Cavendish & Co Limited v Downham Gallery Limited[1]

---

[1] This case study, including the people and events, is a work of fiction. For educational purposes, the mistakes are deliberate.

On behalf of: Claimant
Name: R F Cavendish
Statement: First
Exhibits: 'RFC1'
Date: 14 May

IN THE HIGH COURT OF JUSTICE

KING'S BENCH DIVISION

Claim No: HC186752

B E T W E E N:

ROBERT CAVENDISH & CO LIMITED

Claimant

- and -

DOWNHAM GALLERY LIMITED

Defendant

WITNESS STATEMENT OF
ROBERT FENWICK CAVENDISH

I, Robert Fenwick Cavendish of 8 Ingleby Lane, Parson's Green, London, say as follows:

1 I am the sole director and shareholder of Robert Cavendish & Co Limited, the claimant in this action. The company trades under the name of Lindum Ancient and Islamic Art in Pottergate, Maida Vale. The business has an established reputation for handling early Middle Eastern antiquities. I have been running it for 20 years and it is regarded by my peers as very successful.

2 On the morning of the last Tuesday in November, I received a call from Mrs Chantelle Downham. She is the owner of the defendant company and she has a dubious reputation in the industry. She said

an art world contact had advised her of my reputation as a dealer in Mesopotamian artwork. She said she had just come by an excellent bas-relief. She said 'It's from the lost palace of Sennacherib'. I knew the palace was at Nineveh in northern Iraq. She said 'It's of a soldier and two horses, circa 681–669' or words to that effect. I only wrote down the words 'bas-relief 681–669' but I have lost the note.

3 I had heard of Sennacherib, which was rediscovered in the mid-19th century. It is famous for its enormous bas-reliefs and clay tablets. I had not, however, previously handled any specimens from the site. My main interest lies in the Babylonian cities of Nippur, Larsa and Ur, in southern modern-day Iraq. However, I was interested in the relief because I knew of a wealthy American buyer who collects Assyrian works of art.

4 Assyrian antiquities are becoming increasingly sought after, partly due to their rarity but also because the modern-day conflicts in Iraq and the Middle East have re-ignited awareness in the West of the region's importance to art history and the wider development of human culture. Ironically, the wars that have brought these artefacts to greater prominence have also been responsible for destroying many fine and irreplaceable ancient works. People have a particular interest in Assyrian tableaux of this type because they demonstrate the development of the written form, from early pictorial representations to more simplified and abstract script. There is also excitement that many more sites remain to be discovered.

5 Mrs Downham told me I was welcome to see the carving at any time. It just so happened that I had a meeting of the Classical Art Dealers' Association the next day so I asked her if I could call by and see the relief before lunch. She said, 'Someone will be here'.

6 I think I arrived at Downham Gallery at about 10:30am. Mrs Downham was there with a young woman who appeared to be her assistant. I must emphasise that Mrs Downham is not a particularly likeable woman. She is slim and tall and tries to sound well-bred, but when she becomes excited she lapses into a broad South London accent.

7 She welcomed me and said 'Wait till you see the sculpture'. She led me straight to the bas-relief which was lying down on a layer

of bubble wrap on the counter. She lifted it carefully and leant it up against the wall next to the counter. Just then a man came into the shop. He was attended to by Mrs Downham's assistant. The shop telephone was ringing constantly and was answered by the assistant.

8 On first impressions the relief appeared to be damaged and I was not impressed. The stone also seemed a little too yellow. I was unenthusiastic but Downham worked hard to convince me. She spoke of the archaeological sites at Nineveh and the great excavations of the 19th century by Layard and Smith. She pointed to the late Assyrian cuneiform script, one of the earliest known forms of written expression. She pointed to the quality of the carving and the attention to detail in the harnesses worn by the horses. I remember Mrs Downham commenting on the artistic plasticity and freedom of hand of the sculptor. She also drew attention to the soft limestone from which the relief had been carved, which she said was typical of the stone quarried from the mountains on the borders of the Assyrian Empire.

9 She said she had done a lot of research into Assyrian sculpture, and had concluded there was less variety of style in Assyrian than in Babylonian sculpture. She said there seems to have been only one school, one technique, one style, but that it was possible to distinguish at least two periods of production; one from the beginning up to the reign of Sargon, the other from Sennacherib to the fall of Nineveh. She said a similar bas-relief had sold in Paris recently for €890,000. It was quite clear to me that Mrs Downham knew a lot about her subject. She showed me a copy of the auction catalogue, a copy of which is exhibited at 'RFC1'.

10 She told me the asking price was £850,000 but that I could have it for £820,000. I thought it was a reasonable price in the circumstances so made her an offer. She accepted, saying that she would arrange to have the tablet delivered when the money was in Downham's account.

11 At no time did I say I was an expert on the late Assyrian period or the excavated sites at Nineveh. In fact during the whole episode she appeared to be at pains to show just how much she knew about cuneiform script and the style of carving from the period.

12 The relief was delivered to my gallery about three days later. As I anticipated, a regular American customer of mine, Mr John Arnoldson Jnr, expressed some interest in buying the piece. However, he said that first he wanted it to be checked out by a Mr Worthington who is a trade specialist and expert in the field. As far as I am concerned he is just a gun for hire.

13 Mr Worthington came to my gallery and spent three hours examining the relief. He had magnifying glasses and chemicals. He said it hadn't come from Nineveh at all. He said it was most likely a 19th-century copy. I rang Mrs Downham and demanded my money back but she said it had been a fair deal and I had been given ample opportunity to have the carving checked out. According to Mr Worthington, the relief sold to me by Downham cannot be worth more than £3,000, although I think I could sell it for a bit more.

14 About six weeks after Mr Worthington visited, a cleaner accidentally dropped the bas-relief and it smashed into little pieces. It was not insured because the insurance company and I were arguing over its value.

Dated: 14 May

I believe that the facts stated in this witness statement are true.

Robert Cavendish

....

Robert Cavendish

EXHIBIT 'RFC1'
EXTRACT FROM CATALOGUE

Clifton Barrett
Auctioneers since 1876

LOT NUMBER 263

ASSYRIAN BAS-RELIEF

Late Assyrian, 681–669 BC.
95 x 81 cm
Soldier and two horses
Neo-Assyrian cuneiform lettering
Model for larger relief at Palace of Sennacherib, Nineveh
Excavated by the renowned British archaeologist
A H Layard circa 1846

On behalf of: Claimant
Name: E R Worthington
Statement: First
Exhibits: 'ERW1'
Date: 20 May

IN THE HIGH COURT OF JUSTICE

KING'S BENCH DIVISION

Claim No: HC186752

B E T W E E N:

ROBERT CAVENDISH & CO LIMITED

Claimant

- and -

DOWNHAM GALLERY LIMITED

Defendant

EXPERT WITNESS REPORT OF EDWIN RICHARD WORTHINGTON

To the Court

I, Edwin Richard Worthington BA, MA of 12 McLeod Place, Highbury, London say as follows:

Qualifications and experience

1 For 30 years I have been a trade specialist in works of art from the Assyrian and Babylonian empires of Mesopotamia. As well as running my own successful dealership in Middle Eastern artefacts, for the last 10 years I have been a sometime consultant to the antiquities department at Harling's Auctioneers. I am also a correspondent for the *Antique Merchants' Journal*.

2 Before setting up my own dealership business I was for 10 years the Assistant Keeper of the Late Mesopotamian Collections in the Department of the Middle East at the National Museum.

3 Being a trade specialist, I have a much wider experience than most museum curators because I deal with a far wider range of objects and fresh items pass through my hands all the time.

4 I have given evidence in two High Court trials. In one of them, the judge described my evidence as 'worthy' and in the other the judge thanked me for my assistance.

Synopsis of instructions

5 I have been asked to provide an opinion on whether a bas-relief sculpture, described as 'Soldier and Two Horses', is a genuine Assyrian artefact dating from the seventh century BC.

Background: the development of Assyrian sculpture

6 In order to understand the nature of the reliefs uncovered at the palace of Sennacherib, I think it would assist the court if I were to give a brief outline of the origins and characteristics of Assyrian sculpture.

7 The country of Assyria was established during the second millennium BC. The country began as a narrow strip of land between the Tigris River and the mountains. From the 12th century BC the rulers of Assyria embarked on a sustained period of conquest, such that by the early ninth century BC the Assyrian Empire stretched from the Persian Gulf to Asia Minor. I attach a map to this report to explain the geography of the region.

8 The Assyrian capital of Nineveh became renowned as a centre of art, industry, and commerce. Works of art were brought from surrounding countries and colonies of foreign artists settled and worked there. Assyrian art, with its clearly defined and impressive individuality, exercised an influence that would be spread over the entire East and be carried by the Phoenicians as far as the Greek islands.

9 The Assyrian royal palace was the shrine of art. Every king wished to build at least one palace that should be a memorial of his reign and perpetuate his name forever. The state apartments were more

or less thoroughly decorated with sculptures in relief throughout the main halls and corridors.

10 The Assyrians excelled at bas-relief; that is, sculpture which is not free-standing or in the round, but has a background from which the main elements of the composition project. The sculptors used this method of carving to tell stories. Their work was naturalistic and somewhat narrow in its scope, but it was greatly varied in its detail.

11 They made excellent use of the alabaster and soft limestone quarried from the mountains on the fringes of the Assyrian kingdom. The Assyrian sculptor seemed to revel in the facility with which he could fashion the stone, indulging in the minutest detail work and exaggerating lines, muscular development, and expression. The human figure was represented quite perfectly in profile, but we find no examples of the use of the full face.

12 By the time of the rule of Sennacherib (pronounced Sen-AK-uh-rib), towards the end of Assyrian dominance (705–681 BC), the figures had become more epic, perhaps less lifelike, and the relief much higher. In the art of this time we begin to find scenery and accessories, a multitude of small figures, and detailed representation of the incidents depicted.

Cuneiform script

13 I should also comment on the development of written forms during the Assyrian Empire. The period saw the emergence of the cuneiform script (meaning 'wedge shaped'). This began as a series of pictographs. The symbols were drawn with a blunt reed for a stylus. The cuneiform script underwent considerable changes over a period of more than two millennia, with a gradual move toward spelling out words laboriously rather than relying on signs with a phonetic complement.

The bas-relief: opinion

14 I have examined in detail the relief which is the subject matter of these proceedings. My examination took two hours and 47 minutes. The stone appears to be of a limestone composition, but the lines of the sculptor's tool show that the stone is significantly harder than that found close to the Tigris River in northern Iraq.

15 The sculpture itself is rudimentary. The lines lack refinement and definition. There is no suggestion of muscular exaggeration either

in the human figure or the horses. The design of the harnesses appears to date from a later period. The design was not in use during the reign of Sennacherib.

16 The cuneiform script is also problematic. By the seventh century BC, Neo-Assyrian cuneiform had been further simplified and reached close to a 'pure' form, having almost dispensed with phonetic symbols.

17 Lastly, I note that the dates for the work in the auction catalogue are 681–669 BC. As I have stated above, Sennacherib's reign ended in 681 BC. It is highly unlikely that the relief could be dated as late as 669. The dates given are in fact those of the reign of King Esarhaddon. I acknowledge however that this may simply be a mistake in the catalogue.

18 For the reasons given above, in my opinion the carving is not from the palace of Sennacherib. The stone used and the mistakes in the harness design and written forms suggest it is a reproduction from the 19th century AD, when many similar imitations were made with varying degrees of accuracy.

Statement of truth

19 I confirm that I have made clear which facts and matters referred to in this report are within my own knowledge and which are not. Those that are within my own knowledge I confirm to be true. The opinions I have expressed represent my true and complete professional opinions on the matters to which they refer.

20 I understand my duty to the court and I have complied with that duty. I am also aware of the requirements of CPR Part 35 and its Practice Direction, the Protocol for Instruction of Experts to give Evidence in Civil Claims and the Practice Direction on Pre-Action Conduct.

Dated: 20 May

Edwin Worthington

....

E. R. Worthington

EXHIBIT 'ERW1'
MAP OF ANCIENT MESOPOTAMIA

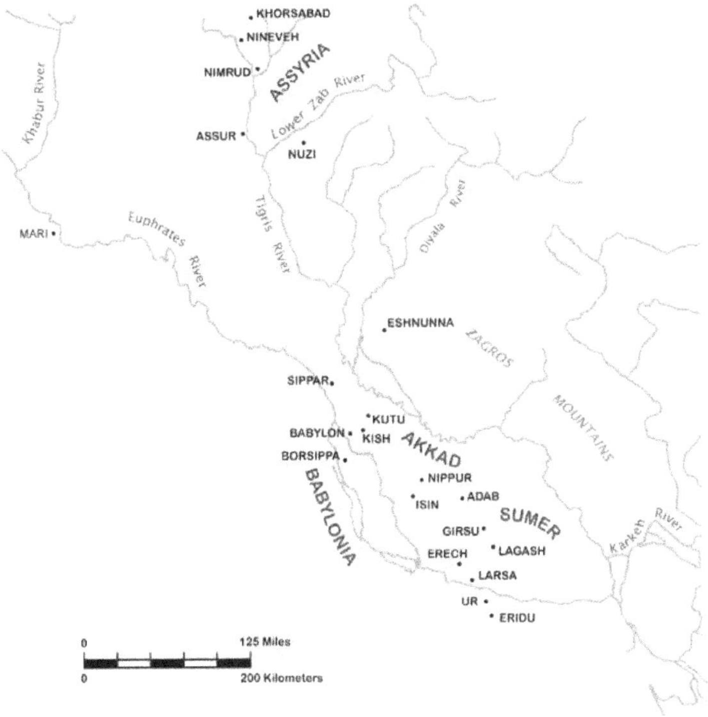

On behalf of: Defendant
Name: C Downham
Statement: First
Exhibits: None
Date: 12 May

IN THE HIGH COURT OF JUSTICE

KING'S BENCH DIVISION

Claim No: HC186752

B E T W E E N:

ROBERT CAVENDISH & CO LIMITED

Claimant

- and -

DOWNHAM GALLERY LIMITED

Defendant

WITNESS STATEMENT OF CHANTELLE DOWNHAM

---

1 I am Chantelle Downham of 26 Pleasance Lane, Putney and I am the owner of Downham Gallery, the defendant in this action.

2 Late last year I bought a bas-relief stone carving which had been described in an auction catalogue as being late Assyrian (681–669 BC), depicting a soldier and two horses. It had apparently been used as a model for much larger reliefs at a palace in Nineveh in modern day Iraq.

3 I specialise in the works of contemporary British artists such as Hepworth, Caro and Moore. However, I had been to the galleries containing Middle Eastern sculpture at the National Museum and had recently been to the exhibition there on Babylon, where I had been taken by the quality of the carving and the beautiful stories

they portrayed. Ancient sculpture is becoming more and more desirable amongst collectors, and is seen as something of a status symbol. It can really set off a room decorated in a minimalist style, with the correct lighting. I believe that a very good piece can fetch several hundred thousand pounds these days. This one caught my eye.

4 Clifton Barrett, the auction house from whom I bought the carving, were reputable and reliable. On 14 November, I took my friend Jonathan Hardwick with me when I viewed the sculpture.

5 We looked at the carving for about half an hour. Jonathan is an expert on Middle Eastern architecture. He had heard of the palace of Sennacherib at Nineveh and told me that there was a dealer in Maida Vale called Robert Cavendish who specialised in artefacts from Mesopotamia.

6 Jonathan said that the palace of Sennacherib was well known but that no artefacts from the site had come up on the open market for a long time. Most of the known pieces had found their way into museums and galleries. He said the Athénée Museum had a particularly fine collection.

7 On the strength of what Jonathan had said and on the reputation of the auction house I offered £790,000 for the bas-relief. It was delivered to my rooms in Brook Street about a week later and displayed in the gallery. I had it insured for the same amount. The insurance company told me to take good digital photos of the sculpture. My assistant Jane Lovering did that for me.

8 In late November I telephoned Mr Cavendish. I did not give any details. I just said I had a Mesopotamian sculpture for sale. He was quite excited and said, 'I'd like to see it tomorrow'. I did not describe it to him. I did not need to. He almost bit my hand off.

9 He was there at 9:30 am apologising because he had misjudged the time. Jane Lovering was with me. Jane has been my assistant for a number of years. We had taken the carving down and it was leaning against the wall on the counter. I remember Mr Cavendish as a slightly older man with a posh voice.

10 When he saw the stone relief he said, 'Do you like it, Mrs Downham?' I replied 'Yes', and he quickly said, 'It has all the features Mrs Downham. Symmetry of composition, precise rendering

of detail and profiling of the figures, while lacking any backgrounds of scenery'. I said, 'You're rather taken with it, aren't you? Would you like to get it checked out?' I always try to be fair with my customers. I said it was £850,000 but that two other people were extremely interested. That was not true but I had stuck my cheque book out to get the sculpture. He sniffed and said 'I'll give you £820,000 here and now'. I waited a few moments, had a private chat with Jane (about her aunt's birthday) and then said, 'Okay'.

11 He said he would pay within 24 hours by BACS transfer and I said he could have the carving as soon as I was paid. It would be sent by special delivery. We shook hands. He looked pleased with himself.

12 The money arrived in my account as promised and I sent the relief to Maida Vale the following day. I did not hear from Mr Cavendish for over a week.

13 He called me at the gallery and said he wanted his money back. I was stunned. I told him he had been satisfied that it was okay and he knew more about these artefacts than I did. I told him that I did not like his manner and that it was a fair sale between two specialist businesses or words to that effect. He said he was going to see his lawyer and I replied, 'It's your problem now'. He hung up.

14 I have since had photographs of the relief examined by an expert in Paris and he has declared it to be genuine. I still believe it was genuine.

Dated: 12 May

I believe that the facts stated in this witness statement are true.

C Downham

....

Chantelle Downham

On behalf of: Defendant
Name: C Fournier
Statement: First
Exhibits: 'CF1'
Date: 21 May

IN THE HIGH COURT OF JUSTICE

KING'S BENCH DIVISION

Claim No: HC186752

B E T W E E N:

ROBERT CAVENDISH & CO LIMITED

Claimant

- and -

DOWNHAM GALLERY LIMITED

Defendant

DEFENDANT'S EXPERT WITNESS REPORT BY CHRISTOPHE FOURNIER

To the Court

I, Christophe Fournier, BA PhD, Professor of Middle Eastern Antiquities, University of Montmartre, Paris, say as follows:

Qualifications and experience

1 I am a senior curator in the department of Near Eastern Antiquities at the Athénée Museum in Paris. I have been the Professor of Middle Eastern Antiquities at the University of Montmartre for 20 years. After graduating I took a PhD. The title of my thesis was 'Austen Henry Layard and the great mound of Kuyunjik'. Whilst in my

current role, I have given evidence in 27 trials concerning art fraud, in the USA, France, Germany, Austria, Italy and the UK.

Material instructions

2 I have been asked for my opinion as to the provenance of an Assyrian bas-relief referred to as 'Soldier and Two Horses', and whether it is genuine. I should say that I do not have the slightest doubt that the carving originates from the palace of Sennacherib at Nineveh.

Context

3 The Athénée Museum is very fortunate to hold many of the original drawings prepared by Austen Henry Layard, one of the principal excavators of Nineveh and the discoverer of Sennacherib's palace in 1849.

4 Nineveh is situated on the eastern bank of the Tigris in ancient Assyria, near the modern-day city of Mosul, Iraq, which lies across the river. Nineveh's mound-ruins, Kuyunjik and Nabi Yunus, are located on a level part of the plain near the junction of the Tigris and the Khosr Rivers. This extensive space is now one immense area of ruins overlaid in parts by new suburbs of the city of Mosul.

5 In 1847 the young British adventurer Sir Austen Henry Layard explored the ruins. In the Kuyunjik mound Layard rediscovered in 1849 the lost palace of Sennacherib with its 71 rooms and colossal bas-reliefs. He also unearthed the palace and famous library of Ashurbanipal with 22,000 cuneiform clay tablets.

6 Layard illustrated many of the antiquities he uncovered, and subsequently published them in various works, including *Illustrations of the Monuments of Nineveh* (1849). Drawings of many of the tablets and bas-reliefs prepared by Layard are within the collections under my curatorship, and formed the basis of my PhD thesis.

Materials reviewed

7 I have read the expert report of Edwin Worthington and I have seen 10 digital photographs of the carving in question. Prints of two of those photographs are attached at 'CF1'. For reasons which

I hope will become clear, I had no need to examine the carving itself. In any event, I now know it has been destroyed. In all, I spent four hours examining the photographs. I used the zoom facility on my computer to see the bas-relief in detail.

Opinion

8 I have compared the digital photographs of the bas-relief (which were sent to me by Mrs Downham) with the drawings made by AH Layard, now held at the Athénée Museum. I believe I have matched the carving in question to an illustration of the carved stone tablets in the state rooms of the palace of Sennacherib.

9 The similarities are striking. The sculpture does indeed lack some refinement and definition, but this was typical of the later Assyrian period when character and sharpness were lost instead of gained by a softer gradation of the surfaces. It is also correct to state that this was a model. The master sculptors appear to have executed models on a small scale both in terracotta and in stone, which were used by the workmen to whom the bulk of the execution was delegated. The production of bas-reliefs was so immense, at the time of the construction of any royal palace, that some such method as this was required in order to ensure uniformity of style and type in the different parts.

10 The cuneiform script appears to match that recorded by Layard, although the sketch is insufficiently detailed to be certain. Contrary to what Mr Worthington says, the mixed method of writing, that is a combination of ideographic and phonetic writing, continued through to the end of the Babylonian and Assyrian empires. The last known cuneiform inscription was written in 75 AD.

11 It is correct that the dates recorded in the auction catalogue are those of the subsequent king, Esarhaddon. However, we believe that work on Sennacherib's palace continued after his death. It is not known who dated the work for the auction catalogue and I agree that little weight should be attributed to it.

12 With due deference to young Mr Worthington, to my knowledge he has never set foot in Iraq. He is a successful and respected dealer in Middle Eastern antiquities but as a result of the very broad range of objects he handles he cannot be considered as an expert in the excavation of the Kuyunjik mound at Nineveh.

13 I am satisfied that the digital photographs of the carving I have studied are those of the genuine bas-relief from the palace of Sennacherib at Nineveh as described and illustrated by AH Layard, and I do not need to see the carving to assure the court that my opinion is sound.

Statement of truth

14 I confirm that I have made clear which facts and matters referred to in this report are within my own knowledge and which are not. Those that are within my own knowledge I confirm to be true. The opinions I have expressed represent my true and complete professional opinions on the matters to which they refer.

15 I understand my duty to the court and I have complied with that duty. I am also aware of the requirements of CPR Part 35 and its Practice Direction, the Protocol for Instruction of Experts to give Evidence in Civil Claims and the Practice Direction on Pre-Action Conduct.

Dated: 21 May

Christophe Fournier

....

Christophe Fournier

EXHIBIT 'CF1'
PHOTOGRAPH 1

EXHIBIT 'CF1'
PHOTOGRAPH 2

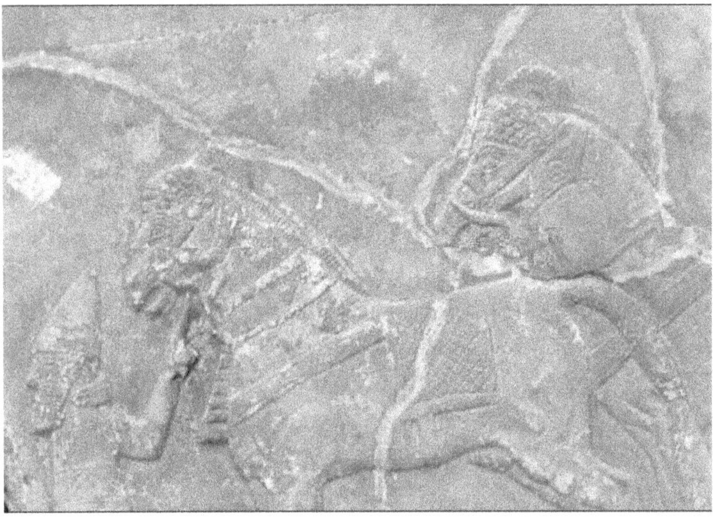

IN THE HIGH COURT OF JUSTICE **Claim No: HC186752**

KING'S BENCH DIVISION

B E T W E E N:

ROBERT CAVENDISH & CO LIMITED

Claimant

- and -

DOWNHAM GALLERY LIMITED

Defendant

PARTICULARS OF CLAIM

---

1 At all material times:

a The Claimant company is and was in the business of dealing in art from premises in Pottergate, Maida Vale; and

b The Defendant company is and was in the business of dealing in art from premises in Brook Street, London.

2 On 28 November Chantelle Downham, acting on behalf of the Defendant, telephoned Robert Cavendish of the Claimant and orally represented that a certain stone carving described as an Assyrian bas-relief ('the Carving') was from the lost palace of Sennacherib in Nineveh in northern modern Iraq, showed a soldier and two horses and dated from the period 681–669 BC ('the Representation').

3 The Representation was made with the intention of inducing the Claimant to enter into a contract with the Defendant to buy the Carving.

4 In reliance upon and induced by the Representation the Claimant entered into an oral contract on 29 November at the Defendant's premises with the Defendant by which the Claimant, acting

through Robert Cavendish, agreed to buy and the Defendant, acting through Chantelle Downham, agreed to sell the Carving for the sum of £820,000 ('the Contract'). The Defendant was acting in the course of its business.

5 The Representation set out in paragraph 2 above was an express term of the Contract.

6 Further or in the alternative, it was an implied term of the Contract, pursuant to section 13(1) of the Sale of Goods Act 1979 (as amended), that the Carving would correspond with the description in the Representation.

7 The Claimant paid the purchase price of £820,000 on 4 December and the Carving was delivered to the Claimant on 5 December.

8 In fact the Representation was false and the Defendant was in breach of the Contract in that the Carving was not late Assyrian but a 19th-century reproduction.

9 As soon as Mr Cavendish of the Claimant discovered the true facts he demanded the return of the purchase price of £820,000 and rescinded the Contract in a telephone call to Mrs Downham of the Defendant on 10 December.

10 As a result of the matters set out above, the Claimant has suffered loss and damage.

PARTICULARS OF LOSS AND DAMAGE

The difference in value between the Carving as represented (£820,000) and its actual value (£3,000): £817,000.

11 Further, the Claimant claims interest pursuant to section 35A of the Senior Courts Act 1981 on the amount found to be due to the Claimant at such rate and for such period as the Court thinks fit.

AND THE CLAIMANT CLAIMS:

1 Rescission of the Contract; and

2 Return of the sum of £820,000

Alternatively:

3 Damages in lieu of rescission; or

4 Damages for misrepresentation; or

5 Damages for breach of contract; and

6 Interest on 2, 3, 4 or 5 above pursuant to section 35A of the Senior Courts Act 1981 to be assessed

STATEMENT OF TRUTH

I, Robert Cavendish, believe that the facts stated in these Particulars of Claim are true.

Signed: *Robert Cavendish*

Dated: 24 January

Served this 30 January by Sewell Barber LLP, Solicitors for the Claimant, of 14 Park Row, London SE3 7HN.

IN THE HIGH COURT OF JUSTICE **Claim No: HC186752**

KING'S BENCH DIVISION

B E T W E E N:

ROBERT CAVENDISH & CO LIMITED

Claimant

- and -

DOWNHAM GALLERY LIMITED

Defendant

DEFENCE

---

1 The Defendant admits paragraph 1.

2 The Defendant denies paragraph 2. The Defendant, by and through its agent, Mrs Chantelle Downham, telephoned Robert Cavendish of Claimant before his visit to the gallery to tell him that the Defendant was offering the carving referred to in paragraph 2 of the Claimant's Particulars of Claim ('the Carving') for sale. Mrs Downham referred to the Carving only as a 'Mesopotamian sculpture'. She did not describe the Carving to Mr Cavendish or give any other details.

3 The Defendant denies paragraph 3. No such representation was made, either during the telephone call or when Mr Cavendish visited the premises.

4 The Defendant denies that part of paragraph 4 which states that any representations were made which the Claimant was entitled to rely on or which induced the Claimant to purchase the Carving. The Defendant admits the balance of paragraph 4.

5 The Defendant denies paragraph 5 for the reasons set out above in paragraphs 2 and 4 of this Defence. Mr Cavendish of the Claimant

was more expert than the Defendant or its agent Mrs Downham. The authenticity of the Carving was not a term of the contract.

6 The Defendant denies paragraph 6. Mr Cavendish of the Claimant was more expert than the Defendant on the authenticity of the Carving, and therefore could not have relied on statements or representations made by the Defendant. The provision referred to does not apply.

7 The Defendant admits paragraph 7.

8 The Defendant denies paragraph 8. An expert, Christophe Fournier, has considered the authenticity of the Carving. The expert's opinion is that the Carving is from the palace of Sennacherib in Nineveh, modern day Iraq.

9 The Defendant admits that Mr Cavendish of the Claimant asked for the purchase price of the Carving to be returned in a telephone call with Chantelle Downham, the Defendant's agent, on 10 December. The balance of paragraph 9 is denied. The Carving is late Assyrian and from Nineveh. Alternatively, the Claimant was not entitled to rely upon, nor did the Defendant cause to be made, any statements or representations about the authenticity of the Carving.

10 The Defendant denies paragraph 10. The Carving was late Assyrian and from Nineveh, or alternatively the Claimant should not have relied on any statements or representations made by the Defendant by and through its agent, Chantelle Downham, regarding the authenticity of the Carving. No actions or conduct of the Defendant caused loss or damage to the Claimant.

11 The Defendant denies the Claimant's Particulars of Loss and Damage.

STATEMENT OF TRUTH

I, Chantelle Downham, believe that the facts stated in this Defence are true.

Signed: C Downham

Dated: 28 February

Served this 28 February by Hartwell Roberts Crisp, Solicitors for the Defendant, of 67 Foster Road, London EC4M 8BZ.

Appendix 2
Further Reading

Books

A good way to obtain some of these books is through https://abebooks.com or the Wildy & Sons bookshop in Lincoln's Inn Archway, London.

Michèle M Asprey, *Plain Language for Lawyers* (Federation Press, Sydney, 1999)

James Baker, *Work Hard, Study ... and Keep out of Politics* (Putnam, New York, 2006)

Garfield Barwick, *A Radical Tory* (Federation Press, Sydney, 1995)

Cicely Berry, *Your Voice and How to Use It* (Virgin Books, London, 2000)

Tom Bingham, *The Business of Judging* (Oxford University Press, Oxford, 2004)

First Earl of Birkenhead, *Contemporary Personalities* (Cassell, London, 1924)

Second Earl of Birkenhead, *FE: The Life of FE Smith, First Earl of Birkenhead* (Eyre & Spottiswoode, London, 1965)

Second Earl of Birkenhead, *Walter Monckton* (Weidenfeld & Nicolson, London, 1969)

Louis Blom-Cooper QC and others, *The Judicial House of Lords 1876–2009* (Oxford University Press, Oxford, 2009)

AE Bowker, *Behind the Bar* (Staples Press, London, 1947)

Fenton Bresler, *Lord Goddard* (Harrap, London, 1977)

John Bryson, *Evil Angels* (Penguin Books, London, 1988)

John Campbell, *FE Smith* (Jonathan Cape, London, 1983)

Winston Churchill, *Great Contemporaries* (Revised Edition, Thornton Butterworth Ltd, London, 1938)

Lord Denning, *The Closing Chapter* (Butterworths, London, 1983)

Patrick Devlin, *Easing the Passing* (The Bodley Head, London, 1985)

Patrick Devlin, *Taken at the Flood* (Taverner Publications, London, 1996)

Sir Owen Dixon, *Jesting Pilate* (The Law Book Company Ltd, Melbourne, 1965)

Richard DuCann, *The Art of the Advocate* (Penguin, London, 1993)

Sir Robin Dunn, *Sword and Wig: The Memoirs of a Lord Justice* (Quiller Press, London, 1993)

Keith Evans, *Advocacy at the Bar – A Beginners Guide* (New Edition, Blackstone Press Ltd, London, 1992)

EW Fordham, *Notable Cross-examinations* (Constable & Co, London, 1952)

Brian Garner, *Legal Writing in Plain English* (University of Chicago Press, Chicago, 2001)

Justin Gleeson and Ruth Higgins, *Rediscovering Rhetoric* (Federation Press, Sydney, 2008)

Thomas Grant, *Jeremy Hutchinson's Case Histories* (John Murray, London, 2015)

Stanley Jackson, *The Life and Cases of Mr Justice Humphreys* (Odhams Press, London, 1960)

Lord Hailsham, *A Sparrow's Flight* (Collins, London, 1990)

Ian Hancock, *Tom Hughes QC* (Federation Press, Sydney, 2016)

Patrick Hastings, *The Autobiography of Sir Patrick Hastings* (Heinemann, London, 1950)

Charles Hennessy, *Practical Advocacy in the Sheriff Court* (Thomson, W Green, Edinburgh, 2006)

Merlin Holland, *Irish Peacock and Scarlet Marquess* (Fourth Estate, London, 2003)

John Hostettler, *Sir Edward Carson: A Dream Too Far* (Barry Rose Law Publishers, Chichester, 2000)

Brian Johnson and Marsha Hunter, *The Articulate Advocate* (Crown King Books, Chandler, 2009)

Michael Kerr, *As Far As I Remember* (Hart Publishing, Oxford, 2002)

Philip Larkin, *Whitsun Weddings* (Faber & Faber, London, 1964)

Sam Leith, *You Talkin' to Me?* (Profile Books, London, 2011)

Edward Marjoribanks, *The Life of Lord Carson* (Victor Gollancz, London, 1932)

David Marr, *Barwick* (Allen & Unwin, Sydney, 2005)

Peter Millett, *As in Memory Long* (Wildy, Simmonds & Hill Publishing, London, 2015)

H Montgomery Hyde, *The Trials of Oscar Wilde* (William Hodge & Co, Glasgow, 1960)

H Montgomery Hyde, *Norman Birkett: The Life of Lord Birkett of Ulverston* (Hamish Hamilton, London, 1965)

Charles Moore, *Margaret Thatcher: The Authorized Biography, Volume One* (Allen Lane, London, 2013)

John H Munkman, *The Technique of Advocacy* (Butterworths, London, 1991)

David Napley, *The Technique of Persuasion* (Sweet & Maxwell, London, 1991)

Nedra Newkirk Lamar, *How to Speak the Written Word* (Revell Co, New Jersey, 1949)

George Orwell, *Why I Write* (Penguin Books, London, 1984)

James Owen, *Nuremberg: Evil on Trial* (Headline, London, 2006)

David Pannick KC, *Advocacy* (Cambridge University Press, Cambridge, 2023)

David Pannick KC, *Advocates* (Oxford University Press, Oxford, 1992)

Edward Abbott Parry, *The Seven Lamps of Advocacy* (Fisher Unwin, London, 1926)

Alan Paterson, *Final Judgment: The Last Law Lords and The Supreme Court* (Hart Publishing, Oxford, 2013)

Michael Pelly, *Murray Gleeson – The Smiler* (Federation Press, Sydney, 2014)

Chester Porter, *Walking on Water* (Random House, Australia, 2003)

Hugh Purcell, *A Very Private Celebrity: The Nine Lives of John Freeman* (The Robson Press, London, 2015)

William H Rehnquist, *The Supreme Court* (Vintage Books, New York, 2001)

David Ross QC, *Advocacy* (Cambridge University Press, Cambridge, 2007)

Antonin Scalia and Bryan Garner, *Making Your Case: The Art of Persuading Judges* (Thomson West, London, 2008)

Mark E Steiner, *An Honest Calling: The Law Practice of Abraham Lincoln* (Northern Illinois University Press, DeKalb, 2006)

Stephen Walmsley, *The Trials of Justice Murphy* (Butterworths, Sydney, 2017)

Articles and papers

Ian Barker QC, 'The Dangerous Art of Cross-Examination' (2013) 84 *Bar News: Journal of the NSW Bar Association*, 28–34

Garth Blake SC and Philippe Doyle Gray, 'Can Counsel Settle Expert Reports?' (2013) 199 *Precedent*, 16–20

Lord Bingham, 'The Judge as Juror: The Judicial Determination of Factual Issues' (1985) 38 *Current Legal Problems*, 1–27 (reprinted in Tom Bingham, *The Business of Judging* (Oxford University Press, Oxford, 2004))

Emma Brockes, 'The Importance of Being Learned', *The Guardian*, 1 November 1999

Geraldine Clark, 'Jonathan Sumption QC on Appellate Advocacy' (South Eastern Circuit, September 2009), https://southeastcircuit.org.uk/education/jonathan-sumption-qc-on-appellate-advocacy

Justice Stephen Estcourt, 'Ethical Advocacy' (Tasmanian Advocacy Convention, 2012), www.supremecourt.tas.gov.au/publications/speeches-articles/ethical-advocacy/

Betty S Flowers, 'Madman, Architect, Carpenter, Judge: Roles and the Writing Process' (1981) 58 *Language Arts*, 834–836

Michel Kallipetis KC and Lady Justice Andrews, 'Skeleton Arguments, A Practitioner's Guide' (The Honourable Society of Gray's Inn, London, 2004)

The Hon Justice John I Laskin, 'What Persuades (or, What's Going On Inside the Judge's Mind)' (2004) 23(1) *The Advocates' Society Journal*, 4–9

Lord Neuberger, 'Lord Erskine and Trial by Jury' (Seckford Lecture, Woodbridge School, 18 October 2012), www.supremecourt.uk/uploads/speech_121018_547b652fdd.pdf

Lord Neuberger, 'Tomorrow's Lawyers Today – Today's Lawyers Tomorrow' (80 Club Lecture, Association of Liberal Lawyers, 19 February 2013), https://supremecourt.uk/speeches/lord-neuberger-at-the-80-club-association-of-liberal-lawyers

Irving Younger, 'Ten Commandments of Cross-Examination' taken from *The Advocate's Deskbook: The Essentials of Trying a Case* (Prentice Hall, Upper Saddle River, 1988)

Conduct guides

Bar Standards Board Handbook, www.barstandardsboard.org.uk/for-barristers/bsb-handbook-and-code-guidance/the-bsb-handbook.html

Equal Treatment Bench Book, published by the Judicial College, www.judiciary.uk/about-the-judiciary/diversity/equal-treatment-bench-book/

SRA Code of Conduct, www.sra.org.uk/solicitors/standards-regulations/code-conduct-solicitors/

Acknowledgements

First Edition

Thank you to Bronwyn Smithies who typed the manuscript with considerable finesse and patience from her home in Sheffield, Tasmania.

Thank you also to my editors Matthew Maguire and Lara Finnegan, young lawyers of such promise who made excellent suggestions, and who pulled me up when I wrote something inappropriate or which did not make sense.

For their encouragement and teaching I am grateful to my highly influential but sadly departed friends, Michael Hodgman QC, Professor Daniel Simons, Keith Beresford, GH Bryan and Governor Peter Underwood.

Thank you also to Fiona Donnelly, Judge Mark Drummond, Robert Jehan, David Kavanagh QC, Dr Torsten Loercher, Ciaran Moynagh, Guy Pendell, Tracey Petter, Lorraine Richardson, Leigh Sealy SC, Carol Sowers, Nigel Savage, Judge Nancy Vaidik, Jim Wilkinson and Peter Wood.

Simon Brown QC, Justice Gregory Geason and Dr Simon Gabriel selflessly read the manuscript and offered suggestions for improvement, but the responsibility for any errors or infelicities of style is mine.

Andrew Riddoch of Wildy & Sons has been patient and helpful with advice and positive comments. Thank you also to his able team.

Lastly, thank you to Chris Taylor, the learned overseer who wrote the *Cavendish v Downham* case study with me and organises everything else with style.

I am grateful to the publishers, authors, individuals and organisations mentioned below who have permitted me to quote from copyright works. Full citations are provided in Appendix 2, 'Further Reading'.

Where some of the books are quite old it has been difficult to contact the publishers, but I have been careful to acknowledge them.

Thank you to:

- Jason Monaghan of the Federation Press for their books on Tom Hughes QC, Murray Gleeson and Sir Garfield Barwick;
- James Stephens of Biteback Publishing for excerpts from the interview with Norman Birkett;
- Cambridge University Press for an excerpt from David Ross QC's book on *Advocacy*;
- Robin Black of The Advocates' Society of Canada for excerpts from Justice Laskin's paper;
- Justice Stephen Estcourt for his paper on advocacy;
- Mrs Justice Andrews, Michel Kallipetis QC and Gray's Inn for their paper on skeleton arguments;
- Gabriel Wendler for the story of his encounter with Sir Anthony Mason, recounted in *Submissions of Law*;
- Akshaya Ganesh of Elsevier for excerpts from *The Closing Chapter* by Lord Denning;
- Hannah Stokes of Orion Books for an excerpt from *Walter Monckton* by Lord Birkenhead;
- Geraldine Clark for her article on Lord Sumption;
- Ingmar Taylor SC of Greenway Chambers for the articles in the *NSW Bar News* about expert witnesses;
- Lord Sumption for a number of observations and suggestions about effective advocacy;

- Lynne Wall and the Editor of *The Spectator* for a story by Charles Moore;
- Maggie Thompson of Allen & Unwin for a quote from *Barwick* by David Marr;
- Oxford University Press for a quote from Lord Bingham in *The Business of Judging*;
- Lord Hailsham and Hoare's, trustees of his father's estate, for *A Sparrow's Flight*;
- Faber & Faber for the lines of Philip Larkin in *Dockery and Son* from *The Whitsun Weddings*;
- David Evans from David Higham & Associates for quotations from *FE Smith* by John Campbell;
- Merlin Holland, who kindly allowed me to quote from his book *Irish Peacock and Scarlet Marquess* about his grandfather, Oscar Wilde;
- Victoria Cliff Hodges, Norman Birkett's granddaughter, who generously allowed me to quote from Lord Birkett's speeches and writings;
- Lord Pannick QC for his very generous and witty Foreword.

Second Edition

Chris Taylor would like to thank Carol Sowers for her generous contribution to the new chapter on Online Advocacy. Thank you also to Dr Simon Gabriel, Nicola Hoskins, Fiona Donnelly and Ruairi Gillen for their ideas and observations about online hearings.

All permissions have been re-sought and renewed, where appropriate, for this Second Edition. As well as those already named above, thank you to:

- Olivia Beattie of Biteback Publishing for excerpts from the interview with Norman Birkett;
- Phoebe Miller of Orion Books for the excerpt from *Walter Monckton* by Lord Birkenhead;

- Boyd Spradbury of Allen & Unwin for the quote from *Barwick* by David Marr; and
- Chris Thurlow of the Ludlow Trust, as executors of Lord Hailsham's estate, for *A Sparrow's Flight*.

Lastly, I am grateful to Lord Pannick KC, Lady Justice Andrews, Michael Kallipetis KC, Merlin Holland, Victoria Cliff Hodges and Robin Black not only for their renewed permissions, but also their kind words about Peter.

Index

References are to page numbers.